*Women*
TRANSFORMING
**POLITICS**

# *Women*
# TRANSFORMING
# POLITICS

## WORLDWIDE STRATEGIES FOR
## EMPOWERMENT

EDITED BY

*Jill M. Bystydzienski*

INDIANA UNIVERSITY PRESS

*Bloomington and Indianapolis*

∞™

Manufactured in the United States of America

Library of Congress Cataloging-in-Publication Data
Women transforming politics : worldwide strategies for empowerment
/ edited by Jill M. Bystydzienski.
    p.    cm.
Includes bibliographical references.
ISBN 0-253-31294-9.—ISBN 0-253-20698-7 (pbk.)
    1. Women in politics.  2. Feminism.  I. Bystydzienski, Jill M.,
date.
HQ1236.W645  1992
305.42—dc20                91-20126

1 2 3 4 5  96 95 94 93 92

*To my daughter, Kate, and the
women of her generation*

# CONTENTS

# Contents

## SECTION 3

## NATIONAL LIBERATION AND DEVELOPMENT MOVEMENTS

# PREFACE

This book is the result of several years' collaboration between me and thirteen other authors who worked very hard to make this collection possible. In this volume we have tried to achieve unity of theme and form as well as to preserve the diversity of women's voices and experiences.

What unifies the following thirteen chapters is a deep concern for documenting women's contributions to the political process—the influence that women the world over have had in affecting the lives of the collectivity. We have also tried to illuminate the strategies that have helped to empower women in different cultures under diverse conditions. Most of the chapters also provide a brief historical overview of women's struggles for empowerment in their respective societies.

While the majority of the contributors are academics, we come from a variety of fields, ranging from political science and sociology to journalism, folklore, and musicology. However, since most of us have been involved in women's studies and women's movements, our perspectives are largely interdisciplinary and feminist. It is important to recognize that in addition to academic training, each author is shaped by different national and cultural experiences and a unique political history. These differences among us affect how we approach our studies of women's struggles; taken together they constitute the collective strength of this book.

All of the contributors are either natives of the countries we write about or have spent extended periods of time living in and studying women's struggles in these societies. Our knowledge of women's conditions in the specific societies on which we focus is thus extensive and profound. Although we make use of a variety of research methods, most of us have relied on firsthand experience, observations, and in-depth interviews. We chose methods that brought us close to the experiences of the women we studied. This is no accident, as most of us by our own admission are both committed scholars and activists, wanting to document and to further the efforts of women struggling for survival and justice. The engagement fostered by qualitative methods was essential to these studies of women's struggles for empowerment. However, most of the chapters also rely on survey data and existing documents to provide a broader societal and historical context.

As I write this, the world is once again torn by war, a war which promises to be extremely costly in human lives and economic and natural resources. I am struck by the observation that, for the most part, women have been excluded from all high-level decisions in the negotiations preceding armed conflict and that they will once again be victims of a male-dominated political process, this time both as soldiers and civilians. I cannot help but think that had women been involved in the process of decison-making, particularly as an interest group with their own agenda, war might have been avoided. Current opinion polls show a gender gap in support for the war, with women significantly less likely to be in favor.

The Persian Gulf War has made the need even more urgent for us all to seek new, peaceful ways of solving human conflicts. It is imperative that women be involved in the resulting transformation process, and I am hopeful that this book can offer some ideas for how that may be possible. After all, as the chapters herein indicate, given the right mix of strategies and conditions, women can make a difference.

This collection would not have been possible without the support of many people who have encouraged our work. I know that each of the authors is thankful to those who are close to them. I am personally grateful to my husband, Hal Pepinsky, and daughter, Kate, who have lived with this book for several years and have given me much needed moral and intellectual support. I also owe special thanks to my parents, Ewa and George Bystydzienski, and Pauline and Harold Pepinsky, whose unconditional love and respect have laid a strong foundation for my life and work.

Numerous friends and colleagues have been helpful in making this book a reality. I particularly want to acknowledge Cynthia Enloe for providing feedback to an early proposal for the book as well as Angela Miles for reading parts of the manuscript and suggesting changes, and my colleagues at Franklin College of Indiana whose interest and encouragement have been an ongoing source of inspiration and support.

My thanks goes also to Gina Doglione for diligently converting chapter files from one computer program to another and for putting together the final copy of the manuscript.

Last, but most importantly, the authors of this book are deeply indebted to the countless women who were and continue to be involved in the political actions which we have described herein. Without their courage and perseverance our studies would have been impossible. Their commitment and work have inspired us to continue the struggle for justice and democracy.

J.M.B.
January 1991

# INTRODUCTION

## Jill M. Bystydzienski

The concept of "politics" as it is generally understood in most contemporary societies denotes the exercise of power in the public realm. According to this view, individual and group involvement in established government structures such as parliaments or congresses, parties, campaigns, and voting, and in the use of control and influence within these institutions, constitutes the essence of political activity. With a few exceptions,[1] all over the world, the public political domain for many centuries has been, and continues to be, defined and controlled by men (usually upper-class).

Concerned about the absence of women from established political structures, numerous scholars have tried to account for this phenomenon. Students of Western societies have pointed to the forces of patriarchy, capitalism, and industrialization that have kept women out of the public sphere, effectively confining their work to the family and to the lowest paid, low-prestige occupations (Schlegal, 1977; Friedel, 1975; Leacock, 1972). Those focusing on the socialist world have suggested that Marx was wrong in assuming that women would achieve political equality with men when the means of production were owned collectively and, furthermore, that as long as socialist nations continue oppressive traditions and pursue policies aimed at keeping women primarily responsible for the family, gender equality in political and other spheres will not be achieved (Miller, 1981; Jancar, 1978). Scholars who study the so-called developing, or Third World, nations often point to colonialism and the "macho" tradition as sources of female exclusion from politics (Swantz, 1985; Andreas, 1985; Obbo, 1980). While such analyses are important, they define political activity exclusively as behavior pertaining to established government in the public realm, and thus tend to reinforce the generally accepted notions of politics discussed above.

The extent to which the term *politics* is used as synonymous with the public sphere of life should not be underestimated. Political science courses as taught in the contemporary academy as well as most standard texts overwhelmingly present this view (Burack, 1988/89; McAdam, 1987; Randall, 1987). Even within nontraditional academic contexts, as in women's studies, the political is frequently conceptualized this way. I recently attended a lecture on women in politics sponsored by a women's studies program at a major U.S. university.

The lecture focused on women "world leaders," that is, heads of governments, and why there have not been any in the United States. Both popular views and those of the scholarly community thus combine to create a narrow definition of the political, confining it to established government structures and the public domain.

With politics restricted to the public sphere of human life and perceived as an area of male activity, the private or personal realm, by contrast, has come to be seen as a sphere reserved for women. The private sphere typically comprises the institution of the family (although it may sometimes include the neighborhood or other units at the local community level) and interpersonal relations between friends and acquaintances. Within this realm, by definition, there is no politics (Randall, 1987: 11). Hence, women's roles, in most societies, have been defined by and largely limited to the private sphere and women's activities deemed essentially apolitical.

In recent decades, with the second wave of the women's movement, came a re-evaluation of many male-created concepts and institutions, including that of politics. Radical feminists in particular have spearheaded this inquiry and stimulated new ideas about politics within the wider women's movement. One of the pioneers in this regard has been Kate Millett. In her now classic *Sexual Politics,* Millett redefined politics from activity taking place within established government structures to relationships based on power whereby one group of persons is controlled by another (1971: 23). Other radical feminists went even further by attacking the notion that there exists a distinct political sphere and proclaimed that "the personal is political" (Bunch-Weeks, 1970: 166; Dunbar, 1975: 46; Eisenstein, 1983: 35–41; Wandersee, 1988: 62–65). As Mc-Williams indicated, U.S. radical feminists, many of whom obtained their political education in the civil rights movement, witnessed a striking conversion of private to public issues: "where one sat on a bus, whom one married, in whose company one ate, where one swam, slept and urinated became questions of public policy" (1974: 160). While at first women made the connection between private lives and public and legal issues in relation to blacks, they soon recognized that every area of life is a sphere of "sexual politics." Since all relations between men and women are institutionalized relationships of power, they constitute an appropriate field for political analysis. Thus radical feminists concluded that such "personal" institutions as childrearing, housework, love, marriage, contraception, and sexual practices, including sexual harassment, rape, prostitution, and sexual intercourse itself, all have deeply political dimensions (Jaggar, 1983: 101).

The breaking down of the traditional dichotomy between the private and the public and the recognition that the sphere of life reserved for women was indeed "political" have led some feminists to examine more closely the activities of women carried on outside the purview of established power structures. Such studies have revealed that women all over the world, both in the past and the present, have been involved in what Randall refers to as "less conventional politics," such as ad hoc or noninstitutionalized politics, including makeshift organizations and self-help projects, protests and related actions, as well as policy-shaping activities of women's associations (Randall, 1987: 58–68). For instance, several recent studies have documented a substantial involvement of women in eighteenth- and nineteenth-century food riots and market disturbances in Europe (Levy and Applewhite, 1980; Stacey and Price, 1981) as well as women's extensive participation in the community action movement in Europe and the United States in recent decades (Gittell and Shtob, 1980; Schoenberg, 1980; Mayo, 1977; McCourt, 1977).

Other feminists have gone further to show women's participation in numerous empowerment-directed activities centered on families and kinship networks, local neighborhoods, and interpersonal relationships (Bystydzienski, 1989; Vickers, 1987). For instance, Lasser documented the importance of fictive kinship networks[2] to the empowerment and support of nineteenth-century middle-class U.S. women (Lasser, 1988), while Dublin (1979), Stack (1974), and Gilkes (1985) showed the significance of such networks in the daily lives of working class, poor and black women. Thus, many feminists have discovered that "until we broaden our definition of politics to include the everyday struggle to survive and to change power relations in our society . . . women's political action will remain obscured" (Bookman and Morgen, 1988: 14). Once feminists redefined politics to transcend the dichotomy between the public and private, women emerged as politically active beings (McAdam, 1987; Stamm & Ryff, 1984; Siltanen and Stanworth, 1984).

Central to the feminist definition of politics is the concept of "empowerment." As used by feminists, empowerment is taken to mean a process by which oppressed persons gain some control over their lives by taking part with others in development of activities and structures that allow people increased involvement in matters which affect them directly. In its course, people become enabled to govern themselves effectively. This process involves the use of power, but not "power over" others or power as dominance as is traditionally the case; rather, power is seen as "power to" or power as competence (Carroll, 1972: 604) which is generated and shared by the disenfranchised as they begin to shape the content and structure of their daily existence and to participate in a movement for social change. An important illustration of this notion comes from the literacy movement.

Feminists within the literacy movement have drawn on the work of Paulo Freire who suggested that "learners are empowered by entering into dialogue with their peers. Through this dialogue they learn to read and write as they name their experience and speak about their world" (Garber-Katz and Horsman, 1988: 118). Feminist literacy work often takes place in local community centers with learners and teachers working together to build a community. As learners progress, they discover that language shapes their experiences, that their experiences need to be represented in the language, and that the language itself needs to be transformed to truly reflect their views. In this process, the distinction between the private and public becomes obscured as learners draw on personal experience and bring it into the public realm by writing about it and making it accessible to their peers and sometimes a wider audience if their work is published (Garber-Katz and Horsman, 1988). In this case, empowerment of the learners is synonymous with a transformation to document their lives: by writing and publishing oppressed people's voices and histories and thus bringing them into the public realm, the established notion of what constitutes "literature" is challenged and redefined. Heretofore unheard from persons—women, blacks, and other racial and ethnic minorities, lesbians and gays, working class and poor people—become empowered through feminist literacy to express their views and to transform traditional literary canons. This process, involving the generation and use of power to bring about social change, is profoundly political.

By going beyond the taken-for-granted notion of politics, feminists have opened up a new way of thinking about what is political and have begun to document the far-reaching involvement of women in politics. This book emerges out of and contributes to such a reformulation. While we recognize that it is important to examine women's attempts to gain power within officially sanctioned political structures, and several chapters in this book do so, our focus is more broadly on strategies developed by women aimed at empowerment. Thus, while we want to explain why in some countries such as Norway, Mexico, or Canada women have been more successful than in other nations in making inroads into established government structures, our emphasis throughout is on nontraditional or alternative sources of strategies available to women in their struggles for empowerment, specifically, the women's culture, women's movements, and national liberation and development movements. Many of the strategies we have discovered are also not typically to be found in books and discussions of "traditional" politics. They include interpersonal networking, grass-roots economic development projects, protests of many kinds, use of traditional women's activities in the cause of national liberation, and involvement in nongovernmental and informal women's groups and organizations.

The definition of politics that we accept and use as a central idea in this volume is that politics includes people's everyday experiences of oppressive conditions, the recognition of the injustice of power differences, and the many and varied attempts to change power relationships at all societal levels. Our specific focus is on women in thirteen different countries and their struggles for empowerment, ranging from attempts to secure a constitutional equal rights amendment to the struggle to attain a measure of economic self-sufficiency in an impoverished village. Each of the chapters also aims to illuminate the various strategies used by women in the process of becoming empowered as well as to evaluate the relative effectiveness of those strategies.

The success or failure of any human endeavor is difficult to assess. By effective or successful strategies we refer to those political means used by women which have resulted in visible or tangible changes within a society, have increased the scope of women's activities, and have allowed a greater outlet for women's voices and views. This is not to say that any means will do as long as women become empowered. For instance, we consider peaceful means to be more effective than violent ones, although we acknowledge that in some cases (see, e.g., the chapter on Uganda) women may have no choice but to join men in an armed revolutionary struggle. Also, strategies which become oppressive of women or other groups cannot be successful by definition. Since empowerment is a process, it needs to be participatory and nondominating if it is to transform societies to include more persons in decision-making at all levels. Finally, while we generally support the strategy of getting more women into existing government structures, we recognize that not all variants of this strategy will be equally effective. For instance, while the election of a few more women to parliament or congress is likely to make no difference for the situation of females in a given society, the election of a substantial number of women supported by a strong women's movement outside the existing system is more likely to make it possible for women in government to speak out on behalf of their sex, to change existing laws in favor of women, and to legitimize the female perspective. (See the chapter on Norway.) While the first situation would exemplify an unsuccessful strategy, the second illustrates an effective means of empowering women.

The chapters in this book are grouped into three sections according to the different sources of strategies for political change and the empowerment of women. The first section focuses on women's culture or values, attitudes and interests which distinguish women as a group from men. Women's culture is a concept developed by feminist historians (see, e.g., Anderson and Zinsser, 1987; Arthur, 1976; Eckstein-Diener, 1965) and applied to the study of women's experience. Not all feminists, however, agree on the usefulness of this concept. Some find it problematic (see, e.g., Randall, 1987: 28–35; Ringelheim, 1985) and some reject it outright (e.g., Grimshaw, 1987). Nevertheless, many radical feminists in particular, recognizing the near-universal oppression of women by men, point to the fact that "women in practically all parts of the world, whether they are working outside the home or not, have responsibility for the cooking, cleaning and child 'raising' chores of the society. This in itself is a cultural split as men go out and mix mainly with other males in the male world outside the home" (Burris, 1973: 337–38). It is this basic division of labor between women and men which is typically used to explain the cultural differences between the sexes (Atkinson, 1970; Jaggar, 1983: 100–105), although some feminists suggest that it is women's biological childbearing function which underlies this split (Firestone, 1970; Rossi, 1977).

Whatever the causes of the cultural distinction between women and men (and I suspect that they are multiple and interactive), numerous studies conducted by radical feminists have shown that as a group, women compared to men tend to be relatively more caring or nurturing of others, to emphasize expressive aspects of relationships, to be cooperative and nonhierarchical (Chodorow, 1978; Gilligan, 1982; Lenz and Myerhoff, 1985; Belenky et al., 1987). Research done on traditionally defined political attitudes of women has shown women to be more supportive of world peace and opposed to nuclear armament than men (Baxter and Lansing, 1980; Brock-Utne, 1985; Randall, 1987; Scott, 1989). Studies on women in elective and appointed offices in the United States and the Scandinavian countries have shown them to be more likely than their male colleagues to take liberal, radical, and feminist stands on many public policy issues (Center for the American Woman and Politics, 1984; Skard and Haavio-Mannila, 1985).

Within this context of women's culture, the chapters in the first section of the book examine empowerment strategies developed by women in four different countries: Norway, the United States, Spain, and Japan. These strategies include electing a substantial number of women into public offices, developing informal networks and coalitions, drawing on existing women's groups and activities, as well as taking part in democratic transformation of public politics in a manner distinct from traditional political participation.

The second section in the volume focuses on women's groups, organizations, and ideologies outside the realm of conventional political structures, broadly termed "the women's movement." While the women's movement has been virtually worldwide, most students of the movement trace its roots and major activities, both in its first (nineteenth century) and second (late 1960s until the present) wave, to the Western countries, especially the United States and western and northern Europe (see, e.g., Banks, 1981; Evans, 1977; Melder, 1977; O'Neill, 1969). In recent years, however, new scholarship in the history of Third World women has revealed that Latin America, Asia, and Africa have had a long history of active and militant feminism as well as early movements for women's emancipation (see, e.g., Bhasin and Khan, 1986; Jayawardena, 1986; Croll, 1980). In this section, the chapter on the women's movement in Mexico contributes to this growing body of knowledge.

Significant differences exist within the women's movement between specific countries and areas of the world. For instance, while Great Britain, Italy, and the Scandinavian nations have had strong socialist feminist branches of the movement, in the United States socialist feminists have had much less influence within the movement (Hernes, 1984; Freeman, 1979). In the Third World, women's movements have been much more closely allied with nationalist and other social justice movements than have those in the West (Jayawardena, 1986). Despite differences, however, some general observations of the global women's movement are possible.

In countries where it exists, the women's movement typically consists of two branches: an established "older branch," which is made up of organizations that have become institutionalized and more or less accepted as the mouthpiece for women's rights; and a "younger," noninstitutionalized branch, made up of small, loose groups outside the mainstream (see, e.g., Bystydzienski, 1988; Freeman, 1979). The older branch usually tends to be ideologically liberal or moderate, essentially struggling for equal rights of women within the existing society. The organizations within this branch are also often, although not always, somewhat hierarchically structured, with some role specialization and formal rules. The younger branch is ideologically radical, aiming to transform existing societies along feminist principles. Its structure consists of small, local groups, often linked by informal networks, that eschew formal rules and individual leadership and prefer to arrive at decisions by consensus.

While the more established branch of the women's movement usually works within the system to change laws and public policies unfavorable to women, the younger branch typically focuses on building alternatives outside the existing system, for instance, cooperatives run and controlled by women including economic enterprises, women's shelters, health clinics, and daycare centers.

The chapters in the section on the women's movement as a source of political strategies explore the relationship between the two branches of the movement in Greece, Great Britain, and Mexico and the various strategies used by them, separately and together, in their struggles to empower women. These strategies range from traditional political forms such as petitioning and lobbying legislators to nontraditional ones such as consciousness-raising and building coalitions by drawing on existing women's networks and creating alliances with other movement organizations. The last chapter in the section compares the strategies used by women's movements in Canada and the United States in their attempts to obtain constitutional equal rights amendments. The only comparative chapter in this volume, it analyzes the different strategies used by women's movements in the two societies and, by placing them in larger societal contexts, shows why Canadian feminists were successful and their U.S. counterparts were not.

The third and last section of this book focuses on women's struggles for empowerment within societies which have long histories of external domination, war, and severe economic problems. Due to such conditions, women's concerns have not been given much attention, and any attempts at improving the status of women have had to deal with national priorities. Since the majority of men in these societies also experience oppression, it is difficult for women to present a case that they are particularly oppressed. On the other hand, as women join with men in struggles for liberation and economic empowerment, they typically discover that unless they find ways to secure their equal rights with men, male domination will continue both within the liberation movements and after the movements have achieved their goals (Jayawardena, 1986; Rogers, 1983).

The chapters in this section deal with five deeply troubled societies: Uganda, Palestine, Nicaragua, Poland, and India. In the case of the first three, national liberation movements are shown to be important sources of strategies for the empowerment of women. These chapters also illuminate the nontraditional political ways in which women contribute to these movements, most notably by drawing on existing women's activities, networks, and associations, and how a feminist consciousness emerges out of women's participation in national liberation movements. The chapter on Poland illustrates what happens when women's specific demands and interests are not included within a liberation movement like Solidarity. Not only have women found themselves left out of the process of creating the new order after the fall of the Communist regime, but the rights they had gained previously also are being threatened. The chapter on India focuses on grass-roots economic development as a source of women's empowerment. While the movement contributes to the national goal of economic improvement, it simultaneously provides women with increased status and changes the character of Indian village life toward becoming more self-sufficient and participatory.

In the conclusion to this volume, I compare the specific cases and countries and identify those conditions under which strategies for empowerment of women are more or less effective. In different societies, various strategies are available to women, some being particularly appropriate to circumstances existing at a given time. What may work in one society may not work in another at the same time or in the same society in a later period under different conditions. It is thus important to examine the combination of societal conditions and specific strategies which result in particularly successful empowerment of women. By undertaking this task in the concluding section, I hope not only to provide analytical cohesion to the book but also to make available to feminist activists some practical ideas for change involving women.

# Notes

1. In some preliterate societies such as the Tasaday of the Philippines and the Iroquois of North America, governance has been shared equally by men and women. In recent years, women have also achieved a considerable share of official governance in the Scandinavian countries, most notably in Norway.

2. Family-type relationships based on friendship rather than biological or marital links.

# WOMEN'S CULTURE

"Women's culture" has been a concept fraught with disagreement and misunderstanding. Yet, as the authors of the four chapters in this section show, it is an important idea to consider in relation to women and politics. There are a number of ways in which women's culture can be defined or approached. As Jill M. Bystydzienski and Susan J. Carroll point out in their respective studies of women's influence on public politics in Norway and the United States, indicators of women's culture are the issues and interests particularly relevant to women's lives as well as women's perspectives derived from their experiences as females living where the sexes are socialized differently and where institutional structures reinforce such differences. Another indicator is explored by Judith Astelarra in her chapter on Spanish women. She examines the particular nature of women's participation in the political realm and concludes that it is a different sort of participation from the traditional male type—it is unofficial, and thus often neglected, yet it has had a substantial impact on the institutional political process; it focuses also on issues and concerns of specific interest to women. Finally, Yuriko Ling, Azusa Matsuno, and Jill M. Bystydzienski show how in a highly sex-segregated society such as Japan a separate set of experiences and values are being drawn on by women in their attempts to change existing political institutions.

The four chapters discuss how women's culture has become an important source of strategies for women involved in struggles for empowerment. While each chapter focuses on somewhat different strategies appropriate to specific conditions of the countries under consideration, all of the authors appear to agree that a feminist consciousness is necessary for women's ways of thinking, organizing, and participating to have an impact on institutional politics and the empowerment of women. Bystydzienski and Astelarra show the importance of feminist movements in Norway and Spain in pushing forward a female political agenda and legislation favorable to women, while Carroll highlights the significance of feminist organizations which function as a link between women officeholders and women's interests. Ling, Matsuno, and Bystydzienski indicate that there is an awareness in Japan among the women who work to elect more women officeholders and the women thus elected that women politicians represent women's interests and perspectives.

The strategies derived from the women's culture include electing a substantial number of women into public offices (Norway, Japan), drawing on existing women's groups and activities (Spain, Japan), bringing specific women's issues and concerns before legislative bodies (Norway, United States, Spain, and Japan), creating and maintaining ties between women in public office and feminist activists (United States, Japan), and developing informal networks and coalitions based upon perceived common interests (Norway, Japan, Spain).

# INFLUENCE OF WOMEN'S CULTURE ON PUBLIC POLITICS IN NORWAY

## Jill M. Bystydzienski

Norway is one of few countries where women have attained a relatively high representation and participation in established government structures. In 1987, the head of government was a woman, women held 44 percent of the cabinet positions, 34 percent of all parliamentary seats, 31 percent of the seats on local councils, 30 percent of all places on governmental commissions and boards, and 32 percent of the positions on municipal commissions and boards (Førde and Hernes, 1988). A new government established in the fall of 1989, headed by a male prime minister, continued to have 44 percent women in the cabinet, while female representation in the Parliament rose slightly to 35 percent (Royal Norwegian Embassy, 1989: 57).[1] Norway, like other Scandinavian countries, has had a history of a substantially higher female representation in decision-making bodies than other Western nations (Van der Ros, 1986; Ås, 1979). However, the recent influx of women into the public political realm has been rather spectacular, tripling in number over a period of about two decades.

In this chapter, I examine first why and how women achieved such high levels of governmental representation, focusing on the conditions that facilitated this increase and the strategies used by women to attain greater representation. Subsequently, I discuss what the increase in female representation has meant in relation to the content of public politics and political discourse in Norway. I attempt to demonstrate that values as well as issues and concerns derived from female experiences and shared by women, which can be termed "women's culture," recently have had a significant impact on the political process in Norway.

### Why Women Obtained High Representation in Norway

Elsewhere (Bystydzienski, 1988), I have documented in some detail the recent influx of women into Norwegian decision-making bodies and the multiple causes of this phenomenon. Here, I shall summarize this only briefly in order to provide a background for the larger question, "can women in public office make a difference?"

Traditionally, access to public offices had been relatively easier for Norwegian women than entry into other spheres, such as paid labor or education. Scandinavian commitment to the values of equality and justice as well as a strong belief in the role of proportionally representative government as the equalizer of economic and social differences (Aubert, 1974) had helped women gain legitimacy for their demands to share political power with men. Moreover, a tradition of organizational involvement and participation in local decision-making bodies as well as relatively open governmental structures (e.g., large number of political parties, flexible electoral procedures, and lack of financial burdens for office candidates) have facilitated the entry of women into Norwegian public politics (Bystydzienski, 1988: 76–81). However, these factors can only partially account for the dramatic recent increase in women's representation—despite the longstanding existence of egalitarian values and participatory government, women began to enter Norwegian public offices in significant numbers only since the early 1970s. This change was related directly to the emergence of a strong women's movement and its concerted drive to get more women into decision-making bodies.

While political actions such as demonstrating, petitioning, lobbying, and attempting to influence public opinion were not new to Norwegian women activists during the 1960s and 1970s, the nature of such actions changed significantly. They became much more intensive, comprehensive, and effective. A larger number of women than ever before devoted a great deal of their time and energy to working together across party, class, and ideological lines, making direct use of the electoral and party systems to get more women elected into public offices. Several major actions took place between the years 1967 and 1981. The dramatic rise in female representation was a direct result of these efforts.

### How Greater Representation Was Achieved: A Focus on Strategies

The most effective, overarching strategy developed by Norwegian women activists during the 1960s and 1970s was the building of a strong coalition between two groups of major significance within the women's movement: women representing traditional women's organizations, "the establishment women," and the "new feminists." The establishment women came from such organizations as The Norwegian Association for the Rights of Women (*Norsk Kvinnesaksforening*) created in 1884, the National Council of Women of Norway (*Norske Kvinners Nasjonalråd*) established in 1905, Norwegian Women's Association (*Norsk Kvinneforbund*) founded during the 1950s, and women's sections in political parties. These organizations represented a longstanding tradition of fighting for sex equality by working within the established political system, were hierarchically structured, and were committed to reform. The new feminists departed from the traditional women's movement both ideologically and practically. They did not want merely equality with men in the existing system but desired to transform it along feminist principles. They organized themselves into nonhierarchical, horizontal structures with emphasis on small, autonomous groups. Rather than working within the system, the new feminists opted for developing alternative institutions such as women's shelters, childcare centers, and consciousness-raising groups.

Despite ideological and structural differences, the two strands of the women's movement in Norway quickly found many issues they could agree on (e.g., abortion, equal pay, treatment of rape victims, and pornography) and developed a mutually supportive relationship. While the new feminists brought forth radical criticisms of existing society's failure to achieve sex equality as well as proposing a fundamental reorganization of major institutions, the establishment women took these criticisms, couched in more "acceptable" terms, to the legislatures and pressed for equal status reforms.

The coalition between establishment women and new feminists developed gradually. At first, the two groups proceeded on parallel courses, one working within and the other outside the system. However, through informal networking and drawing on existing women's associations and groups, women from the two strands of the movement began to form closer links. As representatives of both groups worked more closely together, they came to regard formal political power as an area of priority for Norwegian women and collaborated extensively to elect more women. Eventually, the line between these two groups became blurred as new feminists began to enter public office and establishment women to assert that they did not want equality on men's terms (Førde and Hernes, 1988).

The coalition focused its energies and actions around major elections and used a number of specific tactics, some traditional and others nontraditional, to mobilize women to run for office and both women and men to vote for female candidates. During the latter part of the 1960s and early 1970s, Norwegian women activists concentrated on getting female candidates onto party ballots, teaching women voters how to use the ballot to elect more women,[2] and increasing public awareness of women's issues through public demonstrations and the media. After the mid-1970s, the establishment women and the new feminists created a tightly knit network of committees which worked on getting party nominations of female candidates and their placement in top positions on election ballots. Moreover, a concerted effort was made to develop policies catering to women's interests and to gain acceptance of such policies by political parties.

By the early 1980s, the Norwegian women's movement succeeded in not only getting more women into public offices but also in terms of incorporating a feminist agenda into the platforms of several political parties, as well as affecting some major legislation. The acceptance of sex quotas by the Liberal, Socialist Left, and the Labor Parties, the wording of major portions of the Equal Status Act in favor of women rather than in gender-neutral terms (discussed below in some detail), and changes in laws regarding parental leave are just a few examples of feminist influence.

By the mid-1980s, there appeared a growing consensus among Norwegian activist women that the concept and content of gender equality had to be redefined from women's inclusion in the world of men to changing the dominant ideology and public policy in accordance with women's interests and preferences. "We don't want equality at the behest of men and according to their rules" became a common expression among women of all organizations and political persuasions (Førde and Hernes, 1988: 27). Or, as a well-known Norwegian feminist and peace activist, Birgit Brock-Utne, is fond of saying, "We don't want a piece of the pie; we want to change the basic recipe of the pie." Changing "the pie" includes reconceptualizing and restructuring the major societal institutions according to feminist principles derived from women's experiences.

The Norwegian women's movement's ability to bring women's interests successfully into the public political forums and, in effect, to press for a redefinition and restructuring of the institution of politics owes a great deal to the movement's recognition of a distinct women's culture. Only when substantially larger numbers of Norwegian women found themselves in public offices, however, did women's values, interests, and preferences begin to find expression in political agendas, policies, and legislation. In the following sections, I examine the influence of the women's culture on Norwegian public politics.

### The Significance of a Larger Number of Women in the Public Political Arena

When considering the significant increase in female representation in decision-making bodies in Norway, the question that comes to mind is: Does wider women's representation and growing participation in the public sphere involve anything new or different? Although achieving the democratic principle of equal representation is in itself a cause worth striving for, does a more nearly equal ratio of women to men mean a change in the content and perhaps even the form of established politics?

There are a number of ways in which women as a group potentially can influence and change existing notions and practices in the public political sphere. They can make contributions in areas where their special experiences and abilities derive from their traditional roles, such as in family policies, education, and social welfare. They can focus on specific women's issues and directly promote the interests of women, for example, by working on and supporting childcare legislation or anti-pornography laws (Skard and Haavio-Mannila, 1985: 71). Moreover, as proponents of the women's culture tell us, women can approach issues from the female perspective, i.e., from their experiences as women living in contemporary society which often differ from male experiences (see, e.g., Belenky et al., 1987; Gilligan, 1982; Ruddick, 1988). Women's culture, which places value on cooperation, interdependence, caring, and expressive rather than instrumental relationships, may be able to transform the hierarchical structure of extant political institutions, making it more responsive to human needs, flexible, democratic, and personal (Ås, 1975; Lafferty, 1981: 156–67).

The mere appearance of women in decision-making positions does not guarantee that political change will take place. A handful of women in a predominantly male congress, parliament, or council usually makes little difference in policy-making priorities. Under such conditions, either women "succeed" in obtaining public positions because they act like male politicians, or if they express views reflecting women's interests, they find little support among their male colleagues (Carroll, 1985). However, once women in such institutions achieve a significant percentage of the total membership, they begin to have an impact on the political process.

It is difficult to say precisely when a larger number of women in public office begins to result in empowerment. However, based on the Norwegian case as well as research that has examined the effect of female representation on decision-making in various organizational settings, I have concluded that when female representation reaches at least 15 percent it begins to make a difference.

Yoder, Crumpton, and Zipp (1989) found that in U.S. academic departments where hiring committees consisted of between 16 to 35 percent women, more women faculty were hired than in departments with lower female representation. Studies by South et al. (1982), Spangler et al. (1978), and Yoder et al. (1983), showed that in groups where women composed less than 15 percent of the whole, women did not have enough power to influence group processes significantly. Kanter (1977) pointed out that in groups of between 15 and 30 percent women, minority members "have potential allies among each other, can form coalitions, and can affect the culture of the group" (Kanter, 1977: 209). My research on women in politics in Norway found that in the early 1970s, when women's representation passed the 15 percent mark, women's issues and perspectives began to gain increasing legitimacy at all governmental levels (Bystydzienski, 1987). Both female and male Norwegian politicians agreed that ever since more women found their way into political offices, female incumbents have felt freer to address women's issues, female perspectives have been given growing respect, and matters of special interest to women have been debated and legislated more often. The larger number of women representatives thus may facilitate the expression of women's values, issues, and interests. However, numbers alone may not be enough. Along with substantial representation, women need to be conscious of and to articulate their particular needs and abilities.

## From a Struggle for Gender Equality to a Reconceptualization of the Content and Concept of Equality and Politics

Norway has had a long tradition of well-organized women's groups pressing for gender equality. As early as 1905, Norwegian women's organizations arranged a petition supporting the dissolution of Norway's union with Sweden as an alternative referendum to an official one in which only men could vote (Agerholt, 1973). Norwegian women gradually attained the right to vote by first pressuring male authorities into allowing women to participate in elections to school supervising committees (1889), at municipal liquor referenda (1894), and at parochial school meetings (1903) (Skard and Haavio-Mannila, 1985: 38–39). While women in high income groups had the right to vote by 1901, by 1910 all Norwegian women succeeded in getting the vote in local elections, and by 1913 they became enfranchised in parliamentary elections. At each of these stages, women's organizations were instrumental in obtaining for Norwegian women the right to vote (Agerholt, 1973).

Norwegian women also struggled for increased representation in the public sphere. Beginning with areas where women were considered to have a particular mission by virtue of their traditional gender role, they first agitated for and gained the right to become members of boards of education, child welfare committees, and poor relief boards (Skard and Haavio-Mannila, 1985). Subsequently, Norwegian women's organizations began to press for electing women into government offices. Even though the percentages of women in local level offices did not reach the significant 15 percent mark until the 1960s, Norwegian women had higher representation at this level than did women in all other Scandinavian countries until the 1950s (Sinkkonen, 1985: 83). At the parliamentary level, women held only 1 or 2 percent of all seats from 1913 until 1945 and subsequently began to gain more and more seats, from 5 percent in 1954 to 9 percent in 1961 (Skard and Haavio-Mannila, 1985). Until the 1960s, women were virtually absent from Norwegian corporate committees, boards, and councils, but due to increased pressure from the women's movement, the percentages of women in these bodies began to grow and rose from 7 percent in 1965 to 27 percent in 1980 (Hernes and Hanninen-Salmelin, 1985: 111). Women's representation in the trade unions also increased gradually from 6 percent in 1945 to 32 percent in 1982 (Hernes and Hanninen-Salmelin, 1985: 125–26).

Until the early 1970s, the demands of women's groups who pushed for a greater representation of women in the public sphere centered on achieving gender equality within the existing system. Both the rationale used by spokespersons for the movement and legislation supported by movement women attest to this.

During both the 1930s and the 1950s, lively debates about sex roles and equality took place in Norway. They were popularized by a number of social scientists and activists (see, e.g., Myrdal and Myrdal, 1935; Holter, 1970; Klein and Myrdal, 1956; Skard, 1953). The focus of these debates was on whether women should be encouraged to enter the labor market before motherhood to get an economic foothold, to leave the market during childrearing years, and to be allowed to return to paid labor after their children became independent, or whether they should enter the labor market on equal terms with men (Førde and Hernes, 1988: 27). Women activists argued vehemently for women's right to have the same access to paid labor and to be paid the same wages as men.

Before the late 1950s, reforms ranging from allowing women to unionize to giving women access to traditionally male occupations were made at the municipal and county levels. In 1959, in response to increasing demands made by women's organizations, Norway established the Equal Pay Council (replaced in 1972 by the Equal Status Council) whose members (many of whom belonged to established women's organizations) drafted legislation regarding equal pay for women and men (Ministry of Consumer Affairs and Government Administration, 1985b: 1). Other legislation followed, couched in gender-neutral terms (Førde and Hernes, 1988). As one activist who had been involved for over fifty years in the attempt to gain equal rights for women in Norway stated,

We acted out of a deep conviction that women have a basic right to participate in society on the same footing as men. We wanted to see women in all areas of public life—government, industry, labor unions, all cultural institutions. We also wanted for women to have equal treatment once they entered these spheres. The Equal Pay Act was thus a first very important step. Later came legislation prohibiting sexual harassment and unequal treatment in general.[3]

A woman who had been a member of the Norwegian Women's Association, an organization particularly active during the 1950s and 1960s, had this to add,

We pressed for legislation stated in gender-neutral terms and wanted for it to be strictly enforced without reference to special circumstances of women. We believed that absolutely equal opportunity and treatment of women could only lead to women's emancipation. In retrospect, I think that we didn't realize that if women were not equal to men to start with, equal treatment was meaningless. First, we needed some pro-women changes before equal treatment could become a reality.

With the advent of the second wave of the women's movement and the appearance of new feminists, a gradual shift in activist women's demands began to take place. They started to question the idea of gender-neutral equality pointing out that what it really meant was the assimilation of women into a male-created and -dominated public realm on unequal terms. As a new feminist explained,

How can you talk about "equality" when women are being coopted into the men's world? When women go into organizations and agencies that are antithetical to their previous experience of how they relate to people and what they see as important and are asked to disregard that prior experience and relate to people like men do, that's equality? To me, and my sisters who were just waking up to this realization, equality meant something else; it meant the possibility of each group and person to be actively engaged in a society, to have a say in what that society is going to become. When a minority joins the dominant group on the dominant group's terms, that's not equality.

And a member of a traditional women's organization added:

> I became increasingly disillusioned with the idea of gender equality. As more women began to enter the economy and politics it became clear that we were not getting equal treatment and for many of us the experience of entering men's domains was literally a culture shock. Many of us didn't see the point of competition, of using others to get ahead, and other games that men play. If that's what equality was to be, we didn't want any of it.

Movement women thus increasingly sought an alternative to the dominant view of gender equality. The notion of a distinct women's culture became the source of this reconceptualization.

The idea of a distinct women's culture became increasingly popularized in the 1970s through the writing and public speeches of radical feminists. For instance, a prominent activist, professor, psychologist, and leader of the Socialist Left Party, Berit Ås, wrote and lectured extensively on the female culture as "a necessary counterpart to the highly visible male culture, which suppresses and exploits the female culture for its own purposes" (Ås, 1975: 142). Other activists as well, such as Eva Nordland, Birgit Brock-Utne, and Bett Romstad, seeking an alternative to the dominant views of equality, power, and politics, began to juxtapose their outlook to the predominantly male-dominated view of the world (Sheridan, 1988).

Radical women activists of the 1970s compared their perspective to the dominant way of thinking. They maintained that male-dominated thought is rooted in hierarchical public discourse which places emphasis on control and domination rather than cooperation and interdependence. While men's experiences lead them to channel information from the top of an organization or group downward, making simple matters complicated and isolating men from the realities of the world, women's experiences in the private realm lead them to a caring and interconnected sense of mutual responsibility with the people they live and work with (Sheridan, 1988: 45). Moreover, while men perceive power as capacity to control and dominate, women see it as a process through which people link their daily lives to actions that make their voices heard (Hartsock, 1981). Pointing to women's experiences with friendship relations (Ve, 1984), mothering and caring (Waerness, 1982), and informal networking (Sheridan, 1988), radical feminists attempted to create a different model of values and behavior appropriate not only to the personal but also to the public sphere. Thus it became increasingly common for Norwegian women activists to argue for the necessity of bringing female values and discourse into the public arena where it would offer a viable alternative. This argument was increasingly used as a rationale for getting more women into public offices. Since women had an alternative view of the world to offer, as a group they gave hope for transformation of society to a more democratic one. A well-known male Norwegian political scientist writing in the late 1970s about the relation-ship of the women's movement to the existing political power structure put it thus:

> The feminist movement now stands at a vital historical juncture, where the legal-administrative apparatus of the Norwegian polity has done everything necessary for a full cooptation of women and women's values. It would be tragic indeed if this cooptation into the male game of bargaining, manipula-tive power politics took place before women's values were fully developed into the alternative cultural form they give promise of: a form which both Norway and the industrial-technological world in general may well require for survival. (Lafferty, 1981: 162)

As Sheridan (1988) points out, the contrasting of female and male cultures became a major strategy of the Norwegian women's movement in its struggle to bring about social change favorable to women. By the end of the 1970s, women activists made important connections between feminism, ecology, and peace and brought their message of a distinct women's culture into other social movements (see, e.g., Brock-Utne, 1985; Rolfsen, 1977). As it entered the 1980s, the Norwegian women's movement offered an alternative view of equality in accordance with women's interests and a reconceptualization of power and politics in terms of empowerment of excluded groups. In the following sec-tion, I explore the effects of these paradigmatic changes on established public politics in Norway as a greater number of women entered public office.

### The Influence of Women's Culture on the Content of Public Politics in Norway

In 1978, the Norwegian Parliament adopted the Equal Status Act, the only legal provision of its type in the world because, unlike its counterparts in other countries, it is not neutral according to gender. The first paragraph of the document reads: "This Act shall promote equal status between the sexes and aims particularly at improving the position of women" (Ministry of Consumer Affairs and Government Administration, 1985a: 5). The Equal Status Act ac-knowledges what Norway's women's movement expressed during the 1970s: that it is not possible to achieve equal status between men and women merely by prohibiting discrimination. In order to rectify the discrepancies between the sexes measures need to be taken which will provide women with advan-tages in many areas. The Act also recognizes "that women may acquire certain special rights by reason of their . . . situation dictated by sex. By this is meant special rights in connection with pregnancy, childbirth and nursing" (Ministry of Consumer Affairs and Government Administration, 1985a: 8). This recog-nition of women's situation as different from men's and the incorporation of provisions allowing positive discrimination in favor of women into the Equal Status Act attest to the effectiveness of the women's movement in getting its views across to politicians and the general public.

While mere legal provisions in favor of women do not guarantee that they are carried out in practice, the establishment of an independent "Ombud" (or commissioner) office to enforce the provisions of the Equal Status Act has provided the possibilities for realization of such provisions.[4] Moreover, the Act has allowed for practices in favor of women in various areas, for example, the use of quotas in favor of women in the civil service, differential treatment in job placement and promotions, particularly in male-dominated occupations, and the reservation of places for women in courses, schools, and studies. In 1981, the Norwegian Parliament added another provision to the Equal Status Act aimed at increasing the number of women on all publicly appointed committees, boards, and councils (Ministry of Consumer Affairs and Government Administration, 1985b: 13). This has helped to increase significantly the percentage of women in such decision-making bodies.

The provisions of the Equal Status Act in favor of women helped to reinforce the already strong views of women activists regarding the special situation of women. Having attained some legitimacy for their views in the Act, they continued to press for further changes favorable to women. Thus by the mid-1980s, several political parties in Norway officially accepted sex quotas (at least 40 percent female and 40 percent male candidates in any election) while the rest did so "unofficially."[5] Despite huge spending cuts after the fall of North Sea oil prices, Norwegian government increased its emphasis on women and children. Childcare subsidies have grown, and paid parental leave was increased in 1987 from sixteen to eighteen weeks. Also parents can take off from work up to ten days each (single parents, twenty) for childcare-related crises (Overholser, 1987: 16).

The 1980s have also seen a strong campaign initiated by the women's movement toward creating a six-hour workday. Movement women argue that the shorter workday will allow both men and women to have more time for family, community, and leisure, and that it would be favorable to women by freeing men to do their share of household and childrearing tasks (Førde and Hernes, 1988: 30). The fact that this issue has been widely debated in Norway and has resulted in the government's appointment of a Commission on Working Hours and a growing public support for the six-hour workday (Førde and Hernes, 1988: 30) is an indicator of the effect of women's demands.

The growing responsiveness of the Norwegian government to the ideas expressed by activist women coincides with the increasing number of women in public offices. Thus as more women entered Parliament and county and municipal councils, they made it possible for women's issues, concerns, and values to be discussed, debated, and legislated more openly and frequently. Many of these women received their political training in the women's movement and were sympathetic to the views and demands of activist women. They thus took the feminist agenda developed by the movement into the public sphere of establishment politics, and there it has had a significant impact.

My research in 1986 indicated that women in public offices in Norway contributed to a change in the political agenda and to the climate in government (Bystydzienski, 1987). Once a significant number of women (filling at least 15 percent of the total number of positions) found their way into government, they began to raise women's issues and concerns. Skard (1980) found that from 1960 to 1975 the proportion of issues related to the legal, economic, and social position of women discussed in the Norwegian Parliament increased from 5 to 25 percent. Female representatives initiated over 90 percent of the discussion on these issues (Skard, 1980: 192).

The greater number of women in public office also has made possible the introduction of the female perspective into public issues. What this has meant is that female representatives have been more likely than their male counterparts to consider problems and changes in less abstract terms, focusing on how they affect people, people's relationships to one another, and their everyday lives. This approach to issues has been termed in Norway the "soft" approach as contrasted to the traditional male technical and abstract "hard" approach. Moreover, a growing number of women has also made it possible for both male and female politicians to act differently in respect to their private lives. Whereas fifteen years ago it would have been unheard of for a minister to excuse himself from a meeting because he had to pick up his child from a nursery school, today such an occurrence hardly raises an eyebrow (Overholser, 1987). There is a growing recognition among Norwegian politicians that public and private lives are not totally separate spheres and that how work activities are organized and what one does in public office affects her or his family and personal relationships.

The extent of transformation of the public political agenda, legislation, and atmosphere in public forums in Norway, while significant, should not be overestimated. Sexism and discrimination against women continue to exist in all spheres of life (Førde and Hernes, 1988) with the male perspective dominating the public domain (Sheridan, 1988). During its first three years in office, there was a mounting resentment of the Labor government headed by a female, Gro Harlem Bruntland, and her 44 percent female cabinet, by the more conservative parties. While the government came to power in an economic crisis which it did not create, it was often blamed for the worsening economic situation. I heard Norwegians use the economic crisis to argue that women in government did not make a positive difference. Nevertheless, the subsequent conservative government saw it fit to appoint a cabinet consisting of more than 40 percent women, and when the Labor government returned to power in 1990, led once again by Gro Harlem Bruntland, nine of the nineteen newly appointed cabinet members were women.

Given the presently difficult conditions in Norway, it would be unrealistic to expect that the larger number of women in decision-making bodies can transform public politics in a major way. In addition to economic problems faced by the country, which have led to increasing conservatism and limited experimentation, the structures within which the women must operate are well-entrenched and still largely male-dominated. However, despite these obstacles, women within the established political system and those outside pressing for change have begun to make headway. It may be several generations before more substantial change can take place, but Norwegian women have taken some significant steps in that direction.

## Conclusions

The relatively high number of women in public office in Norway, in addition to bringing the country closer to obtaining sex equality in governance, has also served to create a change in the content of the political agenda and legislation. Since the influx of larger numbers of women into public politics, women's issues, interests, values, and perspectives have become incorporated into political discourse and policy-making.

What the Norwegian case demonstrates is that the strategy of getting more women into public offices can make a difference provided their numbers are substantial enough (at least 15 percent of the total) and that the women entering public politics have an alternative agenda to offer. The importance of a strong women's movement which can articulate that agenda by drawing on women's experiences cannot be overestimated.

While the relative success achieved by Norwegian women in the public political sphere is indeed impressive and might lead feminists elsewhere to consider following their lead, a note of caution is in order. The strategies pursued by Norwegian women should not be generalized to all, or even most, societies. In those countries where access to public offices is relatively open and official ideologies espouse "equality," a well-organized women's movement can take advantage of such conditions to bring more women with a female agenda into the public political sphere. However, where access to government structures is denied to most people (women and men), women may need to pursue other strategies for empowerment.

## Notes

1. By October of 1990, the government resigned due to internal conflict over Norway's approach to the European Economic Community. A new Labor government, headed by the same woman who filled the post of prime minister from 1986 to 1989, Gro Harlem Bruntland, was constituted with a cabinet composed of nine women and ten men. Women's representation in the ruling government thus rose to 47 percent.

2. The Norwegian local electoral system allows for crossing out and writing in names on ballots. While this practice has become restricted somewhat in recent years, a widespread mobilization in the 1971 election to cross out male names and to write in women's names resulted in a landslide election of women in many municipalities (Bystydzienski, 1988: 85–87).

3. This and subsequent quotations come from a series of interviews I conducted in Norway in 1986. For a description of the study see Bystydzienski, 1988: 75–76.

4. It should be noted, however, that the Ombud does not initiate any actions; rather, she responds to complaints of individuals and groups and attempts to accomplish voluntary settlements. If this fails, cases can be submitted to the Equal Status Appeals Board, which is empowered to impose bans and require that measures are implemented (Førde and Hernes, 1988: 29).

5. The nonsocialist coalition, consisting of the Conservative Party, the Christian People's Party, and the Center Party, which came into power in 1989, in effect accepted the sex quota by appointing eight female cabinet members out of a total of eighteen.

# 2

# WOMEN STATE LEGISLATORS, WOMEN'S ORGANIZATIONS, AND THE REPRESENTATION OF WOMEN'S CULTURE IN THE UNITED STATES

## Susan J. Carroll

The reform-oriented wing of the women's movement in the United States has adopted the election of greater numbers of women to public office as a major goal. The election of women to office is viewed as one means for achieving public policy that is more consistent with the preferences of women and more reflective of the gender-specific problems women face.

While the election of greater numbers of women has been a major goal of at least one national feminist organization, the National Women's Political Caucus (NWPC), since its founding in 1971 (Carroll, 1975), the perceived importance of electing women into office increased throughout the 1980s and into the early 1990s. The increased emphasis on electing women to office to represent women has occurred in large part as a result of the failed effort to add the Equal Rights Amendment (ERA) to the U.S. Constitution and the proliferation of state-level legislation pertaining to abortion that took place following the U.S. Supreme Court decision in the *Webster* case.

As the battle to ratify ERA progressed, the National Organization for Women (NOW) and pro-ERA activists increasingly stressed the importance of electing women who were pro-ERA to state legislatures. While pro-ERA men were clearly viewed as preferable to anti-ERA men or women, pro-ERA women legislators were viewed as the safest choice for feminists. Because pro-ERA women legislators had a personal stake in the issue, feminists perceived them as less likely than pro-ERA men to bow to external pressure from constituents, party leaders, anti-ERA activists, or others who might encourage them to vote against the ERA.

In a similar fashion feminist organizations have stressed the importance of electing pro-choice women to office to represent women's interests in the post-*Webster* era. Some women candidates have also appealed to women voters on the basis of their shared concern for preservation of abortion rights. For example, when running against a male pro-choice candidate in the 1990 Democratic gubernatorial primary in California, candidate Dianne Feinstein argued that as a woman she would fight harder for abortion rights than would her opponent (*USA Today,* May 31, 1990, p. 3A).

Although the appeal is frequently made in feminist terms and focused on a single critical issue such as ERA or abortion, a more general assumption often underlies the efforts by feminist activists to elect more women. This assumption is that women officeholders will better represent women's interests on a variety of issues that affect women differently than they affect men. Women officeholders are perceived as more likely than men to represent what might be called "women's culture," which refers to the shared interests women have as a result of the sexual division of labor in society.

This chapter examines the validity of the feminist movement's assumption that the election of greater numbers of women to office will enhance the representation of "women's culture" and argues that women's networks and organizations, both inside government and outside, play a vital role in linking women officeholders to women's culture. Women's organizations and networks help to maintain and support the responsibility of women officeholders to represent women's shared interests and to act as an advocate on behalf of women within the institutions in which they serve.

## Women's Culture

Women's culture is an important, although much debated, concept (see, e.g., DuBois et al., 1980). The concept has its roots both in the historical study of nineteenth-century American society and in the theory and practice of contemporary radical/cultural feminism.

As women's historians investigated the lives of American women in the nineteenth century, they found evidence of resistance to male domination as well as evidence for the existence of close ties and relationships among women (e.g., Smith-Rosenberg, 1975; Cook, 1977; DuBois et al., 1980; Cott, 1977). Women's historians posited the existence of a women's culture, "a set of habits, values, practices, institutions, and a way of seeing the world common to large numbers of middle-class nineteenth-century women and distinct from the characteristic male perspective of the time" (DuBois et al., 1985: 56–57). As Gerda Lerner points out, the political importance of women's culture, whether in nineteenth-century American society or some other society, lies in the fact that it "is the ground upon which women stand in their resistance to patriarchal dominance and their assertion of their own creativity in shaping society" (DuBois et al., 1980: 53).

Within the context of contemporary American society, radical (or what some would label cultural)[1] feminists have also emphasized the idea of a separate women's culture. On the one hand, radical feminists view women's culture as a defining characteristic of patriarchal society. As Alison M. Jaggar observes, "According to radical feminists, the bifurcation between male and female experience means that every society in fact has two cultures—the visible, national, or male culture and the invisible, universal, female culture" (1983: 249). On the other hand, women's culture is perceived as an ideal to be achieved. While rejecting aspects of traditional women's culture that have kept women oppressed, many radical feminists want consciously to create a new "woman-culture" based on the positive values associated with traditional women's culture.

In referring to women's culture as something which women public officials may represent, I have been influenced by women's historians and radical feminists but am using the term in a way that differs in important respects from their conceptions. As employed by women's historians, the concept of women's culture is historically and culturally specific. It applies only to nineteenth-century America and arguably only to white, middle-class women in that society; it describes a society with a more discernible demarcation of gender roles and greater physical and emotional separation between the sexes than exist in contemporary American society.

The radical feminist conception of women's culture is problematic because it is generally rooted in an essentialist, often biologically based, notion of gender difference. Yet, gender differences are not fixed or static. They change over time in response to, and as a result of, changes in the sexual division of labor in society.

Moreover, both the historical and the radical feminist conceptions of women's culture have been criticized indirectly, if not directly, by women of color and others who suggest that conceptions based on the idea of a common, universal women's experience overlook diversity among women and leave out their experience (e.g., Moraga and Azaldua, 1981; Lorde, 1984: 114–23; Hooks, 1981). Neither the historical conception nor the radical feminist conception of women's culture seems sufficiently attentive to variations in the experiences of women from different races, classes, and sexual preferences.

While important differences certainly exist among women, there also must be commonality among women in order for there to be a basis for collective political action. The existence of commonality, however, need not be premised on an essentialist notion of woman nor on the assumption that the experiences of all women are the same. Rather, commonality may stem from the fact that women as socially constructed, gendered beings have certain shared interests resulting from their position in the sexual division of labor and the oppression they face even though the strength and nature of the sexual division of labor as well as the manifestations and circumstances of their oppression may vary considerably depending on race, class, sexual orientation, and other cultural differences. Women's shared interests, which can lead to common values, perspectives, and patterns of interaction, define "women's culture" as used in this chapter.

## Women's Organizations and Networks: Institutions That Link Women Officeholders to Women's Culture

The work of Estelle Freedman demonstrates the importance of women's organizations and networks, what she calls a "strong, public female sphere" (1979: 513), in forging a link between women in male-dominated institutions and women's culture. Although her work examines the relationship between women's culture, feminism, and women's organizations in the United States in the period from 1870 to 1930, it suggests that women's organizations in the contemporary era may play a critical role in helping to insure that women who move into the male-dominated sphere of public officeholding actively represent the shared interests of women.

Freedman argues that decline of feminism in the decades after suffrage was won in 1920 can be explained in part by the decline of separate women's organizations. The attempt by women to assimilate into male-dominated institutions without simultaneously maintaining separate female institutions left them without a base from which to push for greater equality for women. Consequently, their hopes of achieving equality were undermined. As Freedman observes, "they lost the momentum and the networks which had made the suffrage movement possible. Women gave up many of the strengths of the female sphere without gaining equally from the man's world they entered" (1979: 524).

Freedman argues that like the women of earlier decades, women in our time who are entering male-dominated institutions also need access to a separate and alternative women's community to sustain their participation and to enable them to push for gains for women. She concludes:

> [I]t is . . . important for the women within mixed institutions to create female interest groups and support systems. Otherwise, token women may be coopted into either traditionally deferential roles, or they will assimilate through identification with the powers that be. In the process, these women will lose touch with their feminist values and constituencies, as well as suffer the personal costs of tokenism. (1979: 525)

Freedman's work suggests that women in public office, or indeed in any male-dominated institution, who are involved with women's organizations outside or inside government will be more likely than other women and men to represent women's culture and to be advocates on behalf of women. This expectation is examined in this chapter with data from a study of women and men serving in state legislatures throughout the United States.

### Description of the Data Set and Status of Women in State Legislatures

In the summer of 1988 under a grant from the Charles H. Revson Foundation, the Center for the American Woman and Politics (CAWP) conducted a nationwide survey of women and men serving as state legislators. Four samples of legislators were drawn: (1) the population of women state senators (N = 228); (2) a systematic sample of one-half of women state representatives (N = 474); (3) a systematic sample of male state senators, stratified by state and sampled in proportion to the number of women from each state in our sample of women state senators (N = 228); and (4) a systematic sample of male state representatives, stratified by state and sampled in proportion to the number of women in each state in a sample of women state representatives (N = 474). A telephone interview of approximately one-half hour in duration was attempted with each of the legislators, resulting in the following response rates: 86 percent for female senators; 86 percent for female representatives; 60 percent for male senators; and 73 percent for male representatives. Respondents did not significantly differ from all the legislators selected for any of the four samples in their party affiliation, the one variable for which data are available for all legislators.

The study focused on women in state legislatures because state legislatures are the highest level of elective office in the United States where significant numbers of women serve. As of October 1990, women held only thirty-one, or 5.8 percent, of all seats in both houses of the U.S. Congress; only two of the thirty-one women members of Congress served in the U.S. Senate. Only three of the fifty states had women governors, and four had women lieutenant governors. By contrast, 1,273, or 17.1 percent, of the 7,461 state legislators serving throughout the country in 1990 were women. The proportion of state legislative seats held by women ranged from a low of 2.1 percent in Louisiana to a high of 33.3 percent in Vermont (Center for the American Woman and Politics, 1990).

### Women Legislators as Representatives of Women's Culture

Women legislators can represent women's culture through their attention to concerns that have disproportionately become the responsibility of women as a result of the sexual division of labor in American society. Caring for children and caring for the sick and the elderly are two examples of such concerns. While women are not all equally involved in these activities and while some women are less involved than some men, nevertheless women in the aggregate bear more of the societal responsibility for the care of these groups than men do.

Women legislators can also represent women's culture through their actions to end the discrimination and inequities that women face in American society. Women can be considered to have shared interests in alleviating inequities and oppression resulting from their position in the sexual division of labor.[2]

The CAWP survey asked legislators to describe the one bill that had been their own personal top priority for the current legislative session.[3] Of the sixteen content areas into which responses were coded, three were areas where

TABLE 2.1:
**Major Gender Differences in Top-Priority Issues for State Legislators**

|  | State Senate | | State House | |
|---|---|---|---|---|
|  | Women % | Men % | Women % | Men % |
| Women's issues[a] | 9.7 | 3.6 | 8.8 | 2.9 |
|  | $tau_b$ = .12 | | $tau_b$ = .12 | |
|  | $p < .05$ | | $p < .001$ | |
| Health care issues | 15.4 | 8.8 | 14.9 | 6.6 |
|  | $tau_b$ = .10 | | $tau_b$ = .13 | |
|  | $p < .05$ | | $p < .001$ | |
| Children's welfare issues | 5.1 | 0.7 | 6.8 | 3.7 |
|  | $tau_b$ = .12 | | $tau_b$ = .07 | |
|  | $p < .05$ | | $p < .05$ | |
| N = | (195) | (137) | (410) | (348) |

[a]The proportions reported here are for legislators whose top-priority bill seemed feminist in intent. If one also adds the few legislators whose top-priority bill focused on women but seemed anti-feminist in intent, the corresponding proportions are 9.7% for women state senators, 5.1% for men state senators, 9.3% for women state representatives, and 3.2% for men state representatives.

women were significantly more likely than men to have top-priority legislative concerns (Table 2.1). Two of these areas, health care and children's welfare,[4] represent spheres where women have borne disproportionate societal responsibility. Because of the sexual division of labor in American society, women traditionally have been involved more than men both in rearing children and in caring for those who because of illness or age cannot care for themselves. While only a small minority of women legislators had top-priority bills in either of these areas, nevertheless proportionately more women gave top priority to legislation on health care than to legislation in any other content area.

The third area where women were significantly more likely than men to have top-priority legislative concerns was in the area of women's issues (Table 2.1). Women were notably more likely than men to report that a bill focusing on women was their top legislative priority; almost one-tenth of the women legislators gave top priority to legislation on issues such as domestic violence, childcare, equal rights, abortion, teen pregnancy, and parental leave. Only a negligible minority of legislators, whether women or men, who had a women's issue as their top priority appeared to be working on the issue from an antifeminist perspective (Table 2.1, note a); rather, almost all were working to expand women's opportunities or to protect their rights.

In addition to questions about their personal top-priority legislation, legislators were asked whether they had worked on *any* legislation during the current session where the bill itself or a specific provision of the bill was intended to help women in particular. Majorities of the women, and much larger proportions of the women than the men in both houses of the legislature, worked on legislation to benefit women (Table 2.2). Based on responses to

TABLE 2.2:
Gender Differences in Proportions of State Legislators Who Worked on
Legislation to Help Women[a]

|  | State Senate | | State House | |
| --- | --- | --- | --- | --- |
|  | Women % | Men % | Women % | Men % |
| Worked on legislation to help women | 60.0 | 39.4 | 55.4 | 33.3 |
| N= | (195) | (137) | (410) | (348) |
|  | tau$_b$ = .20 | | tau$_b$ = .22 | |
|  | p<.001 | | p<.001 | |

[a]The proportions presented in this table exclude legislators who could not describe how the legislation helped women, or who described a bill that was aimed at helping children but did not seem to benefit women directly. Also excluded are the .5% of women senators, no men senators, 1.5% of women representatives, and 2.0% of men representatives who described bills that were anti-feminist in intent.

this question, large proportions of women legislators can be considered to act as advocates on behalf of women.

### Women's Organizations Outside and Inside the Legislature

Women legislators potentially could be involved with a wide range of women's organizations. There is, indeed, in Estelle Freedman's terms, a "strong, public female sphere" (1979: 513) in contemporary American society that could forge a link between women's culture and women legislators.

Several types of organizations with relevance for women legislators can be considered part of this contemporary "public female sphere." First are the traditional, public-service-oriented membership organizations such as the League of Women Voters (LWV) and the American Association of University Women (AAUW). Naomi Black argues that some of these traditional women's organizations, and the LWV in particular, represent a point of view she labels "social feminism . . . whose most important characteristic is a focus on values and experience identified with women" (1989: 1). Organizations such as the LWV "share . . . a view of women as valuable because [they are] different" and "derive a public role for women from the private role of women" (1989: 3).

Next are the various membership organizations that have developed as part of the contemporary feminist movement; these groups aim to end the inequities women face in American society. Some of these feminist organizations, especially the National Women's Political Caucus (NWPC) and the National Organization for Women (NOW), are active in electoral politics.

In recent years a number of political action committees (PACs) have been created at both national and state levels to provide financial assistance to women candidates. As of 1989, CAWP was able to identify thirty-five PACs that gave money predominantly to women candidates and/or had a predominantly female donor base. While some of these PACs are partisan, many give money to women of both parties. Seventeen of these PACs provided CAWP with information about direct financial contributions made to candidates in 1988; these seventeen PACs contributed a total of $1,139,315 to women candidates (Center for the American Woman and Politics, Winter 1989: 16–20).

At least three national organizations exist specifically for women state legislators—the National Order of Women Legislators (NOWL), the National Organization of Black Elected Legislative Women (NOBEL/Women), and the Women's Network of the National Conference of State Legislatures. These organizations all meet at least once a year and bring women legislators together around shared concerns. The NOWL has a membership of approximately 450 current and former state legislators. All black women state legislators are members of NOBEL/Women. Similarly, all women legislators are members of the Women's Network by virtue of their state's membership in the National Conference of State Legislators. The NOBEL/Women and the Women's Network focus some of their activities on important issues of concern to their members. For example, NOBEL/Women, which chooses one legislative issue to highlight each year, focused in 1989 on at-risk youth while the Women's Network has concentrated its attention on issues such as women's health, leadership training, and gender balance in appointments to state boards and commissions (Center for the American Woman and Politics, Spring 1989: 18–19).

In addition to the many women's organizations that exist outside the state legislature, women in a significant number of states have also organized inside their legislatures. As of early 1989, at least ten states—California, Connecticut, Illinois, Iowa, Louisiana, Maryland, Massachusetts, New York, North Carolina, and Rhode Island—had formal women's caucuses within their legislatures. While these caucuses allow women to socialize and to receive support from one another, members of the caucuses also work together on legislative issues of mutual concern. Most of these issues focus on women's rights, children, the family, and caring for economically or otherwise disadvantaged groups in society. For example, in 1989 the Illinois caucus had as its top priorities enhancing business opportunities for women and minorities, legalizing birthing centers, certifying midwives, and studying the high incidence of cesarean sections. In the same year, the Maryland caucus focused on childcare, domestic violence, and poverty. The New York caucus had as its top priorities a family support act, welfare reform, and prenatal care. In Iowa, the major concerns of the caucus for 1989 were a minimum wage increase, gender discrimination in insurance, and expansion of childcare options. Finally, in Connecticut the women's caucus focused on teen pregnancy, infant mortality, and abolishing the use of mandatory lie detector tests for victims of rape (Center for the American Woman and Politics, Spring 1989, pp. 20–22; Center for the American Woman and Politics, Winter 1989, pp. 14–16). In some states where there are no formal women's caucuses, women legislators meet together informally (Mueller, 1984).

## Evidence of Strong Ties between Women Legislators
## and Women's Organizations

Given the wide range and large number of women's organizations with which women legislators could potentially be involved, one might expect to find strong patterns of connection between women legislators and women's organizations. Indeed, this is the case. A majority of the women legislators in the CAWP study had close ties to women's organizations both outside and inside the legislature.

We asked women legislators whether they were members of two specific feminist organizations (NOW and NWPC), whether they were members of any other feminist organization, and whether they belonged to three major but more traditional women's organizations. (LWV, AAUW, and BPW). A large majority—74.4 percent of women state senators (N = 195) and 72.4 percent of women state representatives (N = 410)—were members of at least one of these various women's groups. The LWV was the organization with the largest proportion of women state legislators as members; about two-fifths of both state senators and state representatives reported that they belonged to the League (Table 2.3). However, all the women's groups fared well, with proportions ranging from one-fifth to two-fifths of women legislators reporting membership in each of the specific groups. Moreover, proportions of legislators belonging to feminist organizations such as the NOW and the NWPC were similar to the proportions belonging to more traditional organizations such as the AAUW (Table 2.3).

However, the ties between women legislators and women's organizations external to the legislature extend beyond mere membership. Furthermore, there is evidence that the ties run in both directions—from legislators to organizations and from organizations back to legislators. In order to measure a level of commitment that went beyond simple membership in women's organizations, we asked legislators if they donated any money (other than dues) to women's groups during the past year.[5] Sizeable majorities, 67.0 percent of women state senators (N = 188) and 60.2 percent of women state representatives (N = 394), reported that they made a financial contribution to at least one women's organization.

Just as most women legislators contribute to women's organizations, most also receive campaign assistance from women's groups. Proportions roughly equal to the proportions reporting that they gave money to women's groups— 67.2 percent of women state senators (N = 195) and 59.3 percent of women state representatives (N = 410)—received either formal or informal support from one or more women's organizations during their most recent election. About one-third of women state senators and about one-fourth of women state representatives reported that they received assistance from NOW, one of the two feminist organizations most active in electoral politics. Virtually equal proportions of women legislators received support from the NWPC, the other major feminist organization that is active in electoral politics (Table 2.4).

TABLE 2.3:
Proportions of Women State Legislators Who Reported Membership in
Various Women's Organizations

|  | Women State Senators[a] % | Women State Representatives[b] % |
|---|---|---|
| League of Women Voters (LWV) | 43.2 | 39.2 |
| American Association of University Women (AAUW) | 20.7 | 20.9 |
| Business and Professional Women (BPW) | 39.4 | 27.9 |
| National Organization for Women (NOW) | 22.1 | 22.6 |
| National Women's Political Caucus (NWPC) | 31.6 | 29.5 |
| Feminist organization other than NOW or NWPC | 24.7 | 24.4 |

[a] Ns range from 187 to 193.
[b] Ns range from 401 to 406.

Women legislators have close ties to women's groups inside as well as outside the legislature. At the time of the CAWP survey, more than two-fifths of
women state senators and one-half of women state representatives reported
that a formal women's caucus existed in their legislature (Table 2.5). Of those
who reported the existence of a caucus in their state, 78.8 percent of the state
senators (N = 85) and 78.0 percent of the state representatives (N = 214) said
they attended meetings of the caucus.

Many of the women who were in legislatures where there was no formal
women's caucus nevertheless reported that women in their legislatures met

TABLE 2.4:
Proportions of Women State Legislators Receiving Campaign Support from
Various Women's Organizations

|  | Women State Senators % | Women State Representatives % |
|---|---|---|
| Received support from: | | |
| National Organization for Women (NOW) | 32.8 N = (186) | 22.8 N = (400) |
| National Women's Political Caucus (NWPC) | 32.6 N = (190) | 29.2 N = (394) |
| Women's organization other than NOW or NWPC | 55.9 N = (188) | 50.0 N = (398) |

TABLE 2.5:
Proportions of Women State Legislators Who Report That
Meetings of Women Take Place in Their Legislature

|  | Women State Senators % | Women State Representatives % |
| --- | --- | --- |
| Women in legislature meet formally or informally | 75.9 N = (195) | 79.5 N = (410) |
| Formal women's caucus exists in legislature | 44.3 N = (194) | 53.0 N = (404) |

together informally. Sometimes these informal meetings included women of both parties; sometimes they were partisan in nature. When asked about informal as well as formal ways of getting together, about three-fourths of women legislators reported that women in their legislatures met together. Most of the women legislators who were aware of these gatherings were also participants in them; 81.8 percent of the state senators (N = 148) and 81.3 percent (N = 326) of the state representatives who reported that women in their legislature met together also reported that they themselves attended the meetings.

### The Link between Involvement in Women's Organizations and the Representation of Women's Culture

Significant proportions of women legislators do seem to represent women's culture in their legislative work. Similarly, large proportions of women legislators are involved with women's organizations. But is there a relationship between these two sets of findings? Are the women legislators who are involved with women's organizations the same ones who are acting as representatives of women's culture? Is there evidence that the connections between women legislators and women's organizations may be enhancing the representation of women's shared interests?

Table 2.6 presents data relevant to answering these questions. The table shows differences between women legislators who were connected to women's organizations and those who were not, with regard to the focus of their top-priority bill and their work on legislation to help women.

Examining first differences between women who were and were not involved with women's organizations in the proportions whose top-priority legislation focused on health care, mixed evidence is found for the idea that involvement in women's organizations may lead to enhanced representation of women's culture. Among state senators, women who were connected in various ways to women's organizations were no more likely than women who were not to have a health care issue as their top legislative priority. The only statistically significant difference occurs between women senators who did and did not get together with other women in their legislature, but contrary to expectations, those senators who did not meet with other women in their legislature were more likely to have health care as a top priority than were legislators who did meet with other women.

Among state representatives, there is somewhat more evidence of a connection between being involved with women's organizations and giving top priority to legislation on health care. Although the differences are not large, women state representatives who were members of feminist organizations, who received campaign support from a women's organization generally or a feminist organization more specifically, and who met with other women in their legislature were significantly more likely than other women state representatives to have a health care issue as their top legislative priority.

Turning to children's welfare as a top-priority issue, mixed evidence is again found for the idea that involvement in women's organizations may lead to increased representation of women's culture. While differences are again small, women state senators who received campaign support from a women's organization or from a feminist organization were more likely than other women state senators to have a children's welfare issue as their top priority. Similarly, women state representatives who were members of a feminist organization, who donated money to a women's group, or who met with other women in their legislature were slightly more likely than other women to give priority to legislation focusing on children. However, on several measures of legislators' connections to women's organizations, legislators who were involved with women's organizations do not differ significantly from those who were not involved with women's organizations in giving top priority to either health care or children's welfare legislation (Table 2.6).

Examining women's issues as top-priority legislation, the evidence is somewhat more compelling, but still somewhat mixed, as to whether connections to women's organizations facilitate the representation of women's culture. Women state senators who were members of a feminist organization, who donated money to a women's group, and who received campaign support from a women's organization or a feminist organization were significantly more likely than other women senators to have a women's issue as their top priority. Similarly, women state representatives who were members of a traditional women's organization, who belonged to a feminist group, who received campaign support from a women's organization or from a feminist group, and who met with other women in their legislature were more likely to give top priority to legislation focusing on women's rights. However, women senators who belonged to traditional women's organizations or who met with other women in their legislature were not significantly more likely than other women senators to have a women's issue as their top priority. The same was true of women representatives who donated money to a women's organization (Table 2.6).

While the evidence for a relationship between involvement with women's organizations and the representation of women's culture as measured by leg-

TABLE 2.6:
**Proportions of Women State Legislators Involved in Various Ways with Women's Organizations Who Represented Different Aspects of Women's Culture**

| | Member of a Traditional Women's Organization[a] % | Not a Member of a Traditional Women's Organization % | Member of a Feminist Organization % | Not a Member of a Feminist Organization % | Donated Money to a Women's Organization % | Did Not Donate Money to a Women's Organization % |
|---|---|---|---|---|---|---|
| *Women State Senators* | | | | | | |
| Health care issue as top priority | 13.2 | 19.7 | 16.3 | 14.6 | 15.1 | 16.1 |
| | $tau_b = -.09$ | | $tau_b = .02$ | | $tau_b = -.01$ | |
| Children's welfare issue as top priority | 4.7 | 6.1 | 6.5 | 3.9 | 5.6 | 1.6 |
| | $tau_b = -.03$ | | $tau_b = .06$ | | $tau_b = .09$ | |
| Women's issue as top priority | 10.9 | 7.6 | 14.1 | 5.8 | 13.5 | 3.2 |
| | $tau_b = .05$ | | $tau_b = .14**$ | | $tau_b = .16**$ | |
| Worked on bill to help women | 65.9 | 48.5 | 70.7 | 50.5 | 69.8 | 40.3 |
| | $tau_b = .17**$ | | $tau_b = .21***$ | | $tau_b = .28***$ | |
| | N = (129) | (66) | (92) | (103) | (126) | (62) |
| *Women State Representatives* | | | | | | |
| Health care issue as top priority | 14.5 | 15.3 | 17.3 | 12.4 | 14.8 | 16.6 |
| | $tau_b = -.01$ | | $tau_b = .07*$ | | $tau_b = .02$ | |
| Children's welfare issue as top priority | 8.1 | 5.1 | 8.7 | 5.0 | 8.0 | 3.8 |
| | $tau_b = .06$ | | $tau_b = .07*$ | | $tau_b = .08**$ | |
| Women's issue as top priority | 10.3 | 6.8 | 11.5 | 5.9 | 9.7 | 7.0 |
| | $tau_b = .06$ | | $tau_b = .10**$ | | $tau_b = .05$ | |
| Worked on bill to help women | 63.2 | 44.9 | 63.5 | 47.0 | 62.9 | 44.6 |
| | $tau_b = .18***$ | | $tau_b = .17***$ | | $tau_b = .18***$ | |
| | N = (234) | (176) | (208) | (202) | (237) | (157) |

$*p < .10$    $**p < .05$    $***p < .01$    $****p < .001$
[a]Traditional women's organizations are defined as the League of Women Voters, the American Association of University Women, and Business and Professional Women.

islators' top-priority legislation is modest and somewhat inconsistent, the existence of even modest and inconsistent evidence may in this instance be viewed as a positive sign. An analysis of legislators' top-priority bills for a single session undoubtedly underestimates the extent to which legislators are involved with legislation in the areas of health care, children's welfare, or women's issues. A single legislative session is a mere snapshot in time, and legislators' top priorities may well vary from session to session. Thus, over the course of several legislative sessions, one would surely find larger proportions of legislators giving priority to health care, children's welfare, and women's issues, and consequently, over a longer time frame one might well find a stronger relationship

| Received Campaign Support from a Women's Organization % | Did Not Receive Campaign Support from a Women's Organization % | Received Campaign Support from a Feminist Organization % | Did Not Receive Campaign Support from a Feminist Organization % | Attends Meetings of Women in Legislature % | Does Not Attend Meetings of Women in Legislature % |
|---|---|---|---|---|---|
| 14.5 | 17.2 | 14.3 | 16.2 | 12.4 | 20.3 |
| $tau_b = -.03$ | | $tau_b = -.03$ | | $tau_b = -.10*$ | |
| 6.9 | 1.6 | 8.3 | 2.7 | 5.8 | 4.1 |
| $tau_b = .11*$ | | $tau_b = .13**$ | | $tau_b = .04$ | |
| 12.2 | 4.7 | 13.1 | 7.2 | 10.7 | 8.1 |
| $tau_b = .12**$ | | $tau_b = .10*$ | | $tau_b = .04$ | |
| 70.2 | 39.1 | 76.2 | 47.7 | 70.2 | 43.2 |
| $tau_b = .30****$ | | $tau_b = .29****$ | | $tau_b = .27***$ | |
| (131) | (64) | (84) | (111) | (121) | (74) |
| 17.3 | 11.4 | 20.1 | 12.0 | 17.4 | 10.3 |
| $tau_b = .08**$ | | $tau_b = .11**$ | | $tau_b = .09**$ | |
| 6.2 | 7.8 | 5.6 | 7.5 | 9.4 | 2.1 |
| $tau_b = -.03$ | | $tau_b = -.04$ | | $tau_b = .14***$ | |
| 10.3 | 6.6 | 12.5 | 6.8 | 10.2 | 6.2 |
| $tau_b = .06*$ | | $tau_b = .10**$ | | $tau_b = .07*$ | |
| 60.1 | 48.5 | 62.5 | 51.5 | 61.1 | 44.8 |
| $tau_b = .11**$ | | $tau_b = .11**$ | | $tau_b = .16***$ | |
| (243) | 167) | (144) | (266) | (265) | (145) |

between involvement in women's organizations and these measures of the representation of women's culture.

Because the measures discussed so far focus on a single priority in a limited time frame, the final measure in Table 2.6—whether legislators worked on any legislation during the current legislative session aimed at helping women—may be the best measure of the representation of women's culture. This measure has the disadvantage of not tapping into concerns such as health care and children's welfare, which have traditionally fallen disproportionately on women's shoulders, and it is still limited to a single legislative session. Yet, it is broad enough to include all the legislation on which a state senator or representative might work during that session. Thus, it reflects a much broader spectrum of a legislator's work and potential impact than does his or her top-priority legislation.

When working on legislation to help women is examined as a measure of the representation of women's culture, the evidence for a relationship between women legislators' involvement with women's organizations and their representation of women's culture is both clear and consistent. For every measure of involvement with women's organizations included in Table 2.6, women legislators who were connected to women's organizations are much more likely than other women legislators to have worked on legislation intended to help women. Women senators and representatives who were members of traditional women's organizations, who were members of feminist groups, who donated money to a women's organization, who received campaign support from a women's group or a feminist group, and who met with other women in their legislature were all significantly more likely than other women senators and representatives to have worked on legislation to help women. Women senators and representatives who were not connected in various ways to women's organizations were only slightly more likely than men (see Table 2.2) to have worked on such legislation. By contrast, women senators and representatives who were involved in various ways with women's organizations were considerably more likely than men (see Table 2.2) to have worked on legislation to help women.

## Discussion and Conclusions

The feminist movement in the United States seems to be correct in its assumption that the election of greater numbers of women to office can be an effective means for increasing the representation of "women's culture," defined as women's shared interests. Most women state legislators do work on legislation aimed at helping women, and proportionately more women than men legislators place top priority on legislation dealing with women's issues, health care issues, and children's welfare issues.

Moreover, most women legislators are involved with women's organizations both external and internal to the legislature. Most women legislators belong to women's organizations outside the legislature, donate money to women's organizations, and receive support from women's organizations when they run for office. Most also meet with other women in their legislature, whether on a formal or informal, partisan or bipartisan, basis. A sizeable minority of women legislators have close connections to feminist groups in particular. They belong to organizations such as NOW and NWPC, and they receive support from these groups when they campaign for office.

Perhaps most important, it is the women legislators who are involved with women's organizations who are most active in representing women's culture in their legislative work. These women are notably more likely than men and than other women to work on legislation aimed at helping women. There also is some evidence, although weaker, that they are more likely to have women's issues, children's welfare issues, and health care issues as their top legislative priorities.

These findings suggest that one of the reasons women's organizations are correct in their assumption that women officeholders more often than men will represent women's culture is that women's organizations help to make this assumption true. Although not commonly recognized, women's organizations seem to function as an important linkage mechanism in representation, connecting women officeholders to other women and to women's interests. In the absence of close ties to women's organizations, it seems unlikely that large proportions of women officeholders would be active advocates on behalf of women and women's culture. As the work of Estelle Freedman reminds us, the pressures toward assimilation and conformity with existing norms are great for those women who move into male-dominated institutions. Women in male-dominated institutions are likely to be able to resist such pressures only if they have alternative arenas in which their identities as women can be validated. Women's organizations, especially feminist groups, provide affirmation and sustenance for women officeholders; they also function as a conscience for these women, providing sometimes subtle, and sometimes not so subtle, reminders that they have a responsibility to represent women's interests within the institutions in which they serve.

It is important for feminists, and for others who are concerned with securing public policy that is more responsive to women's needs, to maintain ties with women who are elected to public office. All too often feminists point to women such as Margaret Thatcher and Indira Gandhi, focusing on the exceptions rather than the norm, and conclude that they should put their energies elsewhere. However, the findings of this chapter suggest that feminists and feminist organizations should cultivate relationships with women officeholders. Creating and maintaining ties between women public officials and other women or women's groups may be one of the more effective strategies for achieving public policies that reflect women's interests.

# Notes

1. Echols, 1989, for example, argues persuasively that by the mid-1970s radical feminism had been supplanted by cultural feminism, which turned away from politics and social transformation and emphasized instead the creation of a female counterculture and personal transformation.

2. Of course, not all women perceive that they have a shared interest in ending inequities. In fact, while they may perceive a sexual division of labor in society, some women (especially anti-feminists) believe that there is nothing inequitable about this division of labor and deny that women are oppressed. Phyllis Schlafly (1977) is a good example of this point of view. Others (see, e.g., Jaggar, 1983: 149–55) argue that those who share Schlafly's views suffer from false consciousness.

3. See Carroll and Taylor, 1989, for a more extensive discussion of responses to this question and other survey results presented in this section of the chapter.

4. In classifying top legislative priorities, health care initiatives targeted specifically at women were placed in the "women's issue" category. Similarly, legislation dealing with both women and children that would primarily benefit women (e.g., childcare) was placed in the "women's issue" category. The "children's welfare issue" category consists of those issues (e.g., child abuse, foster care) where the primary beneficiary seemed to be children.

5. The survey could have asked about participation in the activities of women's organizations. However, legislators' officeholding responsibilities generally leave them with far less time to give to outside activities than is true for most citizens. By contrast, legislators' officeholding activities do not interfere with their ability to contribute financially to women's groups. Therefore, the survey asked about financial contributions as a way to measure a level of commitment to these organizations that went beyond membership.

C H A P T E R

## 3

# WOMEN, POLITICAL CULTURE, AND EMPOWERMENT IN SPAIN

## *Judith Astelarra*

The question of whether there is a specific women's political culture has been raised by many social scientists in recent decades (see, e.g., Duverger, 1955; Flora and Lynn, 1974; Lovenduski, 1986; Randall, 1987). There has been a general agreement that women and men have different ways of defining politics and that differences exist in their political behavior. However, this general agreement does not hold the same meaning for the different observers. For a long time, specific female political traits were defined as negative in light of such standards as rationality, government and voting participation, and modernization. McCormack (1975) suggests that this way of analyzing women's political culture and behavior has been the result of a male conception of politics which is highly biased and assumes women's inferiority. The starting point of this bias, she believes, is the assumption that men and women share the same political reality—structural and symbolic—and that differences between them can be accounted for in terms of different attributes. On the contrary, she concludes, there is an alternative conceptual frame of analysis which implies that there are two different cultures, male and female. Women's political culture is based on differences in political socialization and political opportunity structures (McCormack, 1975).

The reconceptualization of women's political culture has led in the 1970s and 1980s to many studies, theoretical and empirical, which have given a sound basis to the criticism that a male bias has existed in the previous development of political analysis (see Cohen, 1989; Dahlerup, 1986; Evans et al., 1986; Lovenduski, 1986; Randall, 1987; Stacey and Price, 1981). In this chapter, two aspects of women's political culture that have been studied by many of these authors, the relationship between established politics and the private sphere and established politics and the feminist movement will be analyzed in the case of Spain. Neither of these aspects have been considered often as part of political culture and behavior. However, they have been crucial in the development of women's political consciousness and participation and have enabled women's empowerment. This has been the case in Spain, both during the Franco dictatorship and in the transition to democracy.

I will analyze two types of women's organizations: the Women's Democratic Movement (WDM), which mobilized women against the dictatorship during the last years of Franco's regime, and the feminist movement in the years of the transition to democracy. In both cases, a specific form of political culture and participation of women is found; in the first case, this form created the basis for women's mobilization, and in the second, it influenced some aspects of the building of political institutions and parties and aided the empowerment of Spanish women.

## A Short History of Spanish Women's Organizations since 1940

After the civil war in 1940, the Women's Section of the Falange, the organization that had supported Franco, was given official legitimacy to erase all traces of the politics that the Republic had developed in favor of equality of the sexes. Official ideology decreed absolute submission of wives to their husbands and exalted the virtues of obedience, purity, and abnegation for women. These principles were quickly transformed into laws that forbade women's work outside the home, abolished divorce, subordinated married women to their husbands in all respects, punished severely female adultery, and discriminated against children born out of wedlock. In 1940 alone, more than 600,000 women joined the Women's Section, a figure that had never before been attained by any organization in Spain (Duran and Gallego, 1986). At the same time, the Church recovered its influence over women and by the 1950s was able to incorporate hundreds of thousands of women into its organization, the Catholic Action.

Thus, most Spanish women had traditional views concerning women's role, the family, and politics. This model prevailed both in principle and practice throughout the 1940s and 1950s, but it began to be questioned in the 1960s when Spanish society started to change. The sixties was a period characterized by economic growth and a more open society. As tourism began to grow and many Spanish workers emigrated to work in other European countries, new ideas came into Spain that brought modernization and a certain degree of social and cultural liberalization. The need for an increased number of workers led to the revision of legislation barring married women from the paid labor force. Even the Falangist Women's Section proposed some changes, but reaffirmed women's submission due to their "nature" (Astelarra, 1989).

With the reappearance of clandestine organizations and the emergence of opposition groups, a space was created for the participation of women opposed to the Franco regime. There emerged some women's groups that criticized the traditional concept of women's role. Although they mobilized a small proportion of Spanish women, these groups nevertheless launched the first criticism of Spanish patriarchal society.

In 1965, a specific women's organization, the Women's Democratic Movement (WDM), was created, and it became the most active women's organization opposed to Francoism. Although it brought together a large number of independent women, it was closely linked to the Spanish Communist Party, the most active opposition group. The WDM is the first group I will describe in order to show how women developed a specific form of political participation.

The main goal of the WDM was to organize women as part of the opposition to the regime. The idea was that the WDM would serve as a female platform for the political activities that the clandestine groups developed. The organization's initial activities thus were related to propaganda and recruitment. However, the difficulties in reaching women indicated to its leaders that it was necessary to change their strategy and to look at the problems women felt to be important (Threllfall, 1985). Hence, WDM leaders began to analyze problems specific to women at work, in the legal system, and in their homes. The shift in their activities led them to consider the plight of housewives, especially those from the working classes. This new focus subsequently led to contacts with the National Organization of Housewives, created by the Falangist Women's Section many years before. Soon women from the WDM decided to infiltrate this organization in order to recruit more women. After two years of work, the WDM was able to establish local chapters of housewives' organizations in working-class neighborhoods of the biggest cities. However, the Falangist leaders of the National Organization of Housewives discovered that the WDM was behind this work, and the WDM women were expelled from the organization with the collaboration of police forces (Moreno, 1977).

By 1968, the WDM had its owns structure, a national office and local chapters, and was publishing a newsletter. All this, however, was done in secrecy since the WDM was considered an illegal organization. In fact, the WDM's growth was not received well by the male-dominated political organizations of the opposition or by the Communist Party. While they thought the work of the WDM was necessary, they felt that women were becoming too independent. However, given that the WDM now had its own resources, its members continued to develop and to widen their activities. Gradually, the WDM began to add to its demand for liberty and democracy the quest for the end to exploitation of women. Its more immediate demands focused on four points: (1) poor living conditions among working-class housewives, (2) discrimination against women in the educational system, (3) women's access to employment without restrictions and based on the principle of "equal pay for equal work," and (4) reform of the Civil Code, especially those aspects that legalized women's inferior status.

In 1968, clandestine organizations of the opposition to Franco had been very active, and the government decided to terminate their activities. Between 1968 and 1969, the police razed headquarters of the main political organizations, including the WDM and illegal trade unions, and imprisoned their leaders. In 1969, a state of emergency was declared by the government which allowed it to rule by decree, bypassing the judiciary. The WDM survived in spite of repression and continued its activities in the main cities. However, the organization added a new focus—solidarity with political prisoners. Many new members, especially wives and daughters of imprisoned men, joined the organization. Women organized collectively to visit the prisoners, and they began to work for the prisoners' release. National and international campaigns demanding the release of political prisoners were organized, and women were very active in them. Solidarity campaigns became one of the most important tasks of the WDM, while work with housewives continued.

From 1970 to 1975, the year of Franco's death and the beginning of the democratic transition, the WDM established itself as Spain's most important women's organization. However, during those years, in the wake of the European feminist movement, several feminist collectives were founded, introducing to Spain European feminist literature and the debate on the specific nature of women's oppression as well as the need for an autonomous movement independent of political parties.

The appearance of feminist groups raised the issue inside the WDM of its role and its relationship to the Communist Party and other political organizations. Even if some sectors were sympathetic to the newborn feminist movement, the majority of the WDM membership reaffirmed its belief in a joint struggle between women, the working class, and democratic organizations and were critical of the idea of a confrontation between the sexes. Nevertheless, the WDM maintained its separate organization and demands and this often led to disagreements and differences with the parties. In spite of such conflicts, the WDM remained a part of the political platform of the opposition to the regime and maintained its close relationship with the Communist Party.

The year 1975 was crucial for Spain; Franco's illness indicated that the end of the dictatorship was near, and thus the democratic opposition became increasingly active. That 1975 was also the United Nations International Women's Year was a coincidence welcomed by women's groups, which organized a series of activities paralleling the official ones sponsored by the regime. Twenty-four women's organizations together developed their own platform and published a common manifesto that analyzed the situation of Spanish women and the need for profound economic, social, cultural, and political changes. They also demanded the full ratification by government of the U.N. convention for the elimination of all forms of discrimination (Astelarra, 1989).

By the end of the year, the first conference on women's liberation took place in Spain under semi-clandestine conditions. Five hundred women participated in the conference and focused their discussion on women's oppression. A strong debate ensued between the WDM and other women's organizations and feminist groups. The former insisted on a joint action with political parties in support of the demand for democracy, while the latter advocated that women's oppression and specific demands should be given priority (Scanlon, 1978).

Although the debate ended in disagreement, it served to develop the first contacts between feminists and women from the more established political groups and to assert the need for joint actions. Five months later, the first Catalonian Conference on Women's Liberation was organized, and five thousand women attended. This time, an agreement was reached, with all the women supporting the idea that an independent feminist movement was needed. Members of the women's groups linked to political parties accepted this fact, though many of them maintained that even if the movement were autonomous, its participants could also belong to established political groups. Thus the women's movement in Spain developed two main strands: single militancy for the feminists who belonged only to feminist groups, and double militancy for the ones who belonged to both feminist and established political organizations. Feminism was now accepted by all activist women as a legitimate political cause in itself. Women in political parties also expressed the conviction that the parties were patriarchal and had to be changed from within and that this was also a feminist goal (Scanlon, 1978).

The feminist movement grew in subsequent years. Feminist groups, bookstores, publishing houses, and women's studies groups were created. Coordination of these groups was established at both the regional and the national level, and conferences were organized. The main themes for mobilization during the first years of the organized women's movement were amnesty for women convicted of offenses related to their womanhood and the demand for sexual rights, such as abolition of penalties for using contraceptives, the creation of a public system of family planning, and the right to abortion. Both themes are examples of the politicization of demands that had not been considered previously as political and that fit the slogan "the personal is political"—a redefinition of politics that was quickly accepted by Spanish feminists.

The theme of amnesty for offenses specific to women fit into the perspective of the democratic demands that were being promoted by political party organizations. Amnesty was one of the general demands of the day and included all political prisoners, that is, people who had been jailed for activism which was considered illegal. Feminists put forth the message that women condemned on the basis of patriarchal laws should also be considered political prisoners. The dictatorship had approved extremely conservative laws concerning women; leaving home, adultery by married women, the use of contraceptives, and abortion (for women, medical personnel, and any person who helped) were acts punished severely, and there were many women imprisoned for these actions. The feminist movement developed a campaign in support of these women, demanding their freedom along with the rest of the political prisoners. The sensitization of public opinion to the plight of political prisoners drew considerable attention to this campaign.

Abortion and contraception was the other theme that united the efforts of the women's movement. Abortion was a rather important problem since semiofficial figures estimated that around 300,000 illegal abortions took place each year. In 1978, a trial in Bilbao of women charged with having obtained abortions led to a national campaign in their support. An initial manifesto was made public in which a thousand women declared that they had had abortions and demanded that they also be tried. It was followed by a second document in which both women and men stated that they had participated in abortions and insisted that they be judged with the women in Bilbao. This solidarity with the accused popularized the right-to-abortion campaign. Ideological and moral resistance, however, was strong, both in the conservative as well as the more moderate sectors of the population.

Besides the Bilbao campaign, other actions defending the right of women to choose an abortion were organized. Moreover, the movement created channels of support for women who needed abortions and could not obtain them in Spain. (While some clandestine clinics existed in the country, they were very expensive.) Counseling offices were created to help women obtain their abortions in other countries, mostly in England. At the same time, the feminist movement demanded a new law abolishing penalties for abortion.

Abortion was not the only issue related to sexuality pursued by the feminists. Their groups also gave counseling in human sexuality and family planning, aspects of life that had been until that time taboo in Spanish society. Legislation penalized users of contraceptives and the doctors who prescribed contraceptives. Thus, feminists also organized centers where female gynecologists provided birth control information and prescribed contraceptives. Besides this practical work, the feminist movement demanded the abolition of laws that penalized these activities and organized several campaigns in their support.

The WDM and the feminist movement are the two examples I will analyze in order to determine whether their activities can be seen as politically different from traditional ones and whether it is possible to speak of a specifically female political culture. In this analysis I will focus on women's participation as an indicator of political culture. While other indicators, such as women's values and specifically female ways of organizing, could also be examined, data in these areas are scarce for the period considered.[1]

## Women's Political Participation

To assert the specificity of the WDM's and the feminist movement's participation in political life, it is important to compare what the more traditional political organizations were doing at the same time. To begin with, the historical periods during which the two types of organizations were active can be characterized as special periods in terms of existing institutions. The first period, from about 1968 until 1975, was a time of considerable instability. After the civil war, an authoritarian regime was established which was in full control until the improved economy and tourism of the 1960s allowed the introduction of new ideas, thus ending Spanish autarchy and isolation. This, in turn, led to the organization of political forces that opposed the regime and developed actions against it. The second period was a time of change from authoritarian politics to democracy, a process defined as "the transition to democracy" (Astelarra, 1989). The old order had to be demolished and a new one built. This meant the legalization of political parties, free elections, writing a new constitution, changing the existing laws in response to the new constitution, and changing the Spanish system of government from a highly centralized to a federal one.

During the first period, the main activities of the democratic opposition included creating organizations, influencing public opinion against the regime, mobilizing people to demand democracy, and participating in fascist-controlled organizations (such as labor unions) in attempts to change them from within. Some opposition groups believed in armed struggle and carried on actions of sabotage and killing of police officers, soldiers, and other representatives of the regime.[2] As I have indicated above, the WDM was created so that women might participate in these actions. But, WDM leaders soon discovered that women had their own problems and that if the organization wanted to mobilize women, it had to make specific female demands. These specific problems arose from women's role as housewives and from the existence of a special form of discrimination against women, based on the regime's traditional view of women's status in family and society.

The specific nature of women's demands led to the decision that the WDM had to be an autonomous group, with its own chapters and means of communication. This created problems with the members' male colleagues in the Communist Party who did not accept the organization's independence with much enthusiasm. However, in spite of its autonomy, the WDM did accept the idea that it had to work closely with other forces opposed to the regime. Thus, when feminist groups criticized the patriarchal ways of the democratic organizations, the WDM disagreed with this view. However, once the feminist groups grew and established their importance, the WDM changed its position and joined the women's movement. The same pattern was followed by other women's organizations and women's sections in the political parties (Scanlon, 1978).

After 1976, many of the women's organizations became linked with the left, and the democratic opposition defined itself as feminist. Most members of these groups, nevertheless, remained also in their parties and within them started debates about feminism and discrimination against women. In several political parties, the more traditional women's sections redefined themselves as "women's liberation" collectives. This did not happen, however, in the parties belonging to the center and the right. The center, which was the party in government, maintained an ambiguous position on women's issues, and the conservative party was clearly anti-feminist (Duran and Gallego, 1986).

During the period of transition, in which the feminist movement showed a great capacity for mobilization, the activities developed by feminist organizations were clearly different from those of the existing political parties and groups. The democratic transition in Spain, during which the old authoritarian regime had to be dismantled and a new one created, has been described as a combination of mobilization from below and negotiation at the top (Astelarra, 1989).[3] The mobilization helped the process to be more dynamic and the negotiations of the political elites made possible the agreements that led to the legalization of the parties, free elections, amnesty for political prisoners, and finally a new constitution. Women were present in the mobilizations, but with their own demands, even though the political parties thought they were not important and did not place women's demands on the priority lists. There were few women in the political elites who participated in the negotiation process,[4] but most of those few sympathized with the feminist demands and put them forward when the constitution and the new laws were being debated.

Therefore, during the transition period, again women developed their specific activities and discussed issues that were different from the ones being posed and discussed by the parties and other groups. Their emphasis was on sexual demands and on those aspects that had led to women's discrimination: family laws, job discrimination (only 27 percent of the employed population was female), and education.

The feminist groups were never involved directly in the building of democratic institutions; some of them even asked for a vote against the constitution because it upheld several patriarchal features.[5] However, despite their limited input, in fewer than ten years, women attained basic legal reforms that had taken much more time and effort in other countries. The Spanish Constitution, in one of its articles, prohibits sex discrimination and establishes equal rights for women and men.[6]

After the constitution was approved, family laws were changed and the prohibition of information about, and penalties for the distribution and sale of, contraceptives were removed. In 1984, when the Socialist Party had absolute majority in Parliament (which it obtained in 1982), an abortion law, though very moderate, was passed. It made abortion legal under three special circumstances: if the mother's life is in danger, in the case of rape, or in case of malformation of the fetus. Also, a national commission for equality, the Women's Institute, was created. All these changes took place even though feminist groups were essentially absent from the institutional political arena. However, due to the few women who belonged to the political elite as well as to the existence of the feminist movement which modified public opinion and thus could not be ignored by male politicians, changes in favor of women came into being.

In the 1980s, women from conservative parties began to change their views and accepted the idea of equal rights, although they continued to oppose the legalization of abortion. As a consequence, their parties also changed previous conservative platforms (which usually assumed that women's roles lie only within the family), a fact that constituted a significant development in Spanish history (Astelarra, 1986).

The cases of the DWM and the feminist movement show that Spanish women developed their own demands and forms of political participation and were relatively absent from the more traditional political arenas. In fact, if one were to examine what happened in both time periods only in terms of classical political analysis, the conclusion would be that women were not present in the political life of the moment. Only if specific ways that women participated are considered, and also defined as "political," can there be a more accurate picture of women's contributions. This type of analysis also illustrates the need for a redefinition of politics in general to include women's activities (Randall, 1987). Another conclusion that can be drawn is that women's specific political participation not only helped to bring to the political arena women's problems and issues that had to be resolved but, at least in legal terms, the strategy was successful in that it obtained benefits for women which have allowed them some measure of empowerment.

## A Final Remark Concerning Women's Political Culture

The activities I have described here involved only a relatively small percentage of Spanish women. Neither the feminist groups nor the women's sections of the parties have had numerous members. However, recent research done on representative samples of women shows that an analysis focusing on women's culture also can be applied to women's definition of politics.

Two Spanish surveys conducted recently (Instituto I.D.E.S., 1987; 1988) that focused on women's attitudes toward politics and feminism provided some interesting results. When asked about their "political interest" 22 percent of the women interviewed said that they were interested in politics while 56 percent stated that they were uninterested. However, when women were asked their opinion of the feminist movement, 44 percent said that they valued it positively, 44 percent negatively, and 11 percent did not have an opinion. If we consider feminism as politics, then what the above findings mean is that women are more interested in this form of politics than in the more conventional form. When asked how they would define the feminist movement, 43 percent of the interviewees saw it as a movement for the achievement of women's demands, 18 percent as a specific feminine lifestyle, 19 percent as a way to change man/woman relationships, and 20 percent as a form of female chauvinism. Clearly, Spanish women see a political content in the feminist movement. It is important to note that historically Spain has not had a tradition of feminism, as the suffrage movement was weak and involved very few women.

Another important field of analysis is that of women's definitions of their roles in society and which activities they consider to be "male" or "female." The forty years of Francoism certainly had its impact on Spanish women's attitudes. While comparative data for that period are not available, it is apparent that the regime, particularly through the Falangist Women's Section, made a substantial effort to indoctrinate women. Courses in home economics with a strong emphasis on women's traditional role were taught in schools and colleges until the democratic transition took place. Nevertheless, important changes in women's perceptions of their role have occurred during the last ten years. In the surveys cited above, questions were asked also about sex roles to determine whether women considered certain activities as masculine, feminine, or not specific to either sex. The following represent percentages of women who believed that the given activities were gender-neutral or could be done by both sexes: housework, 57 percent; looking after children, 85 percent; being active in politics, 60 percent; practicing birth control, 79 percent; improving the country's economic situation, 67 percent; packing for travel, 56 percent; administering the family budget, 65 percent; dressing with elegance, 75 percent; attending sporting events, 57 percent; driving a car, 75 percent; applying for a loan, 69 percent; buying clothes, 59 percent; and reading the newspaper, 76 percent. These answers indicate a deep change in women's definitions of male and female roles that have taken place recently in Spanish society.

These changes, both in the definition of politics and of women's role, could not have happened without the existence of the women's and feminist organizations whose activities I have described. It can be concluded then that there is a specific form of political participation by Spanish women that attests to a special women's political culture. It is important to redefine politics in order to include these phenomena. Finally, more research is needed to clarify the concept of women's political culture and its impact on political life.

# Notes

1. Little social research was carried on in the 1960s and the first half of the 1970s in Spain since the social sciences were considered dangerous by the regime. Only one sociology department existed then, in Madrid, which was politically controlled.

2. E.g., Carrero Blanco, a minister who was meant to be Franco's successor, was assassinated by the ETA, the Basque nationalist guerrilla group.

3. When Franco was about to die, he said that his regime was "well tied." The main task of the democratic opposition was therefore to "untie" the regime. This meant convincing the Francoist Parliament to resign and call for new elections, a process in which the Spanish king, Juan Carlos, was the main figure. Once this occurred, Suarez, a member of the regime who was the prime minister, to the surprise of the franquists, legalized all parties and called for elections. The newly elected Parliament wrote the new constitution, which democratized substantially the Spanish system of governance.

4. E.g., by 1980, Spain still had less than 5 percent women in Parliament and none in the ruling cabinet.

5. For instance, it did not explicitly approve lesbianism as an alternative to heterosexual marriage and family, and preference was given to male heirs to the throne.

6. This is equivalent to the ERA which was not ratified by the necessary number of states in the United States.

# WOMEN'S STRUGGLE FOR EMPOWERMENT IN JAPAN

*Yuriko Ling and Azusa Matsuno*
*with Jill M. Bystydzienski*

There is a widely held view in many parts of the world that Japanese women are shy, passive, and accept without question their subordinate roles in Japanese society. The fact that recently a woman became the leader of the Socialist Party in Japan and that women are today more visible in the public sphere of politics has surprised many, especially Western, observers. That Japanese women are stepping out of their "traditional" roles, questioning their society, and running for public offices in order to change a system they view as corrupt and unjust is heralded by the world media as unprecedented.

This view, however, is uninformed and ahistorical. Since the late nineteenth century, there has been a growing feminist consciousness in Japan. Going back further in Japanese history, we discover that women held prominent positions in society, as deities, early rulers, literary writers, and teachers. While under feudalism women lost their inheritance and property rights and their roles became restricted, autonomous peasant communities throughout feudal Japan continued to allow women participation in their own egalitarian structures. When modernization and reform swept through Japan in the latter part of the nineteenth century, feminist movements began to flourish.

In this chapter, we begin by chronicling the contributions Japanese women have made to their society throughout Japanese history and their attempts to obtain human rights and to empower their sex from the 1870s until the present. We then focus on the current situation of women and the strategies used by activists in recent years to develop feminist consciousness and to provide women greater control over their lives. We emphasize the importance of a women's culture to these attempts at empowerment. Since Japanese society is relatively homogeneous and women's activities have been effectively segregated from those of men for many centuries, a separate "women's world" has been, and still continues to be, maintained. We show how women have drawn on female values, experiences, and perspectives in their attempts to change existing political institutions in Japan.

The early part of this chapter draws on the work of feminist historians, most notably Sharon L. Sievers, Joy Paulson, Marjorie Wall Bingham and Susan Hill Gross, whose excellent studies have served to dispel myths and stereotypes about Japanese women. The rest of the chapter is based on observations and twenty-eight personal interviews conducted in Japan by the authors, Ling and Matsuno, during the summer of 1990.

## Women in Japanese History

Feminist historians have challenged the image of Japanese women as "doll-like, long suffering, innocent victims who acquiesce to an undeserved fate" and whose status in Japanese society has been shaped by Confucian philosophy— "good wife/wise mother"—imported from China in early times (Bingham and Gross, 1987: 1) As many have pointed out (Bingham and Gross, 1987; Jayawardena, 1986; Sievers, 1983; Paulson, 1978), powerful roles for Japanese women date as far back as the ancient past and continue well into the sixteenth century.

According to early Japanese mythology, the creation of the human race was a joint effort between a male and a female god, and the female sun god, Amaterasu, is considered the original ancestor of the imperial family (Bingham and Gross, 1987: 5). The Shinto religion, which developed out of these ancient beliefs, allowed for important positions for women including those of deities, spirits, and healers (Bingham and Gross, 1987: 21–23). Feminist historians have suggested that earliest Japanese societies were matrilineal, characterized by equality of the sexes (Jayawardena, 1986; Paulson, 1978).

Female rulers were present in early Japanese history. During the years A.D. 147 to 190 civil war prevailed until Queen Himiko restored peace (Jayawardena, 1986: 228). During the period between A.D. 592 and 770 one-half of the rulers were women. These female emperors were compromise candidates, chosen by warring factions who were unable to agree upon a sovereign (Robins-Mowry, 1983: 9). Thus female rulers in early Japan came to be associated with detente and peace. In the eighth century, with the introduction of Confucianism, the Chinese philosophy which espouses the natural inferiority of women, female rule ended with the reign of Empress Koken when women were barred from succession to the throne (Paulson, 1978).

The years 794 to 1185 are known as the Heian period, a time in Japanese history recognized for its literary masterpieces. Almost all the noteworthy authors of the era were women from the aristocratic classes. They wrote in Japanese as distinct from the literary Chinese, which was considered the appropriate language and style for men. The women authors produced a vibrant body of native literature, while the works of male writers at the time were written in highly stylized Chinese and lacked originality (Bingham and Gross,

1987: 39). It was during this period that Murasaki Shikibu wrote *The Tale of Genji*, which achieved fame as the world's first novel and an outstanding literary work (Jayawardena, 1986: 228).[1]

While the growth of feudalism in the Ashikaga period (1338–1500) and the emergence of the masculine *samurai* ethic circumscribed women's roles and reduced their status, women nevertheless continued to hold important positions in Japan until the sixteenth century. Samurai women had to learn not only to manage the family estates while samurai men were off fighting but also to defend themselves and their households (Berger, 1976: 59). Although barred from holding political positions, some women ruled through husbands and sons, and some became known as samurai-like warriors (Bingham and Gross, 1987: 84). Toward the end of medieval times, women also figured strongly in politics by maintaining alliances and advising rulers (Bingham and Gross, 1987: 85), thus carrying on their earlier role as peacemakers.

During the Tokugawa period (1600–1868), a neo-Confucian system took hold in Japan. Confucianism insisted on a strict hierarchy within the family and society where women were to be subordinated to men and peasants to landowners who ruled through a highly centralized government. Even though women lost all legal rights and their physical freedom was increasingly regulated (Bingham and Gross, 1987: 101), there is reason to believe that mostly people of the upper strata (the literate) were effected by the Confucian ethic. Peasants, who constituted the majority of the population, continued to live in relatively autonomous villages (Ueno, 1987). In feudal villages the institution of the *shufu* (or female head of household) and the persistence of a symbolic order and work organization consisting of two independent groups defined by sex gave women a relatively autonomous status (Ueno, 1987: S78). Nevertheless, among the upper and middle classes, the passive, obedient, silently enduring wife and mother increasingly became the norm for women.

With the end of Japan's isolation and the beginning of capitalist growth and policies of modernization during the Meiji period (1868–1913), women's subservient status in Japan began to be questioned. Attacks on the "traditional" Japanese family system and support for women's emancipation came from the Liberty and Popular Rights Movement of the 1870s and 1880s, which not only included liberal male reformers (such as the Meiji Six Society) who supported women's suffrage and civil rights but also produced many women activists (Jayawardena, 1986:230–31).

As Sievers (1983) pointed out, there were two "waves" of the feminist movement during the Meiji era. The first consisted of political activism, where women such as Kishida Toshiko and Fukuda Hideko organized women's discussion groups and lecture societies; joined established political parties working for reform, such as the Liberal Party; or were drawn to socialist and anarchist groups (Bingham and Gross, 1987: 167–69; Sievers, 1983). The women activists spoke up against the oppression of women, advocated women's rights, and the more radical among them supported a restructuring of the family as well as fundamental economic and political change.

This phase of the movement also included labor organizing. By 1876, women accounted for 60 percent of the entire Japanese labor force, with young, unmarried women from poor rural families constituting the bulk of the work force, the greater part of which was in the textile industry (Jayawardena, 1986: 236). The working conditions for these women were extremely harsh, and they quickly learned to organize themselves and to withdraw their labor to protest their exploitation. Japan's first strike took place in 1886, at the Amamiya Silk Mill in Kofu, when one hundred women walked out in response to the owner's proposal to increase working hours while reducing wages (Sievers, 1983: 79). Lack of contact between women in the work force and feminist activists working through the Liberal Party and left-wing groups prevented any changes in the status of working women at the time (Jayawardena, 1976: 237).

The second wave of the feminist movement came in response to the restrictions placed on women by the Meiji Constitution of 1889. Under this new constitution women were not permitted to vote nor were they able to inherit the throne (Sievers, 1983: 51). A year later, under Article 5 of the 1890 Police Security Regulations, it became illegal for women to join a political party, organize a political association, or attend a political meeting (Sievers, 1983: 52). Since women's activities now were severely limited by legislation and police regulations, they began to voice their criticisms through journalism. Two of the most popular journals which appeared during this time were *Sekai Fujin* (Women of the world), edited by Fukuda Hideko, and *Seito* (Bluestocking), whose editors included Hiratsuka Raicho, Ito Noe, and Yosano Akiko (Jayawardena, 1986: 241–47). In these journals, women writers and activists attacked discrimination against women, launched a campaign to remove Article 5 of the Police Security Regulations of 1890, and encouraged women to "rise up and forcefully develop our own social movement" (Sievers, 1983: 127).

While both journals were eventually closed down by the state and many of their writers arrested and some even killed (Sievers, 1983: 180), Japanese feminists continued throughout the early nineteen hundreds and in the post-World War I period to agitate for women's rights. In 1919, Hiratsuka Raicho, Ichikawa Fusae, and others formed the Association of New Women, which campaigned for equal rights, women's suffrage, a labor union for women workers, and the repeal of the infamous Article 5 of 1890 (Jayawardena, 1986: 248–49). In 1921, the law was revised, allowing women to attend and organize political meetings, but still prohibiting them from joining or organizing political parties. The Association of New Women subsequently disbanded and Ichikawa Fusae helped to organize another group, Women's Suffrage Alliance. Meanwhile, the feminist movement had broken up into four factions associated with left-wing parties, and the Women's Suffrage Alliance adopted a position of "political neutrality" in order to mobilize all forces in support of women's suffrage. This, however, led to much criticism of Ichikawa and despite a later "period of hope"—first in 1930 when a bill was passed that allowed women to join political parties and vote in local elections and then in 1931 when the Lower House of the Imperial Diet passed a modified bill on women's rights—Japanese women did not achieve universal suffrage until after World War II (Jayawardena, 1986: 249–50)

The growing repression during the 1920s of all leftist organizations, including the Japanese Communist Party which was formed in 1922, led to increased harassment of their women militants as well as the suppression of feminist activities. The rise of military expansionism and totalitarian policies in the subsequent decade further weakened the women's movement (Jayawardena, 1986: 251). In 1931, Japan occupied Manchuria and continued its expansion into North China, extending its aggression to the rest of South East Asia with the outbreak of World War II. The growth of militarism led to increased anti-feminist sentiment and a reordering of national priorities that made women's suffrage a non-issue (Pharr, 1981: 21). Despite adverse conditions, women continued to resist. For instance, the Third National Women's Suffrage Conference of 1932 condemned Japanese government's military policies (Sano, 1980: 77). Between 1931 and 1933, the Women's Peace Association wrote letters to the women of China deploring the actions of their government (Kawai and Kubushiro, 1934). Taking issue with the government position that expansion was justified in order to make room for the growing Japanese population, feminist leaders opened a birth control clinic in Tokyo to provide an alternative, nonviolent way to deal with the population crisis (Havens, 1975). However, this opposition to Japanese military actions was increasingly silenced by the government. Newspapers and feminist leaders were banned from expressing anti-government opinions, many of the women were arrested, and some were assassinated (Bingham and Gross, 1987: 219). Needing women to "produce the means for aggressive war," the government managed to co-opt many women by appointing leading Japanese females to fill posts on committees involving the war effort and eventually by subsuming the women's movement in the Greater Japanese Women's Association formed in 1942 (Sano, 1980: 78).

It was only after Japan's defeat and U.S. occupation in 1945 that the political prohibitions on women were lifted and they obtained the right to vote. Before the first election in 1946, some of the women activists from the 1920s and 1930s, such as Ishimoto Shizue and Ichikawa Fusae, organized a campaign to get women to vote and to run as candidates. The campaign was enormously successful. Sixty-seven percent of women eligible voted. They elected thirty-nine females (8 percent) to the Lower House (House of Representatives) of the National Diet and ten (4 percent) to the Upper House (House of Councillors) (Robins-Mowry, 1983: 95). While Japanese women have yet to surpass this record,[2] their activism and struggle for empowerment continued and intensified in the following decades.

## Women's Activism in Japan since the 1950s

Once the restrictive climate of the war period was lifted, many Japanese women again resumed the struggle for emancipation. The 1950s was not an easy time to put forth women's issues. The United States during its occupation of Japan provided the country with a new constitution, which in addition to the right of women to vote included a section guaranteeing women equality as a constitutional right (Bingham and Gross, 1987: 248). In practice, however, the occupying forces promoted a model for Japanese women that focused on home, larger families, and housewifely virtues. This, coupled with Japanese men's strong resistance to sex equality (Robins-Mowry, 1983: 103) and the sexual exploitation of Japanese women by the U.S. military, made the legislation on paper almost meaningless. Despite the obstacles, Japanese women continued to fight for the issues they believed in and against sex discrimination.

One focus of female activism during the 1950s, as well as in later decades, was peace and anti-militarism. While a fully fledged peace movement did not develop in Japan until the 1960s, women had carried on their anti-war stance from the earlier part of the century, which was renewed by the nuclear devastation at Hiroshima and Nagasaki as well as the post-war U.S. military occupation of Japan. Women thus staged protests near U.S. military bases, aiming to reclaim lost land and to stop prostitution (Caldecott, 1983). They organized discussions on the effects of militarism on women and in the 1970s and 1980s demonstrated in large numbers against nuclear weapons and the use of nuclear energy (Pharr, 1981).

Many Japanese women found that they could have some impact on their lives and those of their children by becoming involved in civic organizations such as the Parent Teachers Association or the Housewives' Association. Such groups became a fertile training ground for women and an avenue for network-building. Women who had served in civic organizations frequently became involved in further change-oriented activities. Many joined political parties, became involved in political campaigns, and some even ran for public office (Bingham and Gross, 1987: 296).

In recent decades, Japanese women have also been active in environmental and consumer movements. Women led the Anti-Minamata Disease campaign during the 1960s (Bingham and Gross, 1987: 296) and, during the 1970s and 1980s, spearheaded numerous demonstrations and protests against industrial pollution, deforestation, and disposal of hazardous wastes. Since the 1960s, also, women have formed consumer cooperative groups, which at first focused on ways to increase the quality and decrease the cost of consumer goods and services and now increasingly serve as vehicles for recruiting and promoting political candidates (Kubo, 1990).

Since the 1950s, Japanese women have used the formal political system in attempts to improve their status. The voting rate of women has continued to increase over the years, yet the all-time high election rate of 1946 has not been surpassed. Indeed, between the years 1952 and 1980, the proportion of women in parliament averaged a mere 3 percent (Kubo, 1990). A major reason for the relative absence of women in public office is that women have not voted as a block—their votes have been spread throughout the range of political parties.[3] Since 1980, however, when a proportional representation system was introduced in the Upper House, the number of candidates, as well as women elected, increased signficantly.[4] The change coincided with a growing recognition that unless women enter into the formal political process, they cannot effectively alter the obstacles that remain in their path to equality with men (Kubo, 1990). Moreover, Japanese women have become increasingly interested in campaigning against corruption in politics, and many are convinced that women are less likely than men to fall prey to bribery and misuse of public funds. Hence, in the last decade, there have been many campaigns organized by Japanese women to bring more women into politics as candidates and to convince women to vote for their own sex.

Japanese women's political actions have been different from those of men. They are characterized by a focus on specific issues of concern to women, a particular way of viewing politics and of organizing. The strategies used by Japanese women have their source in a women's culture, and it is to this concept that we turn next in order to explain Japanese women's political participation.

## Women's Culture and Politics in Japan

In Japan, as in most other world societies, women live in two cultural realms simultaneously—as members of the general culture and as participants in a women's culture (Lerner, 1986: 262). On the one hand, women live in a different culture from men, a culture based on differences in socialization and opportunity structures (McCormack, 1975), and on the other hand, they exist within the realm of dominant values and norms, which due to their longevity and legal sanctions affect their lives in countless ways. In Japan, the structure of women's lives is different from those of men because not only has Japan been a largely sex-segregated society for many centuries, but also women continue to be responsible for most of the childrearing, family maintenance, social welfare (paid and unpaid), and many cultural activities.

During the United Nations Decade for Women, a nationwide campaign encouraged Japanese women to go out of the home and "participate in society" (Ueno, 1987: S81–82). While for some this meant entering the paid labor force, many took advantage of increasing opportunities to attend local consumer cooperative meetings, civic activities, or adult education classes, and to get involved in leisure activities such as sports. Taking part in these activities helped to create a "renewed 'women's bonding' " (Ueno, 1987: S82), which received support from the traditional sexual segregation and lack of interference from husbands and other men.[5] Hence, while women became increasingly involved in the public sphere outside the home, they did so by participating in women's groups, networks, and organizations. The process of empowerment of Japanese women thus contains a strong emphasis on women's concerns, perspectives, and values. This in turn affects how women relate to and what they want out of politics.

There is strong evidence of a distinct women's culture in the way Japanese women view politics and in the types of issues they bring into public forums, in how they organize themselves, and once elected into public office, how they conduct themselves as politicians. We have found this to be the case when examining the political involvement of women at both the national and the local level.

A major reason for the growing participation of Japanese women in politics as mobilizers of women, political candidates, and voters is a growing concern among women that politics has gotten out of hand. According to the women we interviewed, men have used the political process to accumulate personal power and to get ahead at the expense of collective welfare. Many told us that they joined the efforts to elect more women because, in the words of a member of the Nagoya consumer cooperative, "Men always emphasize profits for themselves and are not concerned about the lives of ordinary people." They feel that the government has become removed from the people and no longer represents common concerns. This was dramatically evidenced by the 3 percent consumption tax that the government of Prime Minister Takeshita imposed in 1989, which was met with disbelief and anger from much of the population, especially the women. Subsequently, in large part due to the efforts of women, the Liberal Democratic Party suffered a stunning defeat in the Upper House parliamentary elections, and thirty-three women (13.1 percent) were elected (Kubo, 1990).

Japanese women, disgruntled with recent sex and stock-for-favors scandals involving members of government and the lack of responsiveness of male politicians to people's needs, have come to believe strongly that women politicians can make a difference. The vast majority of those we interviewed, as well as others we talked with informally, were extremely supportive of female politicians and expressed the view that women can change politics for the better. A middle-aged woman who has been active in the Socialist Party at the local level stated,

> Women have the experience of managing households and running things in neighborhoods. They know and care about the problems of the aged, the children . . . they are aware of what food additives and the contamination of the environment can do to people. They experience all this firsthand in their everyday lives. When they get into public offices they can then try to deal with problems they know exist and people care about.

A member of the Upper House in Parliament expressed a similar view and added,

> Women have certain knowledge and skills that men, because of the way they are brought up, do not have. Women know and understand more about the family, the local community, the real problems of this country. They know how to relate to the common people and how to accomplish goals.

Japanese women's faith in female politicians also comes from the way women view and exercise power and politics. Politics for women in Japan is seen as an avenue for cooperatively achieving concrete objectives. The main reason women run for public office is to "get things done." They recognize a need for public policies at the local and national level that would deal concretely with Japan's pressing problems, such as environmental pollution, welfare of the elderly, childcare, and women's reproductive rights. Akiko Doomoto, member of the Upper House of Parliament put it thus,

> I decided to run for Parliament because I became more and more dissatisfied with the policies of the government made by men without regard to the problems experienced by the people. Japanese government needs to deal with environmental pollution, problems of women's health related to pregnancy, and what we should do about an aging population at the same time as the Japanese family is no longer able to take on sole responsibility for the old. We have to develop concrete policies and to enact effective legislation in these areas.

Women politicians wish to make governing bodies more responsive to the common people of Japan, to realize the democratic ideal of a reciprocal relationship between representatives and those they represent. Power in their view is a resource to be mobilized by politicians on behalf of the people and not to be used for self-aggrandizement and personal gain. Tomako Toguchi, member of the Socialist Party and in the Lower House since February 1990, had this to say,

> I see myself in Parliament as a mouthpiece of the people I represent. For instance, many of my constituents are the elderly, and I know that they need public services. That is why I have been speaking to this issue many times and have put forth arguments for better funding of welfare centers to provide quality services for the aged.

At the forefront of a movement expressing such views is the Socialist Party leader, Takako Doi, who at every opportunity urges Japanese politicians to respond genuinely to the people's needs (Bottorff, 1990).

Such expressions about the role of politics are not idle talk. Japanese women's participation at both the local and national levels of governance has resulted in democratization of political structures (Kubo, 1990). At the local level, where until recently policies have been tightly controlled by elderly businessmen, women have introduced a more balanced sense of life and a more inclusive idea of economy, consisting not only of producers but also consumers. Many of the local women politicians have had extensive experience in consumer cooperatives and other citizens' groups and thus have infused local assemblies with perspectives and problems of the common people and a desire to improve community life. At the parliamentary level, women representatives also address specific problems of concern to their constituents, especially women. Moreover, female politicians have tried to make representatives be more accountable to the people by publicizing the voting record of MPs.

Participation of a growing number of women in Japanese politics has increased public awareness of quality-of-life issues that female politicians have repeatedly brought onto political agendas. Probably most prominent among these have been environmental problems. Many female public officeholders have had extensive training in consumer cooperatives and as members of the environmentalist movement and thus are highly aware of air and water pollution, food contamination, and other related concerns. Being in public office provides these women with an opportunity to do something to solve environmental problems. Thus many are relentless and make their case at every opportunity. One example is Akiko Doomoto, member of the Upper House in the Diet, (cited above) who is attempting to raise the country's awareness of the environmental consequences of Japanese economic development projects overseas. Doomoto conducted an extensive survey in the Philippines and found that toxic chemicals from factories constructed by Japan were threatening the lives of local people. She made a forceful and convincing presentation in the Upper House, which gave her media publicity and prompted environmental legislation.

As we have indicated already, women politicians also have focused on the situation of the aged. Moreover, they have addressed squarely the growing problems of working women. Women representatives in both the Upper and Lower House have been pressing for a Childcare Leave Law and the allocation of funds to local communities for establishment of childcare centers. Women politicians also stress issues related to women's employment, such as protection for part-time workers, equal opportunities in hiring and promotions, and equal pay. Finally, they focus on women's reproductive rights, most recently keeping the male-dominated Diet from passing legislation that would further restrict women's access to abortion.[6]

The issues that Japanese female politicians focus on, more than do their male counterparts, deal with quality of life and include problems that are faced by a growing number of families and individuals in Japan. Their emphasis on concerns of everyday life make politics more understandable to the general public. Mariko Mitsui, a member of the Tokyo Metropolitan Assembly, aptly summarizes this approach: "I want to be a liaison between ordinary people and politics. So I [work toward ameliorating the problems that are important to them and] use direct, everyday language" (Ueda, 1990: 14). Thus the "common people" look with hope toward women politicians, and women in particular can see their specific needs being expressed and supported by their female representatives.

Japanese women's way of "doing politics" is also quite different from the way men operate. Women's political activity occurs within groups that are relatively unstructured, are usually local, place emphasis on concrete goals, and are skeptical of formal rituals. Such groups develop many activities which encourage group cohesiveness and planning, such as special projects and seminars, social events, lecture series, and rallies.

The most successful women's groups in recent years have been consumer cooperatives, which have developed into extensive networks in several areas of Japan. The best known and most effective of these is the Kanagawa Network, which covers the Kanagawa prefecture (population of about three million), not far from Tokyo. The Network consists of women-run local consumer co-operatives which have bases in six cities; the central office is located in Yoko-hama City. The local groups came into being to provide access for people to foods uncontaminated by chemical additives and preservatives. They first be-gan their activities by buying safe and inexpensive consumer commodities for their members. Gradually, as the women members learned about food contam-ination and environmental pollution, they began to make links between gov-ernment policy, regulation of industry, and environmental problems. As a longstanding member of the Network who lives in Yokohama City indicated,

> As I became more aware of how things work, I realized that I needed to become more involved in the world around me and especially in the formal political process. If we were going to make any changes we would have to work through the government also, to make laws prohibiting industry from polluting the earth and air, to restrict the use of pesticides and other chemi-cals. So gradually, I and other women started looking around for political candidates that could represent our views. We realized that it was mostly women who had experience in consumer cooperatives who really knew about the is-sues, so we found candidates and supported them.

Over time, local groups began to form links with others in surrounding cities and thus the Kanagawa Network was born. Today, in addition to providing consumer information by publishing a monthly journal, Network members work on identifying women who can run for political offices and cooperate with other organizations in the system to provide support for their candidates. They also attempt to increase awareness among women about politics by or-ganizing meetings with female politicians and arranging lectures and special events where local women have the opportunity to learn about the issues re-lated to women in politics. The organizational structure of the local groups is nonhierarchical; all members have an equal voice in all matters, participate sometimes in daily meetings, and work collectively toward the goal of getting more women into local government. In the 1987 local election, the Network ran twenty-four women candidates, and fourteen of them were elected. The goal for next year's election is to get thirty women into municipal govern-ment.[7]

While the Kanagawa Network has been successful in its attempts to em-power women, others have had modest success by comparison. The Nagoya Network in Nagoya City, for instance, located in a more traditional, rural setting, has had a difficult time mobilizing women. Author Matsuno was told by several women in Nagoya that while they would have liked to have joined the Network because its products are safe and its political activities commend-able, they feared that the companies their husbands worked for might not promote them as a result. As one woman explained, "People think that the co-op [network] is left-side politics. If I join, my husband's company might pun-ish us by keeping my husband in a low position." Another woman, herself a member of the Nagoya co-op, indicated that "women in this area of Japan have rather low education and do not realize that they have rights to speak out and work for the election of women." Thus while women in Nagoya are generally pleased with the progress women politicians have made recently in Japan, many rejoice privately; publicly, as a female local Assembly member pointed out, they "support their families' conservative male politicians."

Yaeko Nishiyama, professor of sociology, indicated in an interview that the reason why some of the women's networks, especially those in Kanagawa and in Tokyo, have been so successful in mobilizing women is that in these urban areas conditions are changing rapidly, and the family and community are being profoundly affected. The traditional Japanese family is being transformed as more women enter the labor force, and the earlier closely knit neighborhood is being replaced by impersonal ties. "Under these conditions," says Nishiyama, "people are realizing that it is necessary to produce a new society with the incorporation of individuals into a larger whole. Women, who feel these changes more deeply because they are involved more closely in everyday life, are spearheading the movement."

The women's networks have been instrumental in getting more women into public offices not only at the local but also at the parliamentary level. For instance, before the February 1990 election, local groups in coordination with others in their network sponsored public forums where they invited women candidates to speak and to debate male politicians. They also worked with women politicians already in the Diet in a mutual effort of support for women candidates. Takako Doi, the Socialist Party leader, traveled all over the country, appearing at various network-sponsored events in support of female candidates for the Upper House, even though many of the women running were not affiliated with the Socialists.

Women's networks and coalitions have thus flourished all over Japan. Growing out of the consumer and citizen's movement for improvement of quality of life, these groups, which have had a predominantly female membership, have increasingly turned to sponsorship and support of women candidates for political office. Over time, they also have come to cooperate more closely with female politicians and others concerned with increasing women's representation at all levels of government. No doubt spurred on by such efforts, Japanese women politicians have started to develop coalitions across party lines and across organizations and levels of government. For instance, recently women in the Upper and the Lower House of the Diet have pledged to work together to improve legislation aimed at providing social services to children, the elderly, and the handicapped (Kubo, 1990).

## Conclusion

In this chapter we have attempted to show that Japanese women's struggle for empowerment has had a long history and that the recent movement to enter the public sphere of politics has drawn on a distinct women's culture. In their efforts to enter and to change politics the women involved have relied on their knowledge of family and local community needs and concerns and on the organizing skills they have developed in consumer and other civic groups. The women's main strategies have consisted of forming extensive networks and coalitions among women of various ideological persuasions, party allegiances, and experiences in a common endeavor to get more women elected into public offices.

Once elected, Japanese women politicians feel responsible for acting on behalf of their constituents and thus they bring the issues and concerns of their supporters, largely women, onto political agendas. While there is evidence that these women politicians are making a difference at the local and national levels of government, they are still a small minority and thus their impact as a group is not substantial. However, the extensive grass-roots mobilization of Japanese women which has occurred in recent years and the concurrent democratization of local political processes attest to an important transformation taking place in Japanese politics.

# Notes

1. Feminist historians point out that several factors accounted for the relatively high status of women during the Heian age which made it possible for them to achieve literary recognition: matrilocal residence (married couple living with or near the wife's parents), which provided women with economic and social security; the right to inherit property, including the family residence and land; and a sense of mutual sexual enjoyment accepted by the Heian culture (Bingham and Gross, 1987: 54). Thus, while Confucian ideals promoting the patrilocal and patrilineal family system spread gradually throughout Japan since the eighth century, it was not until much later, during the Tokugawa era (1600–1868), that women, and especially those of the upper classes, lost their important place in Japanese society.

2. In all subsequent elections, fewer women have been elected to the Lower House, and only in 1989 was a higher number than ten (twenty-two) elected to the Upper House.

3. There are six major political parties in Japan: Liberal Democratic Party, Japan Socialist Party, Japan Communist Party, Komei Party, Democratic Socialist Party, and Rengo-Sangii, a new party established by a nationwide labor organization.

4. The proportional representation system allows for several candidates from each party and district to compete for a seat, which increases the probability that women will be on the ballots and thus their chances for election.

5. Ueno (1987) points out that Japan did not incorporate the couple culture during its process of Westernization. Since wives do not have to appear with their husbands at social functions or entertain husbands' guests at home, they enjoy relative freedom. With sex segregation of social spheres, the wife can maintain her own relations with other women.

6. In 1988 the government changed Japan's abortion law from allowing women to

have abortions at twenty-four weeks of pregnancy to twenty-two weeks. This was done without any consultation with women's and human rights groups.

7. Another highly successful cooperative, the Tokyo Network, in the unified local elections of 1987 sponsored twenty-nine candidates of whom twenty-three were elected (Kubo, 1990:4).

# WOMEN'S MOVEMENTS

For women all over the world, women's movements have been an important means of empowerment. It is through organizing and joining women's groups and actions that many women have become aware of their oppression and have sought ways to gain control of their lives and to change the male-dominated structures of their societies. Contemporary social science research, particularly in political science and sociology, tends to marginalize women's movements by placing them into "noninstitutionalized" and "social movement" categories, effectively minimizing women's political struggles for emancipation and change. In this section, women's movements are examined as a central political force and major source of empowerment strategies for women.

As all four chapters show, women's groups and organizations outside the realm of established politics function to pressure groups and representatives within the political establishment to take stands more favorable to women and to bring women's issues more openly into public political agendas. Coalitions sometimes form (as in Greece and Canada) between nonpartisan women's groups, women's party caucuses, and other "establishment" organizations. Such coalitions seem to consist of a tacit division of labor where women's groups outside the system formulate issues and work to increase awareness of women's concerns, while women within the system bring these issues into political agendas and discourse.

Yota Papageorgiou-Limberes in her chapter on Greek women's organizations and their relationship to the established political institutions shows that, despite fragmentation within the Greek women's movement, there have been successful attempts in recent years to unite various ideological groups. The strategies which have been effective include mobilizing around central issues of concern to all women, using the media as well as mass-based demonstrations to spread feminist messages, and developing coalitions between women's groups and female members of political parties.

Vicky Randall examines feminist strategies in Great Britain during the 1980s, in light of economic recession and a generally conservative ideological climate. The threats of erosion to feminist achievements of the previous decade and a generally weakened women's movement have led women's groups to take a defensive stand against some current policies designed to undermine women's status, particularly in the area of reproductive rights. At the same time the movement has been trying to forge ahead by pressing for new laws and better conditions for women. Despite ideological divisions within the women's movement and organizational problems, feminists have rallied to the cause of protecting women's abortion rights by building coalitions between various women's groups and effective lobbying of legislators.

Esperanza Tuñon Pablos, in her chapter on the women's movement in Mexico, provides a glimpse of the little-known history of the movement, its ebb and flow in the twentieth century, and recent strategies used by movement activities to attain changes favorable to Mexican women. As she indicates, while in its first phase (late nineteenth century until 1940) the Mexican women's movement sprung from a collective recognition of women's issues and concerns and placed much emphasis on working through the various political parties, the contemporary phase of the movement (since 1970) arose from fragmented ideologies and actions with few links to established parties and other groups. Only since the early 1980s, within the context of a broad-based popular democracy movement, has there been a concerted effort to unite the disparate women's groups, to form alliances with political parties and other social movement organizations, and to press for reform and change. In recent years, the movement has relied increasingly on such strategies as coalition building, using the mass media to spread feminist messages, developing women's scholarship in institutions of higher learning, and on presentation of women's demands in legislative bodies.

Finally, the last chapter in this section examines the societal contexts of the strategies used by women's movements in Canada and the United States in their attempts to obtain constitutional equal rights amendments. Melissa A. Haussman systematically compares the actions of movement women in the two countries and shows how specific societal conditions, the lack or presence of cultural and structural opportunities, and particular tactics combine to create either favorable or unfavorable outcomes. This chapter illuminates how and why Canadian women were successful in obtaining an equal rights clause in their constitution, while their U.S. counterparts failed to do the same.

C H A P T E R

5

# THE WOMEN'S MOVEMENT AND GREEK POLITICS

## *Yota Papageorgiou-Limberes*

This chapter will demonstrate that the Greek women's movement was active in some form historically, and that it managed to change the conservative status quo, albeit weakly. The movement culminated after the fall of the military dictatorship (1967–1974), when women's organizations proliferated, sensitizing and mobilizing Greek women toward greater participation in all spheres of life. These organizations would have been more successful had their efforts been more concerted and unified. Instead, because of the different experiences and achievements of their leaders, as well as external pressure, the movement was split into many, less effective groups. Partly responsible for this fragmentation were the political parties which patronized the major women's organizations (from left to right) and hence managed to diffuse their specific issues, thereby reducing the movement's power.

Some of the women's groups have followed an independent and nonpartisan course. Yet, with all their disagreements, different strategies, and external interference, when genuinely important women's issues have arisen, all women's organizations and groups, regardless of their specific political affiliation, have joined forces to promote such issues. Thus, the family law issue, the abortion issue, and recently the quota system issue found all Greek women's organizations united.

To understand the evolution of Greek women's political activities, it is necessary to examine the role that women's organizations have played in this process. It is also important to present them and their goals in a historical context. In addition, the contemporary situation will be examined in depth, including discussion of current strategies based on interviews with Greek women leaders of women's organizations.

## From Obscurity to Visibility

In the latter part of the nineteenth century and the first part of the twentieth, women's organizations in Greece began to form, aiming to improve women's positions in society. In 1897, the Union of Greek Women was founded by the first Greek woman journalist and feminist, Kalliopi Parren. She published a newspaper called *Newspaper of Ladies,* which was "a journalistic tool that in a period of thirty years served the women's movement in Greece" (Xiradaki, 1988: 100). Parren's main objective was the social and political improvement of women's status. Her strategy was not only to sensitize women through the written word but also to lobby the government and political parties for women's rights. As the head of a group of feminists, she wrote a petition signed by 2,850 women, sent to the government and all Parliament members, asking that: (1) women be given access to paid work; (2) women be given the right to vote; and (3) the government establish public educational institutions accessible to women. In addition, she solicited the Greek prime minister asking for the right of women to vote and to be accepted at the university and polytechnic school. Her extensive writing was influential enough to stir a dialogue among male intellectuals and to convince some of them that Greek women were profoundly oppressed. In the opinion of some contemporary feminist researchers, Parren is the founder of the feminist movement in Greece (Avdela and Psarra, 1985; Xiradaki, 1989).

The main strategies of the organizations established between the period of 1870 and 1920 were to seek the help of prominent men, and to a lesser extent government deputies, in order to introduce and support social and religious solutions in the areas of child welfare, poverty, the handicapped, and the aged. Feminist issues, such as abortion rights, were also a part of these groups' demands. Although the majority of the population was reluctant to listen to such demands, the feminists managed to gain the ear and support of certain prominent intellectual and government people. Forums on emancipation of women and promotion of women's social and political awareness, as a central focus supported by the majority of women belonging to the lower classes, developed a little later, following an economic and social transformation of the country. After 1922, with the influx of the more educated Greek refugees from Asia Minor, the objectives of the women's movement broadened to include women's rights not only within the family but also within society.

The social, economic, and political changes that occurred in Greece during the 1920s allowed many women to participate more actively outside the family. New associations came into existence which attempted to elevate women's role from its secondary social function to one of equal status with that of men. The most prominent of such associations were the Association of Women's Rights established in 1920, and the National Council of Women, established in 1923. (In the same year, these organizations began to publish two important journals *Women's Struggle* and *Greek Women.*) The objective of both organizations was female enfranchisement, and their main strategies were increasing public awareness of women's issues, mobilizing support through the press, and lobbying Parliament members and government officials. They also organized demonstrations outside the Parliament. In 1925, women's organizations signed and presented a petition to the Parliament asking for suffrage, at least in the local elections. This petition was signed by many men as well (Xiradaki, 1988: 117).

The 1920s was an opportune time for discussions, speeches, and heated debates within Parliament and throughout Greece. Feminists gathered in a public place, at least once a week, discussing strategies (Xiradaki, 1988:120).

After long and continuous struggles, women were granted the right to vote in the municipal elections of 1930, on two conditions that were not applied to men: (1) that they had reached the age of thirty; and (2) that they were literate. The rationale behind such conditions was to exclude the majority of women voters, since illiteracy was predominant among women.

During the World War II period, the women's movement became part of a new humanistic movement that was affecting the entire nation. Most members of women's organizations at that time were women who had been active in the resistance movement. For the first time, women's rights officially were supported by the Communist Party (Kalsoyia-Tournaviti, 1982: 12–16). In several parts of Greece, women's organizations had been established with a broader and more popular grass-roots membership than earlier groups had enjoyed. These organizations were mainly concerned with equality of the sexes. For example, the objectives of the Association of Women's Rights were to offer women better skills, better education and higher wages, and to improve their working conditions.

There was a pause of activities during the civil war (1946–1949), but afterwards women's organizations, which until then had a popular base, were dissolved by the reactionary government. The Communist Party was also outlawed, and any association with the party was thought to be suspicious. Secondly, the leftist forces—especially the Communist Party which supported women's rights—became suspect of anti-nationalistic actions and were losing their influence in Greek society. In 1949, women engaged in broad demonstrations and demanded an unconditional right to vote as well as the right to participate in political offices. Finally in 1952, both the right to vote and the right to seek public office were granted to women. During the elections of the same year, the first woman was elected to the Greek Parliament.

With the passage of a new law in 1953, the Covenant on the Political Rights of Women enacted by the United Nations in 1952 was recognized by the Greek state and referred to as the *Political Rights of Women*. Theoretically at least, political discrimination against women was thus outlawed. That very year (1953) may mark the beginning of Greek women's participation in public life, both as members of Greek society and in official Greek politics. They entered the public sector en masse. With these new changes, women's organizations became more active. New organizations were established, such as the Union of Greek Women Lawyers, and the Pan Hellenic Women's Organization (1964). The common characteristic of organizations established during this period was their objective of securing equality for women in economic and political life—equal work, equal wages, and equal representation in governance. These organizations used more systematic strategies to mobilize the Greek public, the government, and elites. They organized campaigns, used the press as a tool for promoting issues, lobbied for women's rights, and wrote to politicians. Greek women's associations, regardless of their weaknesses—such as lack of grass-roots participation in rural areas—were active, forceful, and gradually gained ground. However, with the military coup d'etat that resulted in a change of government in 1967, all public activities stopped, and women's organizations were forced, once again, either to cease their struggle or to go underground.

### Recent Developments

Following the fall of the military junta (1974), a new social and political order began. During the period of military rule (1967–1974), Greek men and women had developed a new political consciousness. This was partly a reaction to the interruption of the social and political changes that Greece was undergoing during the 1960s. Greek political analysts blamed the military intervention for preventing social and political changes which were moving the country toward modernity and democratic development (Mouzelis, 1978; Poulanzas, 1976; Tsoucalas, 1977).

When the Conservative Party (under a new label) resumed power in 1974, it was forced to compromise. Its principles had not undergone any structural change; yet, the new realities forced it to yield to new demands, such as recognition of the Communist Party and of women's rights (Limberes, 1986: 113–37). In the November 1974 election, the conservatives won a large majority in Parliament. In December 1974, a national plebiscite abolished the monarchy (by 69 percent), and a new Constitution was promulgated and ratified (1975), thus formally making Greece a republic.

With the promulgation of the new Constitution and the creation of the new republic, women were accorded several rights and obligations in all aspects of life—public and private. This meant that, at least theoretically, women also should have served in the armed forces.

The new Constitution specified that "All Greek men and women are equal before the Law." In 1983, the government signed and ratified Article 7 of the U.N. Convention on the elimination of all forms of discrimination against women. Thus, according to these laws, women are equal to men in Greek society and have the right to participate equally in all decision-making processes. With such constitutional rights on their side, Greek women's strategies focused on the abolition of institutionalized inequalities against women. Thus, women's organizations demanded institutional reforms such as the modernization of family law, educational reforms, and improved working conditions, hoping that the guarantees of equality encoded in the Constitution could be applied in practice.

Toward this end, in 1974 women with a leftist background came together under an umbrella organization called the Union of Democratic Women (KDG). The KDG was active, decisive, and vocal in making women's demands heard. Its demands were practical and relevant to the position of women. It called for equal work and wages, daycare centers, and greater social and political participation, including the direct participation in decision-making processes at all levels. The KDG's strategies were militant and included protests, riots, and demonstrations.

Political parties such as the Panhellenic Socialist Movement (PASOK) and the Communist Party of Greece (KKE) were seen by women as the sole promoters of their interests because these parties had come to embrace a large array of social issues. However, while these parties endorsed women's issues, they demanded that women submit to the general party strategy. This brought disagreement among women as to which strategy was most effective for accomplishing their cause. Consequently, divisions occurred within women's groups. Thus, in 1976, the KDG had split, and two separate organizations were established. One was EGE (Union of Greek Women), ideologically linked to the Socialist Party (PASOK), and the other was OGE (Federation of Greek Women), which was ideologically linked to the Communist Party. Both groups sided with the strategies of their respective parties. Perhaps the parties themselves were instrumental in splitting women's organizations, but in a period of ten years (1974–1984), many women's organizations and groups had emerged, and the number of organized women had risen by 50 percent in 1984 (Lovenduski, 1986: 104). These organizations were decentralized, creating branches throughout Greece that attempted to mobilize as many women as possible both as members and activists.

The existence of underground women's organizations and the Catholic resistance during the military dictatorship (1967–1974) offered to women members a set of skills which enabled them to maximize their opportunities, expand their organization, and increase their political participation following the military collapse (1974). The contemporary mushrooming of women's organizations is the result of that earlier training. At present (1990) in Athens alone, there are twenty-five women's organizations and twenty women's groups.

In spite of the obstacles to their direct involvement in government politics, women today are exerting considerable influence in the political life of Greece. Responsible for this climate are the activities of women's organizations and smaller groups, irrespective of their ideological orientation. The common intention of these organizations is to promote women's issues and to integrate women as equal members of society. However, as mentioned above, most newly emerging organizations have aligned themselves ideologically and strategically with various political parties and pursue women's demands through them. Their rationale is that by having feminist issues incorporated into the general agenda of the party of their choice, that party will include them in political changes when it comes to power, or at least will articulate the issues more clearly and effectively when in opposition. Thus, some women's organizations have been dependent on, and patronized by, political parties (e.g., EGE by the Socialist Party, PASOK, OGE by the Communist Party, KKE).

The phenomenon of party allegiance is a hotly contested issue at present in Greece and may need some explanation. When political organizations align themselves with a certain party, the general ideology of the party prevails. The party does not facilitate fulfillment of grass-roots needs and demands or promote feminist issues such as promotion of women in decision-making positions. Any pressure on the party to offer political positions to women is of secondary importance. Women's organizations within parties are not likely to push for radical changes for fear that they may alienate the party. While, on the one hand, these organizations become somewhat ineffective pressure groups under the hitherto electoral-list system, on the other hand, by joining political parties and through package deals, women try to promote their issues within specific political parties.

The political parties do respond to some women's issues, or at least make them known to the public and to the decision-makers. Yet, political parties in Greece, by using various issues to mobilize support tend to diffuse the intensity of particular issues. As a consequence, the party cannot emphasize one issue at the expense of another but must present the issues as a package program of its general platform. This makes women's issues only as important as their proportion of the number of total issues involved allows.

There are three important political parties in Greece which are ideologically distinct (the Conservative, ND; the Socialist, PASOK; and the Leftist Coalition), and all three claim to promote women's issues. Women's organizations can, and do, join the party which is ideologically closest to their own views. This diversity, however, is not used as a strategy by women's organizations to pursue the same issues from different angles in a concerted effort. Instead, by advocating the general ideology of a particular party, women's organizations often find themselves in antagonistic positions, both in terms of substantive women's issues (i.e., what are the most important women's issues) and in terms of strategies (i.e., which is the best method to obtain maximum results).

These organizations also model traditional male-oriented forms of organization. They typically have a constitution, a centralized and hierarchical leadership, work committees, an electoral system, and a network of branches (Stamiris, 1986: 106).

While traditional women's organizations' goals and intentions are to change the position of women without disrupting substantially the status quo, there is emerging a new and autonomous movement which seeks a total transformation of the political and social order. Indeed, the last ten years have witnessed the appearance of small, autonomous groups, which are not aligned with political parties and are engaged in consciousness-raising around the themes of sexuality, body, ideology, and prostitution. They challenge the myth of the family unit of Greek society by exposing rape and wife battering and by claiming that these methods are used to perpetuate women's subordination. They also are closer to radical ideology and therefore do not believe in organizing themselves in a hierarchical structure. Their small size, however, makes them less effective in the public sphere than the women's organizations tied to political parties.

In promoting feminist issues these autonomous groups pursue their own strategies. They are inflexible and often refuse to follow the tactics advocated by the better-established women's organizations. However, there are instances where both the groups' and organizations' strategies coincide. For example, the fight to legalize abortion was jointly pursued by both factions with resounding success.

The Greek parties, regardless of their pre-election pronouncements, pay little attention to women's problems. The few women candidates included are listed at the bottom of voting lists while women are excluded from the higher ranks (Papageorgiou-Limberes, 1988: 33). Thus in the parliamentary election of 1990, only 16 (5.3 percent) of the elected representatives were women. At the Euro-Parliament elections of 1989, out of 26 members, only 1 was a woman (4.5 percent). In the local elections of 1986, out of 303 mayors, there were only 6 women (1.9 percent); among 5,697 community presidents only 30 were women (0.52 percent); in municipal councils, out of 4,999 councilors only 412 were women (8.24 percent); in community councils, out of 40,402 only 812 were women (2 percent); and out of 303 presidents of municipal councils only 4 were women (1.6 percent).

The electoral system in Greece fluctuates. For a time it was detrimental to women's efforts to get onto the party ticket. For example, PASOK had introduced a new electoral system, the "list system," in which the leader of the party decided who will run on the party ticket and in what order the candidates will be listed. Therefore, whether to include more women in a party's list of candidates depended on how the party leader felt about the party's chances of winning the election with more or fewer women. But even if the party list included some women candidates, this would not help much: women's chances of getting elected are low if their names are placed at the bottom of the list. Prime Minister Papandreou prefers the list system because it allows the leader to control his or her deputies and prevents defections. On the other hand, because of complaints, especially from small parties, the government has reintroduced the "cross-system." This system depends on the number of votes a candidate receives. Thus, while under the list system one votes for the party, under the cross system the vote is cast for the candidate. If the candidate comes across favorably to the public, she or he is elected. But for candidates to convince people to vote for them, they must make promises that will satisfy the constituency. The list system does not allow for that. However, a study I conducted in Athens found that 65 percent of women voters preferred women candidates (Papageorgiou-Limberes, 1988).

In the April 1990 election, the cross system was employed, and candidates had greater latitude in how they presented themselves. The great irony, however, is that Greek society is politicized in terms of parties, and the candidates were forced to remain close to their general party ideology. A pre-election promise which did not materialize was the "quota-system," where neither sex should exceed 65 percent of each party's candidate list. Women's organizations strongly campaigned for the institution of such a quota system, but the parties would not accept it. Certainly men and women could run as independents, but lately independents in Greece have not done well in the polls; and in addition to competing with established party candidates, they have had to shoulder enormous costs.

Despite the various shortcomings and party hinderances, the feminist movement through its informal network of women has spread throughout Greece and, by systematic and concerted efforts, has promoted and advanced women's issues. By using their personal influence and connections and staying above specific organizational interests, some women have managed to unite the main organizations whose ideological perspectives differ. Their rationale has been that a united front (regarding important women's issues) and common strategies will afford the political parties no alternatives to the women's demands but to go along with them. These feminist leaders have understood that certain issues are very important for women, and therefore they formally proposed the establishment of a common front by women's organizations in order to pressure the political parties more firmly. They also wanted to increase public awareness by presenting important feminist issues to the general population. Women from leftist parties realized the importance of the proposal and campaigned to bring together as many women's organizations as possible. Their efforts brought together twelve major women's organizations under the auspices of SEGES (Coordinating Committee of Representatives of Women's Organizations),[1] which then solicited and lobbied the political parties to take action in favor of women. (The more radical feminist groups, whose work has focused on building alternatives for women outside the established political system, refused to join SEGES.)

Pursuing their goal to remedy institutional inequalities, SEGES organized an extensive mobilization against an old family law which had regulated family relationships for thirty-five years. This law, apart from other inequalities, explicitly perpetuated patriarchy by stating that the husband was the head of the family while the woman did not have property rights or custodial rights regarding her children (Tsouderou, 1981: 20). Under SEGES' pressure, an expert committee was appointed by the government, and the legislation it wrote incorporated some of the women's demands in what was called the Gazis Reform Bill. The bill did not pass when the Conservatives were in power because the propositions were considered revolutionary by the minister of justice (Papachristou, 1982: 20). That made women's organizations intensify their struggle, and through mobilizing public opinion, holding demonstrations, and lobbying for political support, they were successful in securing the pledge of the leftist opposition parties. It was a strategy that paid off.

Indeed, when the Socialists came to power in 1981, the old family law was reformed. The new family law abolished the patriarchal structure and replaced it with the "equal family," in which the husband was no longer the head of the family and family decisions were to be made jointly by both spouses. Children were to be raised without gender discrimination; children born out of wedlock became equal before the law. Civil marriage and "automatic" divorce was permitted; assistance to working parents with children was provided through provisions for parental leave, which established the father's rights to share in the raising of children. But women's struggles did not stop there. "As a principal strategy they continue to lobby the government to adopt progressive policies toward women and to lead public opinion in support of equality. Their final goal is women's full integration into society on an equal basis with men" (Stamiris, 1986: 108). In addition, the Socialist government legally recognized the existence of female inequality and established a national machinery, the Council of Equality (1982), which was later upgraded to the General Secretariat for Equality of the Sexes (1985). Its objectives are to promote equality legislation, to monitor the implementation of existing laws at the national level, and to develop a network of equality bureaus throughout the country in order to secure equality in outlying areas. In 1983, a law that prohibited women's participation in cooperatives was abolished, and in 1984, with the assistance of the General Secretariat for Equality, four women's cooperatives were established. Another achievement of women is that schoolbooks are to be rewritten with the cooperation of women's organizations, to insure that the principles of equality will be included. Also women's organizations are pressing for the introduction of affirmative action programs to secure positions for women in "male" professions.

In 1986, a bill was passed by the Parliament which allows pregnant women to decide on abortion up to the twelfth week of pregnancy or the twenty-fourth week in the case of fetal abnormality, after which individual cases would be examined by a special committee. No restrictions whatever would apply in cases of rape or incest.

Other major issues that women's organizations have been concerned with have been pornography and the image of women portrayed in the mass media. Their strategy has been to press the government to stop the exploitation of the female body. In addition, they have campaigned against pollution problems and for peace. In fact, the Greek peace movement has been growing in the last five years, and women are very active in it.

In the parliamentary elections of April 1990, women's organizations again united under SEGES to pressure the government and political parties to agree to a 35 percent minimum quota to be guaranteed to women running for Parliament. The two major parties had not been very sympathetic to the idea, while the Leftist Coalition had been supportive, without taking any official stand. During the election of April 1990, out of 338 candidates for ND, only 23 (6.8 percent) were women; similarly out of 328 of PASOK candidates, 25 (7.6 percent) were women, while the Leftist Coalition included 60 (18.25 percent) women out of 328 candidates.

In spite of its low number of women in political office, Greece has been rather liberal in adopting legislation favorable to women, not only within the framework of Greek society but also within the European context. To be sure, legal equality alone does not guarantee equality for women in everyday life.

Feminist organizations are cognizant of this fact and realize that they still have a long way to go to secure actual equality of women with men.

## Recent Strategies

Greek women have come to realize that though institutional changes are necessary, they are not enough to change Greeks' cultural orientations. They deem it necessary for women to work toward the change of societal attitudes and values in order to become equal members in every sphere of life. Thus, as part of their strategy, contemporary Greek women's organizations have arranged their activities on a broad scale to sensitize and mobilize women, to lobby for more legislative reforms in favor of women, and, most importantly, to increase the number of women voting for women political candidates.

The mass media, especially television, are considered by feminists the most important means to sensitize people to women's issues. But access to Greek public television, for example, is very difficult. Public television is state-owned and controlled. In addition, it does not air programming focused on feminist issues, and a conservative image of women is projected, perpetuating the notion that women's traditional roles are as housekeepers, babysitters, and sex objects. It is difficult for feminists to have their own programs. As one organization leader stated:

> Mass media, especially TV, are androcratic and controlled by the government. Even newspapers and magazines that are not state controlled have an androcentric viewpoint, and it is difficult for women to penetrate them.[2]

However difficult it might be, Greek women have managed to create a few women's programs, after airing complaints in the press and condemning publicly their ostracism. The managers of the three public television stations, facing strong pressure, have yielded and offered some time to women's programs. The first programs were dedicated to Women's Day and Mothers' Day, and some women's talk shows were aired as well. The programs had a huge viewing, especially in the rural areas, where TV is the only form of entertainment, particularly for women. Subsequently, more women's programs were offered. However, women still have a long way to go in order to be able to create sufficient programs for women. Recently private television has been introduced and thus far the Athens metropolitan area has four stations. No women's programs are being shown yet, but there is hope that if private stations sense a market for feminist programs they will begin broadcasting them.

While private radio and newspapers allow some opportunity for women's news, their ideology is also androcentric. Moreover, both radio and press are ideologically oriented, attached to political parties, and thus are very much controlled by them. Television stations are also ideologically oriented, but because of strong competition they are more open to all types of money-making programs. On the other hand, the women's programs offered on the radio are partisan and aimed at propagandizing party politics, with women used for party ends. The situation is somewhat different with the press. There are two kinds of women's magazines, the typical profit-oriented commercial publications about women, and feminist publications. Commercial magazines (such as *Gynaika* and *Pantheon*) concern themselves with home and family issues, and, as does television, they perpetuate and promote women's traditional roles. There are also other journals and magazines published by women which provide a forum for discussions of political ideas. Although some of these journals may lack sophistication, publications of this kind provide opportunities for feminist consciousness raising. Most of these publications have an activist orientation; few journals (such as *Scoupa*, until 1981, and *Dini*) contain articles "which while brief are filling an important gap in Greek academic political analysis" (Cacoullos, 1988: 8).

Women's organizations have understood the importance of the media and have thus published magazines, newspapers, and brochures enlightening the public about female issues such as birth control, AIDS, and family planning. Realizing the difficulties they have in selling their material on the economic market, they have established feminist bookstores where women can find feminist publications.

A second strategy important for women's organizations is to unite together in "single-issue organizations." As one woman activist put it:

> Pursuing our aim as a single issue is very important for women, because the greater our pressure the more the institutions and parties will be affected, and the greater the challenge of the establishment will be.

Indeed if one women's organization demonstrates or pressures a political party on an issue, it might cause a change of attitude in the given party, but this might not affect the policies of other parties. When organizations act together, they are more effective and can influence the policies of all the parties. This was obvious in the proposed quota system where all women's organizations jointly asked for a 35 percent electoral representation by the political parties. All political parties were forced to take positions on this matter.

A third successful strategy is demonstrations, such as the one about the minimum quota of women electoral candidates. As a prominent organization leader explained,

> At the heart of Athens, women from all organizations as well as political parties gathered together to support our cause. Even some prominent politicians such as Melina Mercouri [minister of culture], were there. It was a peaceful mass protest and became a national event. This event was carried by the evening television news and received much commentary. It had an impact on the political parties because a few days later they were sitting with us at a roundtable discussing the quota system. They knew that if they did not sit with us they would face a mass protest. A few days later, women's organizations had a well-organized massive campaign on this issue. This event also helped them to establish linkages and exchanges between the different organizations. We

know our grievances would not be respected. But at least, we got them to talk to us and received much publicity.

A fourth strategy concerns the cooperation of organizations with female members of political parties. Women's organizations try to make women belonging to the parties aware of women's demands and to convince them to pressure other members of the party to support women's legislation. In fact, every party has its own "women's problem committee" that studies and monitors women's concerns and demands. These committees are very useful and so far have been effective. Often women party members try to sensitize men and also to mobilize around women's issues in order for the parties to support legislation favorable to women. Such efforts, however, are not easily accepted by male colleagues. As a female member of a small leftist party put it:

I had many difficulties with the rest of the members of my party in order for me to continue to press for open dialogue with male colleagues of mine and the leadership, in order for me to pursue and stress that women need special attention since they have special needs. They [male members] were usually ironic, joked, and did not sit down to have a serious conversation on such a topic. Every new idea comes from the female member of the party, and in the case of women, it provokes reaction. That very fact made me more conscious about my sex, and the more I was not taken seriously the more feminist I became.

Another member of the women's problem committee of a leftist party stated:

At the beginning, party ideology was more important for me than the feminist ideology. But the more I stayed in the party the more I changed my ideology to feminism.

## Conclusion

Greek women, throughout their long struggle, have come to realize that to succeed, their strategies must be directed toward public recognition and awareness of their demands. Toward that end, they have pursued a two-pronged attack aimed at formal institutions and at the Greek public by employing standard tactics, such as use of electronic and print media along with door-to-door campaigns and peaceful demonstrations, and by engaging in sit-ins, strikes, and various public pronouncements. As I have indicated in this chapter, Greek society, even with a long tradition of androcratic rule, is gradually giving up some of the male privileges. Partly responsible for the gradual acceptance of women's equality is a more liberal political and social climate but most important are the strategies and resilience of women in their struggle for equality.

At present, there are two streams of the women's movement in Greece. One stream is represented by formal women's organizations, the more established form of the movement, and pursues reconciliation and gradual change.

The other stream is represented by small, autonomous, radical groups, which are absolute in their demands and impatient in their expectations. Even though the strategies of both streams are different, they do complement each other. While the radical women's groups present women's issues in a strident fashion, by mobilizing women at the grass-roots level and thus increasing the general public awareness of women's issues, women's organizations, through moderation, tone down the issues when they present them to the decision-makers. Small radical groups spearhead the new ideas and in so doing allow the moderate organizations who are closer to political power to pursue a less radical and more pragmatic strategy. Greek society is amenable to change provided that change is not overtly threatening. As one deputy put it, "rock the boat but don't capsize it."

Finally, Greek women's organizations must ultimately disassociate themselves from political parties, or at least from the strongly ideological parties, because, as mentioned above, their issues are "packaged" with other issues by parties, thereby making them appear unimportant by themselves and hence are doomed to receive no particular attention. In a sense, by following the party's line and submitting their programs to the general party platform, women's organizations do themselves more harm than good. Often they are forced to accept or allow their issues to be combined with other party issues that may not be compatible.

Alternately, the women's movement must ultimately reach some form of consensus, at least so far as the most important women's issues are concerned, and to pursue a nonpartisan line. In doing so the movement will be able to bargain and influence whatever party is in power and thereby will derive maximum benefits. The Greek women's movement must not allow itself to be "divided and ruled" by any party, and the participants must learn to work together for women's empowerment.

# Notes

1. The coordinating committee of women's organizations included the following organizations: National Council of Greek Women; Union of Greek Women; Union of Women Soroptimists; Mediterranean Women's Studies Institute; Democratic Women's Movement; Lyceum of Greek Women; Panhellenic Union of Women Civil Servants; Union of Housewives; League for Women's Rights; Hellenic Association of University Women; Association of Professional-Business Women; and YWCA of Greece.

2. This chapter is based in part on a study I conducted in Athens and Salonica, during the summer, fall, and winter of 1989. It involved in-depth interviews with women elected to Greek and European Parliaments (N = 30) and feminist leaders and influential cadres of women's organizations and groups (N = 19). This and subsequent quotations are drawn from the interviews.

CHAPTER

6

# GREAT BRITAIN AND DILEMMAS FOR FEMINIST STRATEGY IN THE 1980S
The Case of Abortion and Reproductive Rights

## Vicky Randall

At the risk of sounding a negative note in what is overall an optimistic volume, in this chapter I want to concentrate on identifying and explaining the real *difficulties* for feminism in Britain over the last decade. This is not to deny its continuing achievements on many policy fronts and at many levels: indeed they are the more impressive given the very obstacles that have had to be overcome. These difficulties have been a consequence of the nature of the British women's movement, of its economic and political contexts and the way they have interacted. Some of the problems are longstanding, apparent already in the 1970s, while others are more specifically the result of how the movement has changed and, related to that change, the impact of economic "restructuring" and "Thatcherism."

In the first part of the chapter I shall set out these arguments in general terms. In the second I shall consider developments in the area of abortion policy and reproductive rights. The object is not to give a comprehensive account of these developments but to show how they exemplify the dilemmas for feminist strategy. At the same time, there are features peculiar to this policy area which create particular problems and uncertainties.[1]

While I will concentrate on Britain, this should not be taken to imply that the experiences described are without parallel elsewhere. On the contrary, they have many features in common with feminist struggles in other Western nations, both in general and in the specific field of reproductive rights, which I can only briefly allude to. Nonetheless, the contention is that a particular combination of circumstances has produced a distinctive set of problems for British feminism.

## British Feminism: The Context

Second-wave feminism took hold early in Britain, and by the beginning of the 1970s it was a widespread popular movement. Certain aspects of the economic and political environment at the time had facilitated its development: for instance, rates of unemployment and public sector retrenchment were modest in comparison with their later levels.

But even then any serious attempt to alter policy had to contend with the fact that, among Western democracies at least, Britain has an unusually centralized political system. It is unitary, lacking a significant regional level of decision-making like that in the United States or even Italy or the old German Federal Republic. The closest Britain has come to decentralization is with the introduction of the Greater London Council (GLC) in 1964 and the six Metropolitan Councils in 1974. However, their role was always unclear; strategic rhetoric was unmatched by statutory powers, and they were finally dismantled by the Conservative government in 1984. Even so, GLC initiatives in the early 1980s contributed importantly to the development of "municipal feminism," as discussed below. Otherwise Britain's local authorities, constitutionally speaking, have been more like agents of central government. In the absence of a written constitution, Britain has also lacked a tradition of constitutional interpretation through the courts, which might offer an alternative route for pressure to change policy, as in the United States. One important qualification to this centralized model, especially for feminists, is the policy influence of the European Community (EC). Most relevant to the present discussion, from the mid-1970s the EC has issued a series of directives (not immediately binding but requiring long-term compliance in policy outcome) aimed at enhancing equal employment opportunities for women. The British Conservative government from 1979 has put up the stoutest resistance to these directives of any member country.

Related to this governmental system, especially the absence of a written constitution or Bill of Rights, there has been no strong tradition within the national "political culture" of concern with abstract "rights" or civil liberties which feminists could tap into or which indeed could feed equal-rights feminism (Lovenduski, 1989). In addition, as Meehan (1985) has well described, feminists have had to contend with a distinctive British bureaucratic culture. Even though civil service neutrality is more of a guiding principle than a characterization of everyday practice, it has, for instance in the field of equal opportunities, formed a further barrier to the transmission of feminist pressures and the development of the sort of feminist "networks," linking women inside government with individuals and groups outside, that have flourished in other countries. Feminists are more likely to influence government policy recommendations when they are co-opted in an advisory capacity on the basis of their "expertise," but this of course requires having the right numbers and kinds of women in key places.

The British system is one where Parliament, or government through Parliament, is the main maker of policy. But women's representation in Parliament has been notoriously low, less than 5 percent through the 1970s and only rising to 6.3 percent after the general election of 1987. Since, under the two-party system, policy in fact is largely determined by the ruling party leadership, women's virtual exclusion from such roles[2] puts the final seal on the system's impermeability.

## The Economic and Political Environment for Feminism in the 1980s

Though Britain, as many other Western nations, experienced economic recession from at least the mid-1970s, and the rate of women's unemployment initially rose, by 1983 overall numbers of women employed were growing; and women's employment as a share of total employment has actually climbed continuously since 1971. On the other hand, over 42 percent of British women's employment by 1986 was part-time, and their share of part-time employment, already 94.3 percent in 1981, was exceptionally high for Organization for Economic Cooperation and Development (OECD) countries. Humphries and Rubery (1988) have argued convincingly that this reflected not so much women's ability to choose as their difficulty in arranging childcare, combined with employers' preference for flexible, cheap labor. Overall they conclude: "Contrary to a superficial reading of labour market indicators . . . the adverse economic circumstances and closely related government policies since 1979 have impacted with particular severity on British women, and particularly on unskilled and minority women and single mothers" (Humphries and Rubery, 1988: 102; see also Bakker, 1988).

"Thatcherite" or neo-liberal economic policies alone cannot be held responsible for the "restructuring" that has affected women's employment opportunities throughout the Western world. But a succession of policy measures, aimed at privatization, deregulation, and reducing public expenditure has facilitated the process and whittled away the welfare cushion protecting women workers or would-be workers from its harshest consequences. Deregulation, for instance, has entailed reducing employment protection during maternity leave, weakening the powers of the councils that monitor low pay, and more generally resisting all EC initiatives designed to improve parental leave provision and the conditions of part-time workers. Public expenditure cuts have meant the reduction of the budget of the Equal Opportunities Commission and lower social security benefits. Among their more indirect consequences have been the closing of many family planning clinics and reduced funding for already minimal state nursery provision, for local women's committees, and for women's refuges. Wilson (1987) is surely right in maintaining that it is the impact of these policies which constitutes the real significance of Thatcherism for women.

Writers such as David (1986) and Ten Tusscher (1986) have argued that there is another strand within Thatcherism at least as important for women—

its social conservatism. Indeed for David the core of Thatcherism is an anti-feminist backlash. While such an interpretation is difficult to accept,[3] there is little doubt that the government has made use of the rhetoric of the traditional caring family to legitimize welfare retrenchment.

If this brief account of the environment for feminism in the 1980s has painted a gloomy picture, it is incomplete without reference to one further, paradoxical, and quite heartening development: the establishment of women's committees and units in a series of local authorities, beginning with the London Borough of Lewisham in 1978 and most fully represented in the GLC. Virtually all the host authorities have been Labour-controlled, reflecting both the growing influence of feminism within the party, discussed below, and perhaps such authorities' search for a positive role to offset increasing constraints on their traditional functions by central government. The GLC's women's committee and unit died with the council but despite actual closure in some cases and the threat of closure or severe pruning in many others, overall the number of such initiatives grew throughout the 1980s (see Edwards, 1989). They have provided a real if precarious "window of opportunity" for feminism in these otherwise unpropitious years.

## The "Movement" in the 1970s and the 1980s

The environment of the women's movement has influenced but not determined its character and development, and the options available to it. At the outset, second-wave feminism or "women's liberation" took root among women of the extra-parliamentary left, and accordingly their Marxist-feminist perspective briefly dominated. By the mid-1970s, however, radical feminism was gaining the upper hand and setting the agenda. As in many other countries, this was associated with an insistence on women's separate organization, on absence of hierarchy and formality, on the value of women's subjective experience, on the need for women to gain control of their whole lives beginning with personal relationships and their own bodies, and on the related importance of issues having to do with male violence, reproduction, and sexuality. A third strand, liberal or "reformist" feminism, was always very weak in Britain as compared with its influence, for instance, in the United States, Australia, or Sweden (see, e.g., Watson, 1990).

Although British radical feminists often seemed to have absorbed, quite uncritically, Marxist views about the nature of capitalism, while Marxist or latterly socialist feminists took up issues first raised by radical feminism, tensions between them grew. These reached a peak in 1978, with a major and traumatic clash at what was consequently to be the last movement-wide conference organized on a national basis. Subsequently, a number of socialist feminists, weary of the conflict but also alarmed by the Conservative electoral victory of 1979 and responding to a more sympathetic climate in those local parties where the new "urban Left" was well represented, consciously decided to work for change through the Labour Party.

It would nonetheless be misleading to portray the British women's movement by 1980, or at least that great part of it which was "anti-system" rather than "reformist," as neatly split into a (victorious) radical and a (vanquished) socialist camp. It has always been difficult to pigeonhole individual women and groups. The picture has grown more complicated since. The fundamental issue underlying the 1978 clash was feminists' relationship with men: personally, sexually, in political organizations and alliances, and in the context of the male-dominated state. This issue has continued to divide feminists but not necessarily along the same lines. Often, for example, it has divided socialist feminists who are "aligned" with a left-wing party from those who are "nonaligned." It is difficult to assess the present strength of different currents within the movement. My own impression is that, under the impact of Thatcherism, there has been some marginalization of the more "extreme" forms of radical feminism together with the reassertion of nonaligned "socialist feminism," albeit in a form deeply imprinted by radical feminism. However, the picture varies from one locality to another. This fragmentation and change has taken place in the context of a movement which has been losing momentum, to the extent that many would query its right to be regarded any longer as a movement at all. It is also a movement whose traditional diversity has in the 1980s been accentuated by an emerging "politics of identity," which emphasizes the differences between women. As widening circles of women applied feminist insights to their own situation but found the prescriptions wanting, this has further decreased movement cohesion.

Yet, there have been other developments that partially compensate for the movement's weaknesses. During the 1980s, feminism has continued to inform the climate of opinion, influencing attitudes and identifying new issues. This is related to the increasing numbers of women with a broadly feminist outlook, whether "reformist" or "socialist," who have acquired relatively senior positions in the professions, including law and the media, in trade unions and political parties (especially the Labour Party), in local if not yet significantly in central public administration, and even in business. Some of these were grassroots activists originally; others acquired a more feminist perspective as they pursued their careers. They are in a sense a legacy of the 1970s, raising some concern about how a faltering movement may affect recruitment of their successors in the 1990s and beyond. Even so, given the nature of the British political system, they have constituted a vital conduit for many feminist demands.

## Dilemmas for Feminist Strategy

What are the implications of "Thatcherism" and an increasingly split women's movement for any discussion of British "feminist strategy" in the 1980s? Before considering more explicitly what have been its dilemmas, it is important to examine the sources of feminist strategy and whether there is a single feminist agenda. If, reflecting the increasing theoretical and social diversity of what remains of the "women's movement," there are several different and even at points conflicting agendas, who is to say which one is "true" and, more practically, how are they to be reconciled in action?

The term "empowerment" has recently been widely taken up by feminists as a slogan and a goal to pursue. Empowerment literally means giving power to a person or group. But it is apparent that this in turn means very different things to different people. Thus some feminists may believe that in order to empower women, or a specific group of women, it is necessary to raise their consciousness and to make them more aware of the nature of their oppression so that they can then challenge the oppressor. Others understand empowerment as providing women with the opportunity to come together to discuss and make their *own* choices, even if these reflect a very traditional understanding of women's role. Both of these approaches imply helping women to become self-determining actors. But the sense of "empowerment" espoused by the British Labour Party leadership and even feminists in the Labour Party seems to be more individualized and implies greater passivity. It attempts, through policy changes, to give each woman access to resources such as childcare, improved child and maternity benefits, and parental leave arrangements that will allow her a genuine choice between different life options.

Along with these different views of empowerment are disagreements about what, overall, is the best way to go about "changing things." One approach would be less concerned with empowering others than with discovering oneself as a woman, though usually in the context of relationships with other women. A rationale for this approach could be the need to experience authentic living before knowing what kinds of change are desirable and perhaps also to present the force of this example for other women. Such an approach is often referred to as "cultural feminism." But even when women are agreed on the need to achieve change for women as a whole, and assuming for the moment that they are clear on what that change should be, what is the best strategy? There are a number of questions here, the answers to which are linked in quite complex ways. Should the emphasis be on changing government policy, and if so, nationally or locally? Is the best way to do this to change attitudes of the public at large, to organize effective pressure campaigns directed at the policy-makers, or to get more feminist-minded women involved, as politicians, administrators, or "experts" in the policy-making process itself? How far should feminists be prepared to compromise their principles about, for instance, working with men or organizing hierarchically in order to influence the making or implementation of policy? Or is it more important to reach women, or different groups of women, in the local community, to help them come together and define their own aspirations? If so, then what kind of help is needed—basic resources like a room for meetings or the use of a photocopier, information, or more positive direction? In reality, of course, different kinds of feminists have, at least implicitly, answered these questions differently. The most obvious mismatch, it might be argued, has been between the relatively centralized and insulated nature of the British policy process and the general reluctance of radical and even socialist feminists to become involved in "the system" or workings of the capitalist/patriarchal state. Watson (1990), drawing a contrast with Australia and Sweden, maintains that as a result of this attitude among British feminists in the 1970s, "less energy was put into trying to enter the bastions of power" and opportunities may have been missed. Though socialist feminists have, in the 1980s, shown greater willingness to "work within the system," that system itself has become less sympathetic and accommodating (Watson 1990: 115). Watson may, however, exaggerate the system's receptivity under Labour in the 1970s and at the same time underrate the significance of greater receptivity in the Labour Party, the trade unions, and Labour-controlled local authorities in the 1980s.

The issues raised by the proliferation of local women's committees and women's units need special mention. As already suggested, although established at a time when local government had come under greater pressure from the center than ever before and often endowed with minimal formal powers or resources, these local women's organizations have formed a springboard for a tremendous range of feminist or women-centered activities. They have posed different questions for different groups of women, depending on the nature of the women's relationship to these agencies. For those involved in establishing these organizations, there are questions about the status of a women's committee, its terms of reference, and its composition. Given the customary low numbers of women councilors, it is unusual for the membership of such committees to be entirely female, but they frequently co-opt additional women to represent the wider community or particular target groups within it, either in a consultative capacity or with full voting powers (Edwards, 1988). There are further questions about the location of the women's unit within the wider departmental structure of the local authority, its relationship to other forms of equal opportunity provision, especially those centering on race, and how the unit is organized. Riley (1990) suggests there have been three main internal organizational models: one in which paid women's officers work collectively, consciously incorporating (radical) feminist injunctions against hierarchy; one with two joint women advisers, each working from a particular mandate; and one with a single woman in charge. From the mid-1980s, in practice the last model has been gaining ground.

The women's committee and women's officers face further dilemmas in deciding how to proceed (and may well disagree among themselves). It may be that their jobs have been narrowly specified, but often the problem is the vagueness of their mandates, reflecting the political circumstances in which they were created. Three broad approaches have emerged. One focuses on the Council's role as an employer. British law only allows positive action in the field of training; otherwise equal employment opportunity policy is limited to affirmative action (meaning that employers must demonstrate that members of a given group are considered for employment in proportion to their membership in the pool of those eligible) (Lovenduski, 1989). Second, the unit can try to get the different local authority departments (for instance those dealing with transport or housing) to adopt more "woman-friendly" policies: this raises a further question about whether to tell these departments what the policies should be or to encourage them to draw up their own and to monitor their implementation. Third, the unit can concentrate on distributing resources to different women's groups and voluntary organizations within the community. Going back to the earlier discussion of the meanings of empowerment, this latter approach is rather different from the previous two. Such an emphasis has tended to accompany a preference for collective-style decision-making within the unit and possibly a greater reluctance to get involved in the wider internal politics of the council. Women's committees or units following this approach have faced particular problems of credibility, torn between their role within the council and their role as representatives of women outside. Insofar as they have wanted to elicit the true interests of the women they represent, there have been disagreements about the best way to achieve this. A number of women's committees have held large public meetings, which have at times become very heated. They have been criticized in turn for inviting the wrong women or allowing individual women who were particularly forceful but not necessarily representative to dominate the proceedings.

The other side of the coin has been the dilemmas for different kinds of voluntary women's groups or organizations posed by some degree of "dependence" on the local authority. How far should they accept constraints on their activities in exchange for resources? In the highly uncertain climate of center-local government relations, how dependent should they let themselves become?

Returning to general questions of strategy, these are by no means limited to issues of how given changes are achieved. There are questions about what changes to seek. What *aspects* of policy should be given priority—for instance, employment opportunities or women's control over their own bodies? In practice, the answer has partly depended on what kind of feminist one was, but there has also been an element of serendipity: women might get involved in a particular policy area, such as rape, because of personal experience or simply because a job came up in that field. But then, within the chosen field, what specific changes should one push for? Should one be guided by what women need, and if so, how does one find out? Or does one have to make some kind of decision oneself about what is "best" for women, or a group of women? This might seem particularly necessary where issues are complex, requiring some degree of expertise, for instance legal or scientific, to unravel.

Finally, while the tenor of the discussion so far and certainly of the concept of "empowerment" is a progressive one (i.e., that feminists push the frontier of achievement for women ever forward), in reality in the 1980s, achievements of the 1970s and even earlier have been under threat, whether in the area of employment protection, provision of refuges, or abortion policy. This has led to inevitable strains between the urge to identify and pursue the "best" policies or scenarios for women and the need to defend quite inadequate changes already secured.

Hence the British women's movement in the last decade, ideologically fragmented and weakened by Conservative government policy, has increasingly relied on a variety of approaches and has lacked an overall strategy for change.

Strategies pursued have been determined by different views of empowerment and ways of seeking change, organizational constraints placed on local women's committees and voluntary groups, as well as constant pressure to protect previous gains from the onslaught of central government.

A discussion of some of the developments surrounding abortion and reproductive rights in the 1980s will illustrate many of these more general points.

### Abortion and Reproductive Rights

In the 1970s abortion was almost the definitive issue of the women's movement, bringing thousands into the streets in 1975 and again in 1979. These demonstrations were against attempts to amend restrictively the 1967 Abortion Act. The Act itself by no means conceded the original movement's call for "abortion on demand." It allowed for abortion up to twenty-eight weeks of pregnancy but only if two doctors confirmed that the mother's life or health was otherwise at risk or the baby was likely to be handicapped. It also permitted doctors and nurses to refuse to take part in abortions on conscience grounds. In practice, however, the Act was interpreted more liberally. Through the 1970s in Great Britain around 14 percent of recorded pregnancies were terminated.

The very passage of the Act had stimulated the formation of an anti-abortion organization, the Society for the Protection of the Unborn Child (SPUC); and LIFE, with similar goals though rather different tactics, was established in 1970. Between them they commanded considerable resources: by 1980 SPUC alone estimated its membership at twenty-six thousand with five full-time officers, and by the end of the decade these numbers had risen further. These organizations supported several attempts to amend the Act in the 1970s. It was James White's Private Member's Bill, which in 1975 got through to a second reading (though it then fell), that in turn prompted the formation of a National Abortion Campaign (NAC) as well as an umbrella body, Co-ord, to bring together the different groups and organizations in favor of the 1967 Act. Anti-abortionist John Corrie caused even greater alarm in 1979 when, with a new Conservative majority in Parliament, he drew first ballot in the lottery for Private Members' Bills. The bill eventually fell, due to the disagreements and tactical mistakes of its supporters and the refusal of the government to give it extra time.

After the defeat of Corrie, women involved in running the abortion rights campaign were exhausted but also for a time optimistically believed that the issue had finally been resolved; public opinion had largely been won over, and it appeared that the anti-abortion lobby would not try again (see Berer, 1988). In essence, the NAC was now the main feminist organization. It had been experiencing a number of tensions throughout the campaign, but now, with the relaxation of outside pressures, these came to a head.

There were two main aspects to the conflict, having to do with organization and policy respectively. Although coordinated nationally, like other movement campaigns NAC was largely dependent on the initiative and enthusiasm of its local branches. A number of these were situated within or worked closely with local Labour parties or union branches, though others adhered closer to the radical feminist model of the woman-only collective. While local branches could perhaps more easily ignore these differences, within the national organization and at national gatherings they were too obvious. The women who were eventually to leave NAC were especially unhappy about the inclusion of men and dominance of "heterosexist" assumptions. They resented the influence of Labour Party and far Left party activists within NAC's leadership, claiming that they were trying to impose a more "centralist" style as well as to use abortion as the basis for their preferred strategy of "single-issue" campaigns with which to mobilize anti-government sentiment. A related organizational conflict developed within the campaign between NAC as an employer and its paid workers. It was only toward the end of the 1970s that NAC's financial position improved sufficiently for it to provide employment on more than a very ad hoc basis. A dilemma then arose as to whether to offer these workers generous contracts, on the model being pioneered by the GLC or, in allocating their still meager funds, to give priority to the campaign. Critics of the NAC leadership argued that exploitation of these (women) workers, all of whom were to join the split away from NAC, was typical of Leftist organizations, which expected selfless dedication from their members. Women should not exploit other women, they argued.

These organizational issues overlapped with disagreements about what NAC should be doing. The NAC had always stood for abortion on demand, not simply defense of the Act, but there also always had been a problem about how to pursue the first objective and not allow all the campaign's energies to be absorbed in the latter. The further problem of how to maintain grass-roots involvement in the campaign, between attacks on the Act, was again not new. But as the 1970s wore on, understandings of abortion itself as an issue began to shift. There was a growing feeling that it should not occupy such an exclusive position in the campaign's concerns. The NAC was supposed to be about "a woman's right to choose" and from the start had included, under this heading, the question of contraception, though it did not do much about it. By the 1980s some feminists began to point out that NAC was really about the right of white, middle-class women to choose *not* to have children. This was failing to recognize that working-class, black, lesbian, or disabled women might have no real choice about whether to have children or not. The campaign needed to broaden its focus to "reproductive rights" as a whole.

Where did this shift in perspective come from? A major cause was the emerging "politics of identity" within the British women's movement. Thus although the women in NAC might not themselves be black, they were aware of an increasingly vocal black women's viewpoint which drew attention, for instance, to the pressure often exerted on black women seeking abortions to be simultaneously sterilized. By 1983 there was more awareness of the problems of disabled women, following the formation in 1982 of Sisters Against Disablement. But some women in NAC were also influenced by international developments. An International Campaign for Abortion Rights (ICAR) was established in 1977, which by the early 1980s was itself questioning its original narrow focus. The actual term "reproductive rights" had emerged in the United States in the late 1970s and fed through into the British movement via ICAR.

The culmination of these tensions was a split in the NAC in October 1983. On the one hand, a much diminished NAC persisted, and on the other, a new Women's Reproductive Rights Campaign (WRRC) was launched in January 1984. Some local branches stayed with NAC, and others joined the WRRC.

Both organizations have survived through the 1980s, but neither has flourished. Both have been affected by the general decline in the movement's momentum and morale, which can in turn be attributed to the impact, economic and also perhaps psychological, of Thatcherism, together with internal fragmentation and conflict. In addition they have faced specific problems about priorities and strategies for achieving them.

Following the split the NAC was seriously short of members and resources. It was dependent for accommodation on the patronage of the London Residuary Body, which took over from the GLC, and then of Camden Council, which provided the organization with a tiny office at a minimal cost. With only one part-time worker, it concentrated on producing material for schools. What gave it a new lease on life, ironically, was David Alton's announcement in September of 1987 that he was to introduce yet another Private Member's Bill to amend the 1967 Abortion Act.

But if the NAC was struggling, the WRRC never properly took off either. Initially it consisted of a coordinating committee in London, which issued a newsletter, and a number (which never went into double figures) of local branches. Among the reasons women had left the NAC were a dislike for its alleged "centralist" tendencies and a desire to do something positive at a community level. Increasingly the WRRC local branches "did their own thing," and eventually any residual coordinating functions were distributed among them. One or two of these branches, notably those in Leeds and York, were quite active. For instance, members of the Leeds group submitted evidence to the Warnock Committee of Inquiry on the issue of embryo research, campaigned locally against the use of the injectable contraceptive, Depo Provera, and for better abortion facilities, and, on a more individual basis, were involved in the local Community Health Council.

Like the NAC, the WRRC had difficulty as a campaigning group in securing government or charity funding. It succeeded, however, in setting up the Women's Reproductive Rights Information Centre, which did attract GLC support. Although this agency could not campaign directly, it worked closely with the WRRC, providing information, researching and running different women's support groups. In 1987 it was obliged by its main funding body, the London Boroughs Grants Scheme, to merge with another organization, the Women's Health Information Centre, although it had a rather different set of concerns. Nonetheless, the WRRC has been a valuable resource for the women's movement.

The WRRC has been concerned about broadening its focus from abortion to the whole range of reproductive rights. How has it identified particular issues and what strategies to follow? Issues have been identified largely as a response to new policy developments, such as threats to cut funding for family planning clinics, new medical developments in reproductive technology, or simply new information, as in the use of Depo Provera. In this process the notion of reproductive rights itself has evolved from an emphasis on preventing birth—contraception, abortion, sterilization—to issues around whether and how different categories of women should have children. These issues, which are indeed ethically and often technically complex, rather than clarifying the WRRC's position, have made consensus within the WRRC, as among feminists in general, still more remote.

Responses to the new "reproductive technology" have been particularly problematic. Probably the least contentious question among feminists has been artificial insemination, although access to it for certain groups of women, such as lesbians or single women, could be restricted in the future as the need for HIV testing increases reliance on official agencies. Surrogacy is potentially more controversial but, given the government ban on any commercial transaction, never emerged as a significant issue for British feminists. The greatest concern focused around the area of infertility treatment in general and especially in vitro fertilization. Louise Brown, the first test-tube baby, was born in 1978, and by 1984 around eighty children had been born this way in Britain. The WRRC's early response, as in evidence to the Warnock Committee, showed considerable mistrust. It and many other feminists emphasized that control over these processes remained in male hands and in fact tended to inflate the authority of the male medical profession over women's bodies. Some went on to question the social "conditioning" that made women so desperate to become mothers.

This in turn prompted a response on behalf of infertile women (Pfeffer, 1983). Their spokespersons claimed that reproductive rights should include women's right to choose to have children but that reproductive rights advocates had first ignored the plight of infertile women and then criticized them for wanting children although women who did have children were not criticized in this way. Subsequently the debate was further evolved; British members of the international group, FINRRAGE (Feminist International Networks of Resistance to Reproductive and Genetic Engineering), adamantly reject the new reproductive technology, including amniocentesis and experimentation on embryos (which ironically can be construed to support an anti-abortion position). Among other feminists, including the WRRC, views are less clearcut. Individual feminists, several with a science background, have contributed to the parliamentary debate on some of these issues, but there has been no input from the broader movement as such.

It has not been easy, then, to broaden movement activity from abortion to a whole panoply of reproductive rights. In the meantime, the issue of abortion itself did not go away. There were several minor actual or threatened modifications to implementation of the 1967 Act after Corrie, but the first real challenge to some extent drew on the developments in reproductive technology to which I have been referring. The 1984 Warnock Report and then Enoch Powell's Unborn Child (Protection) Bill not only fueled public concern about using human embryos in medical research but also reported scientific advances that in theory made it possible for the human fetus to sustain independent life at twenty-four weeks.

Against this background, in 1987, David Alton, who had come third in the Private Members' ballot, announced a new bill to amend the 1967 Act. Learning from the difficulties Corrie's overcomplicated bill had run into, this bill would consist of only one clause and would aim to reduce the permissible time-limit for abortion to eighteen weeks. It is easy with hindsight to see the problems Alton's bill still faced, but at the time abortion rights groups believed there was a serious possibility of it succeeding.

I cannot here trace the detailed progress of the bill and its eventual defeat. It must be said feminist interventions were probably less decisive than both the strength of professional medical support for the 1967 Act, as expressed in the representations of the British Medical Association and of the Royal College of Gynaecologists, and the Conservative government's refusal to grant the bill extra time, though both the medical profession and government were increasingly in favor of a twenty-four week limit. The bill did, however, raise important, if in many respects familiar, questions of strategy for the abortion rights activists.

Some of the strategic dilemmas could be summarized as organizational. Besides the NAC, a range of groups, organizations, and individuals, by no means all of them feminist, were opposed to the bill. But what was the best way to galvanize this opposition? The NAC appears to have taken the initiative, contacting Co-ord, the WRRC, and the body which had originally campaigned for the 1967 Act, the Abortion Law Reform Association (ALRA), about calling a national meeting. That meeting launched a campaign, Fight the Alton Bill (FAB), with a coordinating office in London[4] and local branches. The number of groups affiliated with FAB grew rapidly: they included existing NAC and WRRC groups as well as new groups set up by students or, in some instances, local trade unions. However, one problem that arose was that, partly because of the general lull in feminist activity, the local initiative was often taken by far-Left parties. Not only did this rekindle fears that they would use the abortion issue for their own partisan ends, but in some instances local FAB groups became the sites of intense sectarian infighting.

The object of FAB was to mobilize grass-roots support, to write to MPs, and to join in demonstrations, locally and at key stages of the legislative process at Westminster. Like the NAC it aimed to win trade union backing and included men in its membership. Though the WRRC had immediately rallied to the campaign against Alton, it remained uncomfortable with this approach and tended to go its own way, for instance, calling a national meeting of women-only groups. Overall the grass-roots campaign was quite impressive, especially given the adverse political climate, though it was nowhere on the scale of the earlier opposition to Corrie.

How much difference did the campaign make? It certainly gave some new life to the women's movement and won new young recruits. Abortion is not a party issue in the sense of being governed by a party whip in Parliament. Members of Parliament can vote according to their individual conscience and also, it is argued, to please their constituents. This may have been true for the Alton bill in one or two cases, but arguably the key arena was not in the constituencies but Westminster. Here the work of Co-ord was vital. Co-ord was not itself a member of FAB, but FAB was a member of Co-ord and they worked together rather well. As an umbrella group, Co-ord included around fifty organizations, though some were much more active during the campaign than others. Besides the NAC and FAB, these organizations included Pregnancy Advisory Services, Doctors for a Women's Choice on Abortion, Liberals for Choice, and Tories for the Abortion Act of '67 (TACT). Co-ord's function was to align these groups' activities through monthly meetings and less formally to lobby MPs and provide briefings for MPs who support abortion rights, especially during the committee stage of the bill. Co-ord was building here on considerable experience (White and then Corrie) and longstanding parliamentary contacts. Nonetheless, the bulk of the work was done by the equivalent of one and a half full-time workers on a low budget, who committed tremendous time and energy as well as exercised considerable diplomacy in maintaining this precarious alliance (e.g., members of FAB and the NAC felt they had little in common with TACT).

Besides organizational dilemmas, which given the circumstances were negotiated quite well, there was the question of what arguments to employ in order best to refute Alton. The real problem here was that Alton, and behind him SPUC and LIFE, were insisting on the eighteen-week limit; the terms of the debate could not be confined to this option. Instead, the debate was focused around the growing public consensus on the twenty-four week limit. The NAC's response was to say that *any* reduction of the time limit was unacceptable. In fact in 1987 there were extremely few abortions carried out after twenty-four weeks, partly because government already had brought pressure to bear on hospitals in the National Health Service and on private clinics. The real argument was for the need to make abortion in the first trimester available on demand, but this did not fall within the terms of the bill. Thus, however much they denied it, it was extremely difficult for those opposing the bill to come up with a clear and credible slogan.[5] Feminist strategy thus was circumscribed by the terms of debate set by the government as well as the movement's organizational and ideological problems.

This brief account of feminist activities in the area of abortion and reproductive rights illustrates many of the broader dilemmas facing feminism in Britain. As a result of growing awareness and pressures within the movement, there was an attempt to shift the focus of activities away from the national to the local or community level. But initiatives here were weakened both by a more general downturn in movement activism and by the technical and ethical complexity of the reproductive issues encountered. At the same time it was never really possible to abandon the emphasis on abortion rights because of renewed threats to the 1967 Act. Defending the Act against Alton illustrated the importance of influencing policy through conventional tactics, such as lobbying Parliament. It also illustrated the difficulty of pushing abortion policy itself forward toward abortion on demand.

# Notes

1. Material for this section of the chapter has been gathered as part of a broader research project with Joni Lovenduski on the British women's movement in the 1980s, and besides documentary materials and movement journals, includes numerous interviews. Publication of a book, based on this research, by Oxford University Press, is planned for late 1991.

2. A major exception, of course, was Mrs. Thatcher, who demonstrated that women politicians will not necessarily pursue feminist goals. Not to the extent claimed by her more paranoid critics and despite much Conservative rhetoric to the contrary, Mrs. Thatcher presided over a still greater concentration of power in central government in the 1980s. This was most blatant in the sphere of local government, where increased central government policy direction, for instance in housing and education, had gone together with tighter spending controls. There is no reason to believe that the Conservative government under the new leadership of John Major will change its policies.

3. For a fuller discussion see Lovenduski and Randall, 1990.

4. In practice FAB had a shifting address, at one time based with the NAC, at another with a London students' union.

5. During the passage early in 1990 of the Human Fertilisation and Embryology Act, the government actually set aside time for a free vote on the abortion time-limit issue. The outcome was an agreement on the twenty-four weeks, though with no limits at all in cases of fetal abnormality or serious risk to the mother.

CHAPTER

7

# WOMEN'S STRUGGLES FOR EMPOWERMENT IN MEXICO
## Accomplishments, Problems, and Challenges

## Esperanza Tuñon Pablos
### Translated by David and Victor Arriaga

Politics is not exclusively nor primarily the exercise of authority by the state or the participation of individuals or groups in formal governmental and nongovernmental institutions. Politics, seen in a comprehensive way, deals with the definition of a collective will and with the process through which people strive to control the destiny and life of their community.

Politics thus is a twofold concept. On the one hand, it involves a process that encompasses participatory forms. In the case of women, it includes forms which may incorporate them into the public sphere and which allow them to take part in elections. It also covers women's political organizations and the embodiment of their demands. On the other hand, politics can be understood as the construction of a collective identity which allows a group, in this case women, to become a social subject.

We can study the interaction and the close link between these two notions of politics by examining women's struggles and, specifically, feminism. This type of analysis leads inevitably to a new definition of the concept of "politics." By sustaining that "what is personal is also political," the feminist movement is presenting a radical conception of politics which modifies the extant gender relations and the dominant human linkages in societies. The feminist conception also infuses a new dimension into the political understanding of society by taking into consideration a variety of subjective elements that affect behavior in the public sphere.

This reconceptualization has allowed us to go beyond the traditional dichotomy of the "private" and "public" spheres. The dichotomy has been useful in explaining social oppression of women and the reasons for preassigned and accepted roles. The new conception allows a comprehensive view of the two worlds, where politics and culture seem to operate as the articulating agents or elements of social collectivities. The new view questions and exposes how women are relegated to the private sphere as their societal location and how macrosocial considerations determine and influence daily experiences of women's lives. This view also explains how, on the basis of day-to-day circumstances, women truly participate in a broader political and social struggle and that by doing so they add a specific character to political actions.

How do women articulate these two levels in their social and political experience? How do or can they build a gender identity that defines their actions? How are actions embodied in demands, political programs with different sets of objectives, organizations with diverse characteristics, tactics, and strategies; in sum, as a specific form of doing politics? In what follows, I will attempt to address these questions in relation to the feminist movement in Mexico.

It is my objective in this chapter to present some of the characteristics of women's struggles in Mexico since the turn of this century, and especially during the last twenty years, as well as the effects of these endeavors on the political institutions and agenda. I will discuss briefly also some of the challenges the Mexican feminist movement is likely to face in the future.

## A Brief History

Women have had an active presence in the social and political struggles in Mexico since the last decades of the nineteenth century. In the present century, from the 1920s until 1940, through mobilization and organized movements with clear feminist demands, women's presence reached its peak. During the 1930s, the United Front for Women's Rights (FUPDM) was founded and comprised more than fifty thousand women members from different social classes representing several ideological and party viewpoints. This organization allowed women to develop a common set of demands and actions, to exert their influence and visibility in society, and to define governmental policies related to women.

This period, however, ended on a rather paradoxical note. Due to the country's specific historic moment, the most radical and best organized sector of the women's movement was incorporated into the official party, *Partido de la Revolución Mexicana* (PRM), the predecessor of today's *Partido Revolucionario Institutional* (PRI). At the time, the party's corporate scheme was based on the assimilation of the most important social movements in the country (Tuñon, 1986).

As a result of this political situation, the dynamics of women's social struggle and feminist demands underwent substantial change. Women became one of the groups that tried to maintain their demands and fought to earn their own spaces within the official party's internal organization. The historical period and the economic cycle of the country from 1940 to 1970 (known as the stabilizing development period) did not allow women involved in this type of participation to preserve their demands, specific methods of struggle, or their collective identity. The struggles of women and also those of other groups, including workers and peasants, were mediated and controlled in the interest of political stability, an essential objective of a state that needed to redefine the incorporation of the country into the world capitalist system.

During this period, women faced adverse national and international political conditions which represented an obstacle to the evolution of their organizations and the attainment of their objectives. Nevertheless, as a group, they did receive the benefits of economic growth, largely manifested by their inclusion in the labor market and in access to education.

Between 1940 and 1970, women from the popular sectors joined, and on several occasions played an important role in, social movements that were part of general political struggles. In particular, their decisive support in teachers', miners', and railway workers' strikes must be recognized. However, women did not participate in these movements with specific feminist viewpoints but as part of a social conflict that revealed the tensions of the economic model embraced by the country.

This model generated the unquestionable growth of a middle class. Nevertheless, in spite of their social ascent, a lack of opportunity to participate in political institutions hindered middle class people's abilities to express their own existence and interests. The presence of the middle class on the national scene had important repercussions in several guild movements such as those of physicians and public servants during the 1950s and 1960s, but they reached a peak with the student and popular movements of 1968.

The Mexican movement of 1968 was part of the worldwide social movements that represented the counterculture, student rebellion, feminism, and several other expressions of anti-capitalist struggles against any kind of hierarchical power, including that of state bureaucracies. The movement also responded to specific national circumstances. The development model had reached its exhaustion, and it was imperative for the system to modify its power structure to recover the fractured political and social consensus. Nineteen sixty-eight was so significant to the country's development that changes in government policy actually took place—though the party in power remained the same—and the search for a new economic model was undertaken (Zermeno, 1985; Monsivais, 1987).

## The Seventies

After 1970, President Echeverria's regime (1970–1976) stressed the importance of "national unity," the urgent need to achieve a "shared development," and a "democratic opening" in the political system (Monsivais, 1987:

14). The administration actually began a dialogue with groups of the opposition who were willing to join in the newly created political framework. Opportunities to participate in that framework were opened to intellectuals and professionals who volunteered to become part of, and were willing to collaborate with, the state. The government enforced legal reforms to reduce voting age and to allocate mass media space for party propaganda.

In a context of international unrest, numerous and varied social movements, and emerging ideas from intellectual elites and leftist sectors, Mexican feminism developed new forms. Women began to search for their own channels of expression, while new political parties and social organizations appeared.

This process gave Mexican contemporary feminism a distinct and specific identity. It appeared jointly or as a parallel expression of leftist political parties and social organizations and not as an appendage to them—a major difference from developments in European countries and the United States (Gicolini, 1987).

As was often the case in the West, the most important characteristic of Mexican feminism in the early 1970s was the creation of the small, consciousness-raising group as its organic form of representation. In the small group the scenario was set to discuss, develop, and spread feminist concepts from each and every woman's particular situation. The purpose was to establish a direct link between women's daily life and their oppression in the private sphere with their overall societal situation and, finally, to help every woman understand that "what is personal is also political."

The consciousness-raising groups allowed women who joined to destroy old prejudices, and although invariably members belonged to the educated middle class, they began to appeal to the general public regarding women's specific problems. However, since the group was much more infused by a therapeutic spirit rather than a public political one, it could not respond to the needs of a movement that was growing and demanding action, communication, and coordination.

The consciousness-raising small group helped many women develop their own concept of reality and gain enough strength to build their self-identity. After going through this process, it was not uncommon for members to leave the group to search for wider political action in the public domain (Gicolini, 1987).

The small group thus gave way to larger groups that faced the challenge of defining feminist policy, broadening ranks, and acquiring a public image. It was a challenge that led to the appearance of more than a dozen groups, which united and then broke up during the 1970s. Each of these groups had distinct goals, political strength, and public appeal. All contributed to building an identity for the feminist movement during these years, an identity nourished by different ideological positions ("Feminismo y Movimiento Popular en Mexico," 1986: 137–58; Jaiven, 1987). Thus, all sort of groups appeared, ranging from those based on a liberal type of feminism with a more hierarchical and legal structure (such as the National Women's Movement—Movimiento Nacional de Mujeres—that was formed as a civil organization in 1973) to others such as Women in Solidarity Action (Mujeres en Acción Solidaria) in 1971, and later the Women's Liberation Movement (Movimiento de Liberacion de la Mujer) in 1974, and Revolt (La Revuelta) in 1975, which represented and allowed for radical and Marxist feminism. There were also groups related to Christian and political party activism that contributed new ideas about communitarian and militant activities regarding feminism.

The task of elaborating a specific policy to influence public opinion made the groups and the movement as a whole face serious difficulties at different levels. Many of the women who had joined the feminist movement for personal reasons lacked organizational and other skills needed to mobilize other women and to influence public policy. The movement was fraught with basic ideological negation regarding certain organizational structures and forms of representation that led women with greater political awareness to reject positions of natural leadership. In addition, the movement had difficulty linking gender demands that might lead to approaches, contacts, and unification with women belonging to other than middle social classes, and thus creating a common plan of action. Finally, obvious and sometimes acute internal differences regarding age, marital status, and sexual orientation influenced the degree of involvement of women with their groups and also affected several political confrontations and divisions among the groups.

The subject of demands as the political expression of the women's movement is quite substantial because it helps to explain the specific mechanisms and the particular dynamics of the Mexican woman as social subject. Mexican feminism of the 1970s arose as a response to the recognition of women's immediate oppression. It was only later in the process that women looked for unifying elements in their struggle. This search for common issues influenced and explains the evolution of three main demands held by the feminist movement: legalization of abortion, stricter penalties for rape, and support for victims of rape. Several groups fought most vigorously for the first goal even though, of the three, it was the least possible to attain during the 1970s.

Beginning in 1972, several women's groups began to struggle for abortion rights as a specific demand. During the decade, the struggle acquired different forms of expression. These ranged from debates and discussions in public institutions that dealt with population, health and female labor, to demonstrations, meetings, and conferences. As a result of these activities, in December of 1979, the Leftist Coalition Group (Grupo Parliamentario de Izquierda) presented an abortion bill in the Chamber of Deputies.

Despite substantial mobilization, and the fact that in 1976 the National Population Council (CONAPO) published the officially recognized figure of 800,000 annual abortions—making this a major public health issue—the bill was not approved. Several factors contributed to the bill's defeat. For one thing, since it was presented by recently legalized leftist parties, its approval would have altered the government's plan for a process of "gradual democratization" (Monsivais, 1986: 52). Moreover, the proposal expressed a feminist perspective on maternity which clashed with the state's population and birth control policies. Also, legalization of abortion would have affected powerful economic interests of clandestine clinics and hospitals. And finally, and most importantly, legalized abortion also would have affected the interests of important conservative sectors in the country, particularly those of the Catholic church and religious organizations.

The defeat of the struggle for voluntary maternity temporarily stalled the feminist movement. Feminist activists realized that there was little support for the demand for abortion rights from women of popular sectors. The movement thus shifted to the two other claims (related to rape) for which there was somewhat more public sympathy. Yet, support on this issue also was difficult to mobilize.

The celebration of International Women's Year in Mexico City in 1975 was an important moment for the Mexican feminist movement. It affected not only its structure and internal consolidation but also offered possibilities for the establishment of ties with other social movements.

The previous year, the state had reformed the Civil Code and the Federal Labor Law with a clear intention of eliminating the more discriminatory aspects of women's conditions, promoting its population policy, and improving its international image. These factors, in combination with the International Women's Year, provided Mexican feminism with new perspectives. These included the possibility of meeting Latin American women from popular classes and the organization of a counter-conference—the celebration of parallel activities—or participation in the event organized by the United Nations. As a result, the movement experienced important growth.

The most evident sign of this growth was the opportunity to create unification among the different groups within the movement. The option chosen was to promote front-like organizations that could understand the new needs of the women's movement and could reach a clearer position regarding not only demands but also possible alliances with other social sectors and political groups.

There were two efforts undertaken during the 1970s: the Women's Coalition (Coalición de Mujeres), founded in 1976, which represented the efforts of groups to mediate, on the basis of their similarities and differences, and to elaborate a common program; and the National Liberation Women's Front (FNALIDM), established in 1979, which searched for approaches and possible alliances with leftist political and democratic unions that already had an important feminist presence.

The Women's Coalition was successful in promoting public debate and in encouraging the search for consensus and the desire to join—through FNALIDM—with other political organizations, which at that particular time faced a favorable (open) national situation. Militant party women formed links with female union members, aware of the great potential of realizing feminist demands.

The dynamics of the groups that constituted FNALIDM generated serious confusion as to what an alliance organization should be. Some wanted it to respect the autonomy of each participating organization and to facilitate the search for common actions. Others saw it as a unified organization that would establish exclusive mechanisms for wider political participation and consensus.

The disagreement led several of the women's groups, particularly members of unions and guilds, to withdraw from the Front when party and sexual orientation proposals were made. Others left when leadership gradually shifted from the original founding feminist groups to women belonging to political parties (the Communist Party and the Trotskyite Worker's Revolutionary Party).

The unfortunate erosion experienced by the FNALIDM pointed to the difficulties in achieving wider alliance activities while lacking widespread support for the movement and strong, effective organization capable of sustaining such alliances. Nevertheless, even though FNALIDM failed to attain its goals, its existence had an important impact on the movement. For one thing, women's specific problems became introduced as issues in political parties. Women also became more aware of their possible relations with political parties. Debate intensified within the movement regarding this issue and several viewpoints developed. These ranged from positions that aimed at regaining total independence for the feminist movement refusing any kind of alliance, to those that argued in favor of the need to preserve autonomy on organizational level but also to support alliances that would build a wider political base, including political party feminist cadres, and promote internal debate in women's organizations.

During these turbulent years, several ideas concerning possible strategies, growth, and stability of the women's movement also appeared. They included the recovery of the small, consciousness-raising group and the search for ways to join women from the popular sectors (working class and peasant women) and the struggle for democracy that was taking place throughout the country.

These main points of discussion and organizational possibilities became the core of the movement during the following decade. They gave it a new shape and posed new challenges for its future development.

## The Eighties

The decade of the 1980s in Mexico was characterized by the intensification of the economic crisis since 1982 and a difficult situation regarding political legitimacy. It also witnessed the eruption of new social actors on the public scene, which modified the traditional dynamics of the struggle of the worker, the peasant, and the urban dweller.

Some of these new actors included women from the popular sectors whose participation had become essential. Some political organizations such as the National Coordinator of the Popular and Urban Movement (CONAMUP) have stated that women are the backbone of these organizations (Monsivais, 1986). The economic crisis has exerted a decisive influence on women's job opportunities, purchasing power, and on general living conditions. In addition, on the basis of their assigned and assumed social roles, women are immersed in a struggle aimed primarily at guaranteeing and satisfying social reproduction. Thus, groups of women workers, peasants, and above all, urban dwellers have played an important role in the struggles focused on working conditions, the initiation of agricultural projects, increasing food supplies, establishment of state-owned stores in marginal sectors of the bigger cities, and the provision of public city services such as sewage, electricity, and transportation. It is important to point out that these women face an extremely difficult situation because of their political participation. In addition to the cultural and ideological recrimination received from the males in their families, they work double and triple shifts at their places of employment and must fight the sexist discrimination they encounter in the political organizations they share with men.

Influenced by the 1970s style of feminism, which attempted to reach out to diverse groups of women, and supported by groups that in the 1970s had created ties with popular sectors (e.g., Mujeres para el Dialogo—Women for Dialogue), this popular movement set out to establish its own organic women's structures within the larger organizations (e.g., women's commissions, women's regional organizations). Another goal has been to establish communication between such groups. In recent years, women who participated in popular movements have organized eight national, regional, and local meetings.

This process had led to the development of a popular type of feminism. It has provided a medium for women of different social sectors to stamp some of their class demands with a feminist viewpoint and a gender orientation. Feminist groups, on the other hand, have also been able to include issues of national, regional, and class dimensions in their platforms.

During the 1970s, the feminist movement, with its small consciousness-raising groups, consolidated organizations, and attempts to achieve national coordination, was unable to articulate a comprehensive political agenda. In contrast, in the 1980s, the need to develop such an agenda acquired a new and decisive momentum.

During the first half of the 1980s, the movement's means of expression had expanded. The movement sought new forms of expression and insertion due to the difficulties it experienced in attempting to achieve unity and organization in the previous decade. In an effort to develop a unified agenda, many groups have geared their activities toward academia and the transmission of women's issues and problems through the mass media. Teaching programs and research centers dedicated to women's concerns have appeared in the major national institutions of higher education,[1] and feminist debate and discussions have received TV and radio coverage.

Academic and political participation has broadened throughout the country. Many women's groups have appeared in the states of Nuevo Leon, Sinaloa, Colima, Michoacan, Oaxaca, Morelos, Puebla, and Chiapas. Interest in these groups and the need for contact and communication first led to the creation of the Coordination of Autonomous Feminist Groups (Coordinadora de Grupos Autonomos Feministas) in 1982 and, later, the National Women's Network (Red Nacional de Mujeres) in 1983. Both were formed to maintain communication among groups that worked independently from each other.

The Network is evidence of a new situation in Mexican feminism which can be characterized as "the blooming of a thousand flowers." Still, the feminist movement lacks the ability to voice common demands, to establish a central axis for its struggles, or to settle effectively ideological differences that appeared in the 1970s and were augmented by such factors as age, marital status, and sexual orientation.

The part of the feminist movement linked to proletarian women gained great strength during the 1980s. Joining the previously existing groups, five new ones (Cidhal, Mas, Apis, Gem, and Emas) appeared between 1980 and 1984. They have been an important sector within the movement. Not only have they supported working class and peasant women but also their establishment as nongovernmental groups (NGOs) that rely on financial aid from international agencies has allowed for links between the global feminist movement and such groups.[2]

An important landmark in the process of creation of the proletarian women's groups was the earthquakes that shook Mexico City in September of 1985. Social consciousness and solidarity both sprung out of tragedy and destruction to such a degree that political identity in the huge city was transformed greatly. Groups of women who lost their homes joined the common struggle for democracy based upon their own living, working, and gender conditions. This was exemplified especially by the seamstresses' guild which arose from the ruins of the clandestine workshops to build a national, independent, and democratic union with a feminist perspective (Informacion Costureras, 1986).

The size of the disaster modified the political thinking and dynamics of social movements, political organizations, and of the government itself. The spontaneous and self-organized response of the citizenry as a whole in reaction to the state's inefficiency and authoritarianism produced what has been called the "tremor of civilian society." The organizational ability shown by the city dwellers at the time of the earthquakes is quite possibly related to and also present in the political events that occurred during the presidential election of 1988 (Mayer, 1989).

During the second half of the 1980s, three factors were of particular importance for the further development of Mexican feminism: an economic crisis, a political crisis in reference to the ruling party's legitimacy that stimulated the development of new options, and the growth and consolidation of social movements. Among them, the women's movement held a special place.

Between 1986 and 1988, Mexico experienced an intense eruption of broad and massive participation. One of its central points of action was the search for a democratic alternative that would limit the establishment's power and exert political pressure on the ruling government. During the process, the ruling party, PRI, underwent a severe internal crisis which affected its structure, social composition, and its ability to produce the necessary social consensus to govern. Having the support of the right-wing party, Partido de Acción Nacional, (PAN), produced within the government very conservative positions on economic and social issues. At the same time, however, liberal and leftist opposition managed to overcome a longstanding tradition of sectarianism and presented a united front. The National Democratic Front (FDN) consists of five political parties and several organizations, thus creating a social democratic alternative for political expression.[3]

This open and democratic period in Mexico prompted women to once again consider the need to define their movement goals. This had to be done not only in relation to the sectors within which they participated but also more generally in relation to what the movement as such might achieve in the future (Mayer, 1989).

Besides the discussion of possible political alliances, the debate now also included the topic of democracy and the specific forms in which it could be linked with feminist demands, the contributions that feminism as a worldwide movement offered to democratic struggles, and even partisan inclinations of women within the current political party context.

The need to create a clearer set of goals and to design guidelines for participation in the search for democracy explains the appearance of three new front-like women's organizations within the past two years. One of these is Women in Struggle for Democracy (Mujeres en Lucha por la Democracia) with a membership of about four hundred women, including professionals, intellectuals, and politicians. Another is Coordinator Benita Galeana, named after a well-known woman union organizer, and includes thirty-three women's organizations from unions, urban dwellers' organizations, feminist groups, and political parties. And Network Against Violence and for Women's Rights (Red Contra la Violencia y por los Derechos de la Mujer), which focuses its action on gender demands and summons many of the participants from the other two organizations.

Women from diverse social and economic backgrounds and with different political ideologies assemble in these three organizations. Unlike their predecessors of the 1970s, however, in spite of their differences, they have been able to reach agreements and design actions following internal discussions and debates.

In the last year, there has been a renewal of old demands for more severe penalties for rape and for legalization of abortion. Attitudes toward rape have undergone significant changes in the last decade. Although a victim is still considered guilty until she can prove her innocence, Mexicans condemn rapists morally and legally and generally express support for rape victims (Lovera, 1990).

Groups within the women's movement have pushed for a new bill on abortion. Various organizations and political groups outside the movement have supported it, and female deputies from different political parties have presented the bill in Parliament. Presently, acknowledgment of clandestine abortions as a major public health issue (in 1990 a total of 1,200,000 abortions were performed), the greater political presence of women, the consolidation of their organizations, and a growing support for women's issues from important sectors of the society create a more favorable climate for the attainment of legalized abortion.

Nevertheless, abortion rights advocates face the challenge of important conservative and religious groups who totally oppose the measure. The Catholic church hierarchy has expressed its opposition and a pro-life group (Provida) has gone even further to reject sexual freedom through violent actions against cultural expression.

The situation of the present regime's shaky legitimacy has driven it to search for a new consensus and to design public policies to regain social credibility, while simultaneously undermining the images and identities of the new participants on the public scene from different social sectors and left-wing parties. Since the economic crisis and governmental policies have severely deteriorated women's standard of living, the Salinas administration has pushed for public policies, including a Presidential bill to increase the penalty for rape to twenty years in prison; the establishment of centers to help raped women and a Bureau of Investigations for sex-related crimes; programming of public debates on women's issues and the inclusion of the issues in the National Development Plan; denunciation of clandestine abortions by public officials who consider them a public health problem and debate on the subject at high governmental levels; and finally, the future establishment of a Public Defender's Office for Women as a specific government agency where women may file charges and defend their rights against any form of aggression or discrimination.

The possible implementation of these government policies as part of its modernization scheme has generated political debate within the women's movement regarding its own political agenda and its alliances and strategies for the achievement of goals. Supporters of the policies (including prominent members of the ruling party who have traditionally pushed for openness and advocated women's demands, such as Beatriz Paredes and Gloria Brasdefer) and women from feminist or leftist traditions (who are afraid that the implementation of the measures might affect the future independence and collective identity of the movement) have entered into discussions about the advantages of the government's proposals.

Groups of women who believe that it is important for the women's movement to present its own public policy proposals on the basis of feminist perspectives feel that consolidation and fulfillment of demands that give the movement its character is a condition for maintaining its autonomy (Lamas, 1989). Following this notion, several groups of women linked to popular activism *(trabajo popular)* have made alternative proposals and have lobbied the legislature in the nation's capital in areas of safety, health, and food supply. Their proposals reflect the accumulation of years of experience in the establishment of support centers for raped women, abortion and mother-child medical care centers, development of community mechanisms to control prices of basic consumer goods, and the creation of consumer cooperatives. While some of these women's proposals have been debated in the Asamblea de Representantes del

Distrito Federal, some already have become incorporated in the Presidential bill discussed above.

The women's movement has undergone growth and relative consolidation during the 1980s. As evidence, on March 8, 1990, a mass demonstration brought together a great diversity of participants (approximately eight thousand housewives, urban dwellers, blue-collar workers, and students) in Mexico City's Zocalo (central plaza). The initiative to legalize abortion and to increase penalties for rape has received broad support. More than a thousand sympathizers, including many famous and distinguished personalities from the cultural and political spheres, have expressed their support publicly through paid advertisements in newspapers.

Another indicator of change is the discussion in many sectors, including workers' and urban organizations, political parties, and educational and research centers, on the need for women to go beyond performing specific tasks in these organizations and to fill positions of greater responsibility and influence. This has made some groups call for either the elimination or the expansion of women's committees within organizations. In the academic context there is a call for inclusion in research and teaching of interdisciplinary scholarship on women and gender.

## Challenges for the Future

This historical overview of the experiences of the feminist movement in Mexico indicates that women organized to attain gender demands face several challenges for the future.

There appears to exist a real potential to grow and develop as a broad social movement and to exert influence on the democratization process the country is undergoing by providing specific gender viewpoints. This will be possible if demands can be formulated and developed which express the collective feelings of women and if a wide-ranging political agenda is outlined that takes into consideration the varied backgrounds of the participants.

Even though an outline of a political agenda already exists and includes provisions to focus the struggle and establish goals for the short, medium, and long range, it must be firmed up and further clarified. Such clarification involves an extended ideological debate that would lead to a better understanding of the historic moment, would help plan possible alliances, and would formulate a lucid position on democracy. It also implies the exercise of participatory democracy within the movement, an evaluation of the different areas and expressions of the struggle, the need for patience and understanding of political and personal differences, recognition of natural leadership, and the development of imagination and creativity regarding organizational structures.

The road traveled thus far, the experiences accumulated, and the challenges met lead me to believe that in the future the women's movement in Mexico will consolidate, progress in its demands, and help modify gender relations. The future is an open road.

# Notes

1. The National University, the College of Mexico, the Autonomous Metropolitan University, and some other public state universities have developed women's studies programs and have provided funding for research on women.

2. It is important to point out that problems have arisen in the area of relations between the proletarian women's groups and other organizations outside the women's movement. This has led to discussions about power, alliances, and autonomy, as well as political projects and welfare activities.

3. The official presidential and legislative election results of 1988 produced a substantial rearrangement, with 51 percent of the voters supporting the PRI, 30.5 percent for FDN, and 18 percent for PAN.

C H A P T E R

8

# THE PERSONAL IS CONSTITUTIONAL

Feminist Struggles for Equality Rights in the
United States and Canada

*Melissa H. Haussman*

In the United States in 1982, proponents of the Equal Rights Amendment (ERA) conceded defeat after sixty years of effort on its behalf. They had fallen three states short of the three-fourths required for ratification. That same year, Canadian feminists celebrated the inclusion of two gender equality clauses, Sections 15 and 28, in the Charter of Rights and Freedoms, after little more than one year of effort. Of central focus to this chapter are the conditions which enabled Canadian feminists to achieve constitutional equality for women and those that hindered the ERA endeavor in the United States. The present work is based on a larger, extensive study I conducted for my doctoral dissertation, which included personal interviews with U.S. and Canadian women activists involved in the struggles to obtain their respective equal rights amendments as well as interviews with those opposed to ERA guarantees.

The ERA was first sponsored for introduction in the U.S. House of Representatives by the National Woman's Party in 1923. Neither of the two established political parties would touch it until the 1940s—the Republican Party adopted it in its platform in 1940 and the Democratic Party followed in 1944 (Klein, 1984: 13–20). It took the ERA nearly fifty years from its introduction to achieve passage in both Houses of Congress. The time period for the ERA I will examine here most closely is the ten-year ratification struggle, beginning with the Amendment's 1972 passage in Congress. Originally slated for seven years, the ratification deadline was extended in 1978 until June 1982, a unique occurrence in U.S. constitutional history (Freeman, 1983: 60).

The Canadian process was part of an attempt to "patriate" its Constitution from Great Britain in 1980. It began with Prime Minister Trudeau's introduction of a bill to this effect in the Canadian House of Commons. Negotiations among the federal government, provincial governments, and interest groups, including feminists, were complete, when in December 1981 the constitutional resolution, containing the Charter of Rights and Freedoms, was submitted to the House of Commons for approval. In April 1982, Queen Elizabeth signed the Canada Act, giving Canadians the power to amend their own constitution without having to go through the British Parliament.[1]

The strategies used by the women's movement in each country to include gender equality clauses in their respective constitutions played an important part in the outcome. However, as I intend to show, the political, structural, and cultural framework within which each equality struggle was waged was of great importance to whether feminists were successful, as in Canada, or unsuccessful, as in the United States. I will examine first the universe of political discourse and the political opportunity structure in each country to indicate the extent to which such factors facilitated or impeded women's efforts to achieve constitutional equality. Strategies utilized by the Canadian and the U.S. women's movements will be discussed subsequently.

## The Political Process Model for Studying Social Movements

In the 1980s, a new theoretical approach to social movements was developed which acknowledged structural and cultural constraints within which social movements must operate (Jenson, 1989; Tarrow, 1989; Piven and Cloward, 1979). Termed the "political process" model, this approach recognizes that not all options are open to social movements at the same time. It also assumes that a movement may use the same strategies and rhetoric an infinite number of times, but may not always be successful with a particular strategy. The political process model also indicates that receptivity by state elites is a crucial intervening variable to social movement success; it assumes a feedback loop between the actions of a particular social movement and the state, which affects how the two will interact in the future. Present actions may foreclose future strategic options on the part of movements and future government policy opportunities.

Within this framework, Tarrow (1989) developed the concept of "political opportunity structure" to explain when "cycles of protest" involving social movements were likely to lead to success or failure for the movements. He identified four main groups of factors, common to the political process approach: "the degree of openness or closure of the polity; the stability or instability of political alignments; the presence or absence of allies and support groups; divisions within the elite or its tolerance or intolerance of protest" (Tarrow, 1989: 34, 102–103). Tarrow uses the political opportunity structure to explain at what point will social movement efforts conjoin with state reformism to enact, partially or completely, social movement goals into public policy.

The political opportunity structure is a useful concept for analyzing periods of likely social movement success and failure. However, as Tarrow himself has noted, a favorable political opportunity structure is a necessary but not sufficient condition for success. It is not enough to examine the political structure within which social movements exist—the cultural context within which social movement struggles take place must also be taken into account. The necessity of adding factors other than the "shape" of the polity into an explanatory political process model is illustrated in part by Piven and Cloward's work. While locating the success of "Poor People's movements" within a situation of access to the state, Piven and Cloward also identified the "power of beliefs . . . which defines for people . . . what is possible and what is impossible;" and "the behavioral imperatives that follow from these beliefs" (Piven and Cloward, 1979: 1).

This emphasis upon the power of beliefs and meanings in society and state is central to Jenson's conceptualization of the "universe of political discourse" (Jenson, 1985; 1987; 1989). It is defined as "beliefs about the ways politics should be conducted, the boundaries of political discussion and the kinds of conflicts resolvable through political processes" (Jenson, 1987: 65). Jenson's concept is a valuable addition in that it allows an understanding of the "cultural loadings" assigned to social movement rhetoric across both polities and time periods within the same polity. This may help to explain why the mere formulation of a strategy does not guarantee success. A strategy successful at one time may not be so at another. It also enables one to see that "changes in the universe of discourse make that discourse available to enemies as well as allies, so that the former may extend the discourse in a negative fashion" (Jenson, 1985: 15).

The political process model, including Tarrow's concept of political opportunity structure and Jenson's universe of political discourse, lead to the recognition that movement mobilization and success are not simply dependent upon the nature of the resources possessed by a group or the particular strategies developed. Factors exogenous to a movement, such as timing, cultural context, and the state structure directly affect the outcome. I will examine, therefore, the universe of political discourse and the political opportunity structure within which the women's movements worked for constitutional equality in the United States and Canada.

### The Universe of Political Discourse

The universe of political discourse in Canada was more favorable toward the formulation of a Charter of Rights and Freedoms and the inclusion of women's rights therein in the early 1980s than was the case in the United States toward amending the Constitution to include gender equality in the 1970s.

Of significant importance to the process in Canada was that Prime Minister Trudeau's Constitutional Resolution, put before Parliament in October 1980, already contained one guarantee of equality for women. It was the clause taken from the Canadian Bill of Rights, operative since 1960, in which women were assured of "equality before the law and protection of the law without discrimination" (Brodsky and Day, 1989: 15). The Resolution added to the 1960 version the word *equal* before "protection of the law without discrimination," and a second section, stating that it did not "preclude any program or activity that has as its object the amelioration of conditions of disadvantaged persons or groups" (Brodsky and Day, 1989: 15). Thus, the government took the initiative of incorporating some form of women's rights into the Charter, which put Canadian feminists in a position of reacting to the government's proposal and assessing what the next step was to be. It also served as a positive first step for women, for when anti-equality groups made presentations in Parliament, "it was clear that the MPs were not listening to them."[2] By contrast, the U.S. Congress, the President and national parties never played such a shepherding role.

Indicative of cultural differences between Canada and the U.S. were aspects of the universe of political discourse which affected women's position within the public sphere at the time of the constitutional equality effort. A political-cultural description of Canada includes a collectivistic orientation, a role for the state in promoting social welfare and economic efficiency and equity, and an acceptance of multicultural diversity, as reflected, for instance, in the languages of government operations.[3] The collectivistic ethos is manifested in the Canadian legal code, which recognizes group rights in addition to individual ones; indeed group rights were a major building block for the Charter of Rights and Freedoms (Burt, 1988: 75; Christian and Campbell, 1989: 51).

Canada's three major parties at the federal level[4] have been committed, throughout the twentieth century at least, to a role for the state in fueling the motors of capitalism and alleviating its inequities. There has been some degree of consensus among Canadian voters and elites of the three major parties on an interventionist role for the government.

Not surprisingly, the collectivist vision has made itself felt in the Canadian women's movement. Canadians have tended to view the State as an extension of their communal values; similarly, most Canadian women espouse some type of feminist values (Vickers, 1986). Thus women in Canada have felt justified in demanding rights from their federal government that their U.S. counterparts may not have felt able to put forth.[5]

The more favorable climate for the representation of women's interests in the Canadian Constitution may also be traced to governmental policy predating the Charter. With respect to women's issues, Canada has generally acted in advance of its neighbor to the south. For instance, with the statement that "the government has no place in the bedrooms of the nation," Prime Minister Trudeau's Liberal Party in 1969 began reforms in the areas of abortion, contraception, and sexuality (Dubinsky, 1985: 7–8). Thus, such issues were not available for would-be opponents of women's equality in Canada to make the linkages between equal rights and widespread social change. Given that the timing of a social movement's struggle is an important part of the universe of political discourse, the fact that many of the most contentious women's issues had been dealt with legislatively in Canada a decade prior to the feminist equality struggle helped that struggle a great deal.

Related to the differences in timing of the two constitutional equality struggles were each country's judicial and federal traditions. The Canadian traditions of judicial restraint and legislative supremacy made some provincial premiers fearful that the Charter would erode provincial powers. The issue was raised during the final stage of negotiations in which the premiers expressed their desire to retain their historic control over human rights legislation, and the fear that they would lose this control by including women's rights in the Charter. In the end, the urgency to patriate the Constitution expressed by the federal government, and the fact that it could not occur without the amending formula contained in the Charter, resulted in a compromise.

Similar to the provincial premiers, U.S. conservatives feared the loss of the constitutional tradition of "states' rights." They viewed the origin of this loss in the federal legislation on social issues, beginning in the 1960s. Since ratification occurred in state legislatures conservative arguments that the ERA would enable the national government to perform all sorts of "mischief" were particularly effective (Felsenthal, 1982: 235). Without an urgency to amend the U.S. Constitution comparable to the Canadian government's patriation desire, there was therefore no need to silence subnational discontent.

The universe of political discourse within which feminists tried to ratify the ERA in the United States in the 1970s posed overwhelming obstacles to the extension of women's rights. The U.S. political culture, grounded in classical liberalism, traditionally has denied women the right to participate in the public sphere. An inherent contradiction thus arose between the liberal political culture of the United States, based upon the belief that women are citizens only of the "private" realm of home and need to be "protected" if they venture out of this realm into the workplace, and women's claims to equality as stated in the ERA (Jenson, 1989). The tension between the views of women as "equal" and "different" historically has not been part of Canadian political discourse to the degree it has in the United States (Vickers, 1986: 11–12).

Protectionism for women in the United States became federal policy through the 1908 Supreme Court decision of *Muller v. Oregon*, limiting the amount of weight women could lift and the number of hours they could work daily. The decision was reflective of a time in which "liberalism was at its height in American legal doctrine" (Jenson, 1989: 243). The protectionist position continued throughout this century, chiefly expressed by labor unions and their allies. This view of women as "wards of the state" constituted the main obstacle to the ERA until its congressional passage in 1972. A key assumption was that, in mandating equality of treatment, the ERA would eradicate differential labor regulations for women. While both the Republican and the Democratic parties endorsed the ERA in the 1940s, several attempts were made to water it down in Congress (Mansbridge, 1986: 9; Klein, 1984: 20).

Surrounding the passage of the ERA in 1972 were changes at the margins of the universe of political discourse which made available greater support for the amendment. The addition of Title VII to the Civil Rights Act of 1964 and succeeding lawsuits by the National Organization for Women (NOW) to get it enforced, resulted in extending labor "protections" to men instead of removing them for women (Mansbridge, 1986: 10).[6] However, unlike the legal reforms instigated by the Canadian government in the 1960s, the U.S. changes sparked a backlash with the mobilization of the "New Right" and Phyllis Schlafly's STOP ERA campaign (Freeman, 1983; Felsenthal, 1982).

The place accorded to liberalism in the U.S. political culture can also be found in the emphasis on individual rather than group rights (Mandel, 1989: Ch.1). In this tradition, individuals theoretically possess "equality of opportunity" and do not need government help to improve their lives.

Part of the universe of political discourse surrounding the two constitutional equality struggles was the definition of the equality issue by proponent and opponent forces. Canadian feminists were able to define their struggle in terms of "role equity" (Gelb and Palley, 1987), claiming that women were deserving of equality rights in the Charter on the same basis as other groups. In contrast, Phyllis Schlafly, principal leader of the opposition to the ERA in the United States, effectively portrayed the amendment as promoting widespread "role change" of the sexes, leading to "change in the dependent role of wife, mother, and homemaker, including . . . perceived threats to existing values" (Gelb and Palley, 1987: 6). As Gelb and Palley point out, "when an issue is perceived as one affecting role equity rather than role change, success is most likely" (1987: 5).

## The Political Opportunity Structure

A structural obstacle to the constitutional equality efforts of U.S. feminists was the difficulty of amending the U.S. Constitution, as opposed to the relative ease of writing a new one in Canada. The framers of the U.S. Constitution included many safeguards against future alteration of their handiwork. Each amendment requires passage first by two-thirds of the membership of each House of Congress. There have been nearly ten thousand amendments proposed in Congress to date; only twenty-two of them have passed both Houses in one session and been submitted to the states for ratification (Hoff-Wilson, 1986: vii).

After passage by Congress, an amendment must be ratified by three-fourths (thirty-eight) of the state legislatures. In contrast, opponents of change need only to prevent ratification in thirteen states to stop the amendment's passage. The nature of the amendment process can lead to a situation in which majority opinion is held hostage to the interests of a concentrated minority (Mansbridge, 1986: 34).

The intent of the framers of the U.S. Constitution and the British North America Act in Canada was to have a strong central government with clearly delineated powers (Van Loon and Whittington, 1981: 257). However, since each nations' founding, the central government has lost powers to the subnational levels. In comparative terms, Canadian provinces have gained more rights than U.S. states and are more powerful vis-a-vis their federal government. Canadian provincial divisions reinforce regional and ethno-linguistic particularisms. Instrumental in the Charter formulation were federal-provincial conflicts as well as regional conflicts among the provinces. To some degree, toward the end of the Charter process, Canadian feminists were able to take advantage of these divisions, playing provinces and regions against each other, and securing "reinstatement" of their rights in the Charter after the Prime Minister "traded them away" in the First Ministers' Conference of November 1981.

In the United States, regional differences were capitalized upon by ERA opponents. By concentrating their efforts on state legislatures dominated by conservatives, opponents were able to keep the necessary thirteen states from ratifying, and ultimately prevented ratification in fifteen states.

At least two factors in the Canadian governmental system helped feminists enormously in their effort to attain constitutional equality guarantees: the parliamentary system of government and the logic of party competition in multiparty democracies. The parliamentary form of government encourages the existence of more than two parties. The parties put forth ideologically distinct platforms, and the elected MPs are responsible for these programs in Parliament (Duverger, 1964: 229–31). Voters then reward the parties for their ideological distinctiveness by supporting the party platforms rather than individual candidates (Downs, 1957: 117–27).

In Canada, at the time the Charter was fashioned, the three federal party organizations contained women's caucuses, "formally committed to improving the status of women within the parties rather than providing support services for the mainstream organization" (Bashevkin, 1985: 99). During the ERA ratification process, only the Democratic Party in the United States had a women's caucus (Freeman, 1975). Moreover, Canadian women were represented federally at a rate more than twice that of U.S. women, at thirteen percent (Gray, 1983: 19). During the state ratification process for the ERA, women's representation was quite low, averaging about eight percent in 1975 (Darcy, Welch, and Clark, 1987: 47). Canadian women MPs were of invaluable help at all stages of the feminists' equality struggle (Kome, 1983: 53–70, 89–97), while the relative lack of women in the U.S. Congress and state legislatures made the atmosphere surrounding presentations made by female lobbyists on the ERA seem "surreal and circus-like" (Boles, 1979: 135).

While a multiparty system promotes distinct party positions on issues, the logic of competition in two-party systems tends to lead to programmatic convergence of the two parties in hopes of attracting the "median voter." This shows why neither U.S. national party organization gave much more than lukewarm support to the ERA throughout the state ratification campaign—neither party wanted to be perceived as more radical on the issue than the other. The only difference was to be found in 1980, when the Republican Party dropped the ERA from its platform and the Democratic convention pledged not to give campaign support to anti-ERA candidates or to hold meetings in unratified states (Klein, 1984: 157).[7] In Canada, the Conservative

Party was officially against the inclusion of women's and other group rights in the Charter and some MPs from the New Democratic Party took this position as well. However, women MPs from both parties supported the feminists in their equality struggle (Kome, 1983).

The relationship between the women's movement and the state in each country also formed an integral part of the political opportunity structure. The Canadian women's movement has had a more "state-aligned" nature as evidenced by the funding of its major organization. The National Action Committee on the Status of Women (NAC), an umbrella organization containing more than five hundred groups, receives funding through the Department of State (Women's Program). This arrangement puts the Canadian women's movement in a similar situation to that of Scandinavian women's movements, which also have experienced a heavy reliance on public funding (Haavio-Mannila et al., 1985).

Membership in the largest U.S. "mainstream" women's movement organization, the National Organization for Women (NOW), takes place on an individual basis. Funding sources are also individually-based, in that NOW receives its funding primarily from membership dues, public fundraising, foundation grants, and sporadic government allotments, in that order (Freeman, 1975: 91). The more state-aligned character of the NAC gave it a degree of "insider" status during the Charter negotiations that NOW clearly did not have in the ERA ratification process. The closer alliance between the Canadian women's movement and the state also effectively ruled out an organized opposition to the inclusion of equality clauses in the Charter.[8]

The universe of political discourse and the political opportunity structure set the environment in which Canadian and U.S. feminists worked to obtain constitutional equality. Undoubtedly the most important factors aiding the Canadian women's movement were the fact that the Trudeau government had an overwhelming desire to patriate the Constitution, cultural norms that mandated the protection of group rights, and the parliamentary system which aided group representation. The favorable Canadian universe of political discourse was based in part upon a collectivist political culture as well as a fortunate lag in timing between the points at which the Canadian Parliament addressed the most contentious issues seen to affect relationships between the sexes. Finally, the women's movement had a more institutionalized relationship with the political parties and the state at the time of its equality struggle which allowed it to use certain strategic options reserved for insiders.

In the U.S. case, lack of access to the state in terms of a desire for constitutional change and the difficulty of amending the Constitution, no effective alliances with political parties as well as the cultural emphasis on individual rights, and a protectionist attitude toward women hindered the efforts of feminists to obtain equality rights. While in Canada no effective opposition to inclusion of women's rights in the Charter was mobilized, in the United States the opposition not only defined the issue but also used regional divisions, and the provision that only a minority of states needed not to ratify the amendment, to stop the ERA.

## Feminist Strategies for Equality in the United States and Canada

To a large degree, the strategies undertaken by the feminist movements to attain constitutional rights in the United States and Canada had a debatable influence upon the outcome. In some ways, feminists in the United States could do virtually "no right" after 1973, and, to a certain extent, given the Canadian government's initial willingness to include gender equality in the Charter and its overwhelming desire to achieve constitutional patriation, Canadian feminists were in a charmed position. The thirty states that ratified the ERA within one year of its Congressional passage did so largely without the influence of feminist coalitions. However, once STOP ERA mobilized in 1972, U.S. feminists were able to do little to overturn negative votes in state legislatures (Boles, 1979; 1982). Conversely, Canadian feminists were able to have an impact throughout most of the process leading to the inclusion of gender equality clauses in the Charter (Kome, 1983).*

The more favorable contextual factors allowed Canadian feminists to pursue successful strategies. In addition to the helpful structural, cultural, and time factors, Canadian feminists possessed another advantage: the Canadian constitutional patriation process began eight years after the U.S. Congress passed the ERA, and Canadian feminists were able to learn from the strategic errors of their U.S. counterparts.[9]

After Congressional passage of the ERA in the United States, its shepherding through the state legislatures was to be undertaken by a nationally-based ERA Ratification Council, including groups such as the National Federation of Business and Professional Women's Clubs, American Civil Liberties Union, National Council of Negro Women, YWCA, AFL-CIO, UAW, the League of Women Voters, and organizations from the "younger" strand of the women's movement, including NOW and the National Women's Political Caucus (Rawalt, 1983: 52–68; Boles, 1982: 573; Klein, 1984: 27).

In 1976, the ERA Ratification Council gave way to another organization, ERAmerica. While successful in fundraising, it lacked the resources to play the central role in ratification, and its function became to disseminate information about the amendment and to coordinate press conferences for ERA advocates (Boles, 1982: 573).

While the national framework was established early, largely as a carryover from the group which spearheaded congressional passage, proponents did not set up coalitions in unratified states until 1974. This has been called the "key

---

*This chapter was written during 1989–90. In June 1991, I had the benefit of interviewing Eleanor Smeal (President of NOW, 1977–81), and other NOW activists who influenced the ERA strategy and interpretation. In addition, in June 1991 I spent two weeks researching the NOW files in the Schlesinger Library at Radcliffe College. In the interviews and archival research, I found much evidence to undercut claims of previously published ERA studies. Among the most important findings are those that suggest that NOW had a much more active presence in the state coalitions than previously suggested. It appears that NOW had a serious commitment to the ERA from the beginning of the ratification effort, but due to both internal and coalitional constraints, was unable fully to demonstrate this commitment until 1977.

strategic error of the entire campaign" by at least one ERA scholar (Boles, 1982: 575–76). Proponents likely assumed state coalitions were unnecessary as thirty of the thirty-five states which ultimately ratified did so within one year of the ERA's passage in Congress.

In Canada, an umbrella group, the National Action Committee on the Status of Women (NAC) was charged with the same coordinating functions as ERAmerica in the United States. Within a few months of the government's introduction of the Constitutional Resolution in Parliament, leadership in the struggle for women's equality became narrowed down to a small group of about thirty, named the "Ad Hoc Committee on the Constitution" also known as the "Ad Hockers" (Burt, 1988: 77). The Ad Hoc Committee was comprised of feminists from Toronto and Ottawa, most of whom were members of the NAC, some who belonged to the National Association of Women and the Law (NAWL), and many who were drawn from the legal profession.[10]

In the United States, one organization, NOW, ultimately came to spearhead the ERA fight, although not until 1980 (Boles, 1982: 574). In Canada, the opposite process occurred—the number of proponent groups widened as time went on. In the latter part of the process, some of the women's organizations representing the "older" branch of the women's movement, including the National Council of Women and the Federation of Women's Institutes, became involved (Hosek, 1983:43).

The effort to amend the Constitution in the United States to include women's rights consisted of three stages. The first comprised an attempt to develop an interpretation of the ERA acceptable to the state legislatures and with which to lobby legislators. The second focused on a national appeal for support of the amendment, and the last incorporated more confrontational tactics such as protests and rallies.

At the beginning of the ERA state ratification process, proponents defined the ERA in terms of "role equity" issues, in which the ERA would "eliminate the most prevalent form of discrimination in the American legal system" (Boles, 1979: 40). In the first stage, covering the period 1972 to 1977, the strategy of the ERA Ratification Council and its successor ERAmerica, focused on legislative lobbying tactics, including "presentation of research, testimony at hearings, contacts by constituents, letter and telegram campaigns, public education, and election activities such as contributing time or money to a pro-ERA candidate's campaign" (Boles, 1982: 573).

While it may not seem that waiting two years to establish ERA coalitions in all the states should have mattered much, it is clear that in retrospect it did. Phyllis Schlafly formed STOP ERA in 1972; not until 1974 did the ERA Ratification Council have "formal pro-ERA coalitions containing up to 100 groups set up in virtually all the unratified states" (Boles, 1982: 575). The ineffectiveness of ERA proponents' attempts to use interest-group lobbying at the beginning of the campaign may be seen in that they did not take the initiative in contacting legislators, and eventually did so only after a legislature had consistently failed to ratify the ERA in more than one session. By the time proponents went to the state legislature to lobby, they confronted a hostile environment in which STOP ERA had defined the amendment as causing unwanted "role change" in the relationships between the sexes. Proponents thus had to spend more time in answering STOP ERA's accusations than in putting forth an interpretation of the ERA as bringing about "role equity."

The ERA proponents and opponents began to use a more "national" appeal from the beginning of the second phase of the effort in 1977. In 1975, President Gerald Ford signed an Executive Order establishing the National Commission on the Observance of International Women's Year (IWY) to "support U.S. participation in the U.N. conference for International Women's Year," to be held in June 1975 in Mexico City (Tinker, 1983: 19). The Commission made the passage of the ERA its top priority and planned to hold a conference in Houston in 1977. In response, STOP ERA brought a lawsuit in Illinois to stop the distribution of the Commission's report and organized a pro-family counter-conference in Houston at the same time that the IWY conference was held there (Tinker, 1983; Ferree and Hess, 1985: 123). The appearance of women holding banners identifying themselves as members of socialist and lesbian groups at the Houston conference, highlighted in the media, provided STOP ERA with further ammunition for the charges that the ERA was fundamentally linked to drastic role change.[11]

During the second stage of ERA proponents' efforts, strategic efforts were geared toward persuading Congress to extend the ratification deadline for another three years. Although feminists were successful in getting the deadline extended, the final outcome was not affected since no state ratified the amendment during the 1979 to 1982 period.

Toward the end of the second stage, NOW intensified its national focus. One tactic introduced was an economic boycott of the fifteen unratified states, where NOW would not hold conventions. The third stage was necessitated by the observation that "our opposition is national" (Boles, 1982: 574). NOW also stepped up the use of confrontational tactics designed to put the ERA's unratified status into the national limelight by organizing rallies, nonviolent protests, and an ERA Walkathon.

At the close of the second phase, NOW also changed the issue definition of the ERA. Stressing that issue which nearly all post hoc analysts agree would have constituted the most successful interpretation, NOW highlighted the "economic equity" advantages of the ERA (Boles, 1982; Ferree and Hess, 1985; Tinker, 1983).

While ERA proponents shifted both to new tactics and issue definition toward the end of the ratification campaign, STOP ERA retained its strategy of lobbying legislators but shifted its issue emphasis somewhat. Gone were the earlier claims that the ERA would require unisex toilets; from 1980 on, Schlafly concentrated on abortion, draft, and combat issues (Mansbridge, 1986: 86). Keeping focus on such issues ultimately overrode the effects of the proponents' strategic changes, and the ERA expired with the state ratification deadline on June 30, 1982.

As with the U.S. strategies, those of Canadian feminists consisted of three stages. The first, between October 1980 and February 1981, entailed presentations to the Special Joint Parliamentary Committee on the Constitution, aimed at strengthening Section 15, as originally contained both in the Bill of Rights and in Prime Minister Trudeau's Constitutional Resolution. The second stage consisted of formulating an overriding guarantee of equality in addition to Section 15. It took place from February until April of 1981, when the overriding guarantee, which ultimately became Section 28, was included in the Charter by the House of Commons as an amendment to the Constitution Bill (Kome, 1983: 77). The final part of the feminists' struggle was concerned with the reinstatement of Section 28, after Trudeau traded off jurisdiction over that section to the provinces at the November 1981 First Ministers' Conference on the Constitution.

The first part of Canadian feminists' effort vis-a-vis the Charter involved the recognition that "equality before the law," a phrase that became operative through the 1960 Bill of Rights, had not been sufficiently strong to protect women's rights in various cases heard by the Supreme Court (Brodsky and Day, 1989: 12–17). A provision protecting women's rights under the law, in the substance of the law rather than just in its application, was deemed necessary. Thus the Canadian Advisory Council on the Status of Women (CACSW) commissioned studies by feminist lawyers on the ramifications of the Constitution for women (Kome, 1983: 29). The means used to transmit women's concerns to the policy-makers at this point were twofold. First, CACSW sent out flyers to Canadian women asking them to return the portion that demanded the wording of Section 15 be changed. A conference on "Women and the Constitution" was planned to discuss the results. Second, feminist lawyers who conducted the studies commissioned by the Advisory Council made presentations to the Special Joint Parliamentary Committee on the Constitution, stressing the importance of changing the wording of Section 15. These presentations were well received, for revisions of Section 15 of the Constitution Bill were announced in January 1981. Changes included the addition of "equality rights under the laws" and "equal benefit of the law" (Burt, 1988: 76).

Part of the Ad Hockers' agenda in setting up the "Women and the Constitution" conference was to stress to Canadian women that a companion clause to Section 15 was needed in the Charter. A more sweeping guarantee of equality, stating that "the rights and freedoms in the Charter are guaranteed to men and women equally," was viewed by the Ad Hockers as a requisite addition.

While attendance at the conference on "Women and the Constitution" was expected at two hundred to three hundred participants, thirteen hundred women came from across Canada. The conference endorsed the Charter of Rights and a proposed amendment guaranteeing all rights therein equally to both sexes. Support of this proposal did not come without cost, however, as the Federation des femmes du Quebec (FFQ) withdrew from both the conference and NAC membership.[12]

After formulating the proposed amendment, the next step was to lobby MPs to include it in the Charter. In their efforts to lobby MPs, Ad Hockers were helped by women MPs who lent offices and the perquisites contained therein, such as telephones and photocopying equipment, for the purpose.[13]

In order to demonstrate that this effort was being undertaken on behalf of Canadian women in general, the Ad Hockers also mailed literature to Canadian women asking for their support.

In March 1981, some of the Ad Hockers and members of the National Association of Women and the Law met with the justice department, and the overriding statement of gender equality was hammered out. It eventually became Section 28 of the Charter, stating that "not withstanding anything in this Charter, the rights and freedoms referred to in it are guaranteed equally to male and female persons."

Although members of the Ad Hoc Committee and the general feminist lobby felt that all would be "smooth sailing" after April 1981, when the Parliament's House of Commons approved the Constitution Bill, unexpected complications arose. They took the form of the Supreme Court's decision in September 1981 that the federal government could not proceed unilaterally with patriation. To achieve provincial accord, the First Ministers' Conference on the Constitution was held in November 1981 in Ottawa. Its outcome was a "watering down" of the Charter by the introduction of a provincial override clause, Section 33, which enabled provincial legislatures to exempt themselves from portions of the Charter for a period of five years, subject to renewal by the provincial legislature (Milne, 1989: 142–60). Section 33 was said to apply to Sections 7 through 15 of the Charter. When asked in the House of Commons on November 6 whether Section 28 was also subject to provincial override, the Prime Minister said he "didn't know," but on November 9 he confirmed that Section 28 could be overridden.

Trudeau's statement touched off the most intense, public portion of the women's lobby (Kome, 1983: 84). The Ad Hockers immediately mobilized Canadian women to flood MPs with phone calls and letters; however, women were told they had to go to the provincial premiers to seek reinstatement.

A key difference between the final part of the feminists' struggle and earlier strategies was that, for the first time, help was available to the women's lobby not just from opposition women MPs but also from members of the Liberal government. Judy Erola, Minister of Mines, who also received the portfolio of Status of Women in September 1981, "made it clear to the Cabinet that she would support the women's lobby."[14] Others followed, and both liberal women MPs and bureaucratic staffers "felt free to participate in what had become a federal-provincial feud" (Kome, 1983: 89). Pauline Jewett and Margaret Mitchell from the NDP and Pat Carney and Flora MacDonald of the Conservatives, who had been helpful previously, were equally accessible at this stage (Kome, 1983).

In this final part of the campaign, lasting from November 16–22, 1981, the Ad Hockers and the larger NAC membership lobbied each of the ten premiers individually, getting them to agree to "reinstate" Section 28, by removing it from the list of provisions subject to Section 33. Direct contacts by women in federal and provincial government, telegram and telephone barrages, and an all-night vigil in thirty-degree-below-zero temperatures in Regina, Saskatchewan, worked effectively so that on November 24, 1981, Justice

Minister Chretien announced in the House of Commons that the Constitution Bill was complete with a reinstated Section 28. Passage in the House of Commons was, to all appearances, a formality.

## Conclusion

The universe of political discourse and the political opportunity structure within which Canadian feminists waged their efforts to obtain constitutional gender rights clearly was much more favorable than the context within which the U.S. women's movement took up its struggle. The widespread legitimacy of demanding group rights, a parliamentary system, and a federal government desiring to promulgate a new constitution, which partially took its language from the 1960 Bill of Rights, helped Canadian feminists. In contrast, U.S. feminists worked within a framework of individual rights, a two-party system, and the great difficulty of amending a longstanding constitution. Canadian women's movement's inclusion in the party and political organizations also gave it an insider's status in the bargaining process that the U.S. movement did not possess. Finally, Canadian feminists' efforts could take advantage of a better timing than that of their neighbors to the south. In Canada, the more contentious women's issues had at least been placed on the public agenda, if not resolved satisfactorily, nearly one decade before the Charter process began in 1980, while the ERA was sent to the U.S. states during a period of social turmoil on which STOP ERA was able to capitalize.

While the universe of political discourse and political opportunity structure favored Canadian feminists' efforts to strengthen the equality guarantees in their Constitution, the Canadian strategies themselves also appear to have been more effective than those used by U.S. feminists. Although it was the Canadian government which initiated the formulation of constitutional equal rights in the Charter, Canadian feminists were quick to respond. They were able to define the equality issues and then to lobby effectively, first to get the language changed in Section 15 and then to add Section 28. When Section 28 became threatened, they managed to get it reinstated in a remarkably short period. In contrast, Boles (1982) claims, U.S. feminists did not establish lobby coalitions in the unratified states until two years after the ERA passed Congress. By that time, STOP ERA had managed to set an image for the ERA as causing profound role change and was able to use regional conservatism in its favor. Hence, while the structural and cultural context within which feminist strategies were used was of great importance, the strategies themselves have also had a significant effect.

While the Canadian equality struggle was more indicative of an interest-group lobby than the one in the U.S., both aroused the interest, if not the participation, of a majority of each country's population. The costs and benefits of each effort are as yet unmeasured, although there are some strong indicators. In both countries, the debates during and following the equality struggles have raised the consciousness of many people and have, no doubt, contributed to some favorable changes in women's status. On the other hand, in the United States, the "New Right," which mobilized in response to the congressional passage of the ERA, continues to have strong hooks into U.S. social policy. In Canada, the Charter lobby brought about a fission between French and English-speaking feminists, which continues to persist. The feminist movement of each country thus faces some very formidable obstacles to future policy success.

# Notes

1. This discussion stops at the point at which the Constitution was considered "patriated" in 1982, and does not include attempts to amend it under the Meech Lake Accord of 1987. For a summary of developments since 1987 see, e.g., Latouche, 1990.

2. Telephone interview with Gwen Landolt, Toronto, 10/19/89.

3. Canada officially considers itself to have two "founding races," French and English, guaranteeing citizens' rights to receive government services in either language.

4. The three parties include the social-democratic New Democratic Party (NDP), the Liberal Party, and the Progressive Conservative Party also known as the Tories.

5. One example comes from a discussion seven years after constitutional patriation, in which the justice minister for the Trudeau government, Jean Chretien, noted that "we funded groups to lobby against us." (The Struggle for Democracy. Video. Chicago: Democracy Films. Summer, 1989.) This included the women's movement which was active in formulation of the Charter.

6. Other reforms included *Roe v. Wade* in 1973, Title IX of the Education Amendment of 1972, and the Equal Credit Opportunity Act of 1974.

7. This effort came too late to save the ERA, however, since no state ratified after 1977.

8. The conservative, largely anti-abortion rights REAL Women group, which has become the chief opposition to the Canadian feminist struggle for equality, did not become well organized until 1984, two years after the Charter took effect.

9. Interview with Prof. Catharine MacKinnon, Osgoode Hall Law School, Toronto, 10/24/89; interview with Toronto members of the Ad Hoc Committee, Toronto, 10/30/89.

10. A precipitating factor leading to the creation of the Ad Hoc Committee was the widespread perception of interference by the Minister Responsible for the Status of Women, Axworthy, in the affairs of the Advisory Council on the Status of Women (CACSW). CACSW had planned a conference to be held in Ottawa on "Women and the Constitution," for the purpose of polling Canadian women as to what they wished to see included in the Charter. First scheduled for September 1980 and canceled due to a translators' strike, the conference was rescheduled for February 1981. In January 1981, Doris Anderson, President of CACSW, was informed that Minister Axworthy preferred that regional conferences be held. When put to a vote, other members of CACSW's Executive Board upheld Axworthy's decision, and Anderson resigned (Kome, 1983: 39–41). Within the next few days, women in Toronto started meeting and communicating with like-minded feminists in Ottawa, and the Ad Hoc Committee was born.

11. Phyllis Schlafly claimed that the reason no state ratified the ERA after 1977 was the Houston Conference and its news coverage (Eagle Forum Video, 1984).

12. Feminists who supported the separatist Parti Quebecois had at least two reasons for opposing the Charter. The first was that they believed they had a "better deal" under the provincial charter adopted by the P.Q. government. The second was that due to their loyalties to that government, they could not support an effort by Ottawa which was seen by Quebec as an attempt to usurp its powers. (Interview with Mme. Charlotte Thibault, President, Federal des Femmes du Quebec, Montreal, 9/14/89; interview with Mme. Ginette Busque, former President of the FFQ, currently Vice-President, Conseil au Statut de la Femme au Quebec, Montreal, 10/6/89.)

13. Interview with members of the Toronto Ad Hoc Committee, Toronto 10/30/89; interview with the Hon. Pauline Jewett, Vancouver, 11/14/89.

14. Interview with the Hon. Judy Erola, Ottawa, 11/7/89.

# NATIONAL LIBERATION
# AND DEVELOPMENT MOVEMENTS

The attempts to attain women's emancipation described and analyzed in this section are set in the context of nationalist struggles aimed at achieving independence, asserting a national identity, and improving or "modernizing" economies. The five societies under consideration, Uganda, Palestine, Nicaragua, Poland, and India, have long histories of external domination, occupation or aggression, as well as severe economic problems. In this context, the specific difficulties experienced by women due to the highly patriarchal nature of these societies have not been given priority. Yet, women have participated alongside men in the struggles to achieve autonomy and democracy and have, in the process, discovered the importance of asserting their demands. Thus, while tensions between nationalism and feminism remain, there is a growing recognition in all of these societies that women's concerns and demands need to be incorporated into the national agenda.

The first three chapters in this section emphasize the difficulty of separating the "women's question" from the "people's question" where long years of oppression have left women little choice but to join men in national struggles. In her chapter on women's participation in the Ugandan resistance movement, W. Karagwa Byanyima highlights the difficulties experienced by Ugandan women in getting their concerns incorporated into the movement's objectives. Nevertheless, as a result of taking part in the national struggle, women developed a feminist consciousness and were able to use the movement's commitment to democracy and equality to gain recognition and improve their status.

Orayb Aref Najjar, in her chapter on women's contributions to the Palestinian efforts to create a nation-state, shows that recently formed women's committees, while organically tied to the national movement, have been successful in incorporating women's demands into the women's political agenda. Najjar also illustrates that many activities of Palestinian women done for the nationalist cause which have been regarded as "nonpolitical" need to be redefined and that women's involvement in the national struggle has been a strong impetus to the development of effective strategies for the empowerment of women. These include mass recruitment, the creation of democratic structures which encourage participation in decision-making, providing education and employment for women, building community solidarity, recognizing women's achievements, and unifying the women's movement.

Barbara J. Seitz examines the participation of women in the revolutionary struggle in Nicaragua. She points out that while some quite radical changes in the status and role of women had been advocated by the Sandinista regime, attempts at female emancipation have been in tension with traditional views and self-images of women. Nevertheless, women were active in all aspects of the Nicaraguan revolution from its beginning, held important positions in the Sandinista government, and attained equal protection under the law after the revolution. Seitz attributes this to a very high proportion of working and head-of-household women in Nicaragua as early as the Somoza regime. However, the recent change in government in Nicaragua poses a threat of setbacks to the gains women had made under Sandinista rule.

In the chapter on women in Poland, Joanna Regulska focuses on the period since the Second World War, the recent changes toward democratization, and the struggles women have begun in order to be included in the political process. While Poland was under Communist government its policy toward women was characterized by a contradiction between ideology (which ensured women equal rights) and practice (which kept women in inferior positions). While many Polish women joined the Solidarity movement, they were not its leaders or spokespersons and did not enter the movement as an interest group with its own goals and demands. This lack of a "women's agenda" ensured that women's issues and concerns were not given attention by the newly elected government in 1989. On the contrary, the Solidarity- and Church-allied, male-dominated government has introduced legislation which aims to limit women's rights. Nevertheless, the collapse of one-party rule, a nascent democratic process, and the government's attempt to outlaw abortion, have created opportunity and motivation for women to begin struggling to change their situation.

The last chapter in this section, by Dorane L. Fredland, describes a local community project in India which, like many others in that country, has arisen in opposition to, or in spite of, the "development" strategies of the State. While Indian government, in its efforts to catch up with the Western world, has focused its energies on technological modernization, local initiatives involving women have tried to cope with pressing needs of the poor, such as health care, rights over forests, and other community resources. In the process, women have become empowered as they have gained greater control over their day-to-day activities and created marked improvements in the quality of life of the community. As this chapter illustrates, the very content of politics has been redefined by such development projects, as issues which previously were not seen as amenable to political action (e.g., people's health and women's rights) now fall within the purview of political struggle.

CHAPTER

9

# WOMEN IN POLITICAL STRUGGLE IN UGANDA

## W. Karagwa Byanyima

In the twentieth century, the East African country of Uganda has undergone massive upheavals—from colonization by the British to independence, followed by several brutal dictatorships, to a five-year civil war, and finally to recent attempts at reconstruction. During these many years, the fate of Ugandan women and men had been closely tied together—both had lost their self-determination under colonial rule and both suffered massive injustices under fascist dictators; also both saw no alternative but to join an armed resistance to end the years of atrocities and to regain human dignity. However, women suffered more than men under colonial and dictatorial rule. Under the former, they lost all influence in local affairs and under the latter became frequent victims of rape. For women, an armed resistance aimed at national identity, equality, and dignity met their basic interests to improve their material conditions and to achieve equal status with men.

In this chapter, I examine the situation of women in Uganda from precolonial to contemporary times. My main focus is on the armed struggle during the guerrilla war of 1981 to 1985, when women joined men to overthrow an oppressive, dictatorial regime. I attempt to show that by joining the National Resistance Movement women were able to address and resolve some of the problems associated with their oppression by men in the larger context of a nationalist, anti-imperialist struggle. For Ugandan women in the early 1980s, there was no alternative for emancipation but to unite with men in an armed resistance. In the process, they acquired a sense of competence, self-confidence, and opportunity for self-determination. Women's involvement in the resistance struggle in Uganda thus constituted an effective strategy for their empowerment.[1]

## The Pre-Colonial Period

The area now known as Uganda has for many centuries been inhabited by several different groups of peoples, whose customs and traditions grew from diverse roots in the past. Before colonial rule, these groups lived as separate and independent states with different forms of political organization. The kingdoms of Bunyoro, Buganda, Toro, Nkore, and others had clan systems based on lineage and blood kinship. There also existed "segmentary" societies (where the elders had most authority), such as the numerous states of the Luo-speaking people and the Bakiga. Migrations of the different groups sometimes brought about a blending of kinship concepts and segmentary politics of consensus of the elders (Dunbar, 1965).

To understand how, and to what extent, women exercised power in these pre-colonial societies, it is misleading to make clear-cut distinctions between political, economic, and religious power, as these were usually fused. The Western notion of a public sphere, which is male and within which politics takes place, and a private sphere of the family, reserved for females and where there is no politics, is inappropriate to the Ugandan pre-colonial experience and submerges women's political action. In Ugandan pre-colonial societies the extended family and the clan comprised both the public and the private spheres, and women had important roles within this realm. Moreover, if we avoid globalizing the Western context of male domination and understand its specific nature in Uganda, then we can appreciate the broad extent of women's political participation in this period. For instance, women had (and many still have) more decision-making authority as sisters and clanswomen than as wives.

The political/juridical structures of Uganda's decentralized clan-states were uncomplicated, easily accessible, thoroughly understood, and their services were free. These structures depended upon personal relationships which women could, and often did, influence. If politics is about how people affect the distribution of resources, then there is no doubt that this was the period in Ugandan history when women were closest to political power.

Ordinary women wielded indirect power through their relationships with brothers, sons, clanspeople, and, to a lesser extent, husbands. They also acted in groups based on kinship, age, or common tasks to affect decisions and to support each other. The relationships developed between themselves and their menfolk and amongst themselves allowed these women to influence decisions affecting their lives, their families, and their communities.

Although there were fewer women than men in positions where they could contribute effectively to the process of governance, it is now well known that during the pre-colonial period women in Uganda (and Africa in general) were closer to and better served by the political systems that existed then than in subsequent periods (see, e.g., Kiwanuka, 1972; Obbo, 1980).

## The Colonial Period

Colonial intervention caused the collapse of the small-scale, personal structures of Ugandan states, leaving women in a particularly powerless situation. To establish an efficient system of control and exploitation, the colonizers concentrated power in the hands of a British governor. Clan power was usurped, and the political/juridical role of elders, clan leaders, and kings was taken over by the governor's representatives—collaborator chiefs. The treaties and laws the British made to consolidate their authority reinforced patriarchal rule. The wholeness of communities, ensured by elders' councils, was replaced by separate, unintegrated, and complicated government departments (law, security, administration of land, animals, forests, etc.), all headed by men who were, more often than not, strangers in the areas where they worked. The centers of the new system were located too far for most women to utilize. Their services were not free and thus they led to a segregation between the rich and the poor, and between women and men. (Most peasant women in Uganda historically have had little or no control over money.)

With the new system came the notion of some matters being for the "public" sphere, that is, the government departments, and others being for the "private" sphere of the family. The colonizers promoted and encouraged the ideal of a nuclear family and tried to discourage extended family systems, especially in urban areas. The means through which women had acted to change their conditions—the extended family—thus became disempowered. Women, more than men, had little access to and no influence in the new structures. Many important issues which they had previously brought forward, and in the resolution of which they had participated, were now pushed out of the newly defined "political" or "public" arena. For instance, wife beating ceased to be a social problem solved publicly by the extended family. Instead, Ugandans adopted the colonizers' view that wife abuse was an essentially "private" or "domestic" problem to be solved within the home by a husband and his battered wife. Seeking recourse under the law was, and still is, for many women, a complicated, expensive, and unsatisfactory matter. Most importantly, the law was more concerned with punishing the offender than protecting the victimized woman. To this day, violence in the home has not recovered its public political dimension of pre-colonial times. Women's power to create peaceful communities thus became undermined effectively during this period. African women's loss of power to affect their lives and their communities during the colonial period has been a main theme for several writers (see, e.g. Boserup, 1970; Sachs, 1983), and Ugandan women were no exception.

The colonial period lasted sixty-eight years, after which a constitution was drawn up (at the inevitable Lancaster House) which ensured that power was transferred to those groups which could be trusted to serve British interests in Uganda after independence. The British government made sure that Uganda was to continue providing a market for British manufactured goods and to be a source of raw materials and primary commodities such as copper, coffee, tea, and cotton. The British found collaborators in a new class of Ugandans who wanted to maintain the old system in order to inherit the privileges of the departing colonial administrators. In 1962, the British withdrew, having secured Uganda's neo-colonial state, leaving the country as a whole, but in particular its predominantly peasant population, vulnerable to and yet heavily dependent on the international coffee market with all its vagaries.

Upon independence, the Ugandans adopted a parliamentary structure based on the Westminster model. The new Constitution guaranteed universal adult suffrage. The new government claimed to be committed to equality of the sexes as laid down in the U.N. Universal Declaration of Human Rights. In the first Parliament after independence there were even two women ministers. The government was anxious to show the world that it was prepared to meet the Western standard of a nominal female participation in mainstream institutional politics. The reality, however, was that parliamentary democracy was a mere disguise; actual power remained firmly in the hands of foreign nations and their Ugandan allies in high public offices.

Under colonialism a gradual but sure transformation of the old systems of governance had taken place; by separating "politics" from other human activities (social and economic), and centralizing political power, women's local initiatives and men's control of community affairs had given way to national control. The main beneficiaries of the new system were men who were co-opted or chosen as the new officials.

### Years of Dictatorship and Fascism

Within three years of independence, the British-style parliamentary democracy had collapsed, and by the fourth year, the Constitution was abolished. Women's right to vote was meaningless, because "parliamentary democracy" was not only undemocratic and male-dominated but also elections simply were not called when they were due. As external exploitation increased (infiltration of the army, police, and intelligence service by foreign powers; fluctuating international markets; institution of trade barriers, etc.) and internal contradictions deepened, the elite leaders continued to compete among themselves for the privileges of official positions. The people's discontent was answered with coercion, and for this purpose a brutal and repressive machinery was built.

Women's organizations such as the Mothers' Union and the Young Women's Christian Association (YWCA), which insisted on their "unpolitical" nature, survived under the first dictatorship.[2] Although these organizations, led by elite women (usually the wives of local notables), taught Victorian and Christian values which reinforced male domination, some women were able to develop leadership and organizational skills through participation in them. However, membership in women's organizations kept declining as the climate in Uganda grew more and more tense—states of emergency were being declared in many parts of the country, detentions without trial were routine, and meetings were viewed suspiciously by government officials. Also, as the economic situation worsened, many women found that they had less and less time and energy after a long day's work to devote to activities of women's organizations.

Excluded from the post-independence political institutions and economically weakened by land laws which favored men, peasant women saw in education a way out of powerlessness for their daughters. The 1960s in Uganda witnessed women's struggles against the traditions of keeping girls at home and sending boys to school and of taking daughters out of school in order to marry them off.

The civilian dictatorship of Milton Obote was brought to an abrupt end by Idi Amin's military coup d'etat. It is estimated that 500,000 women, men, and children were killed during the eight years of Amin's fascist regime. Yet, in essence, Amin's regime was similar to the one it had replaced—both were, as it became increasingly clear, agencies of one or several foreign powers, most notably Great Britain (Mamdani, 1983).

How Amin's rule affected women's lives and their actions depended on their class, religion, ethnicity, and other factors. However, it is undeniable that, in general, women peasants and workers were the regime's worst victims. They were terrorized in the same ways as men but also had to endure rape. In fact, rape by soldiers became so common that a raped woman was often told she had only herself to blame for getting caught—soldiers were rapists and women were expected to know how to avoid them. Corruption, which had started in the colonial period, reached epidemic proportions under Amin's rule. When poor women could not raise enough money to bribe corrupt officials (in order to obtain an essential service such as health care), they were forced to pay with their bodies.

Every type of prejudice was used by Amin to divide the people and to stall the growing opposition to fascism. Women were a perfect group to target. In the name of morality, Amin, through a series of decrees, banned women from wearing certain clothes, using cosmetics, and from having abortions. Amin's list of prohibited female appearance and behavior was so long that a woman walking on the street could never be certain that she might not be arrested at any time for breaking the law (Mamdani, 1983). Amin's decrees served to reduce the social status of all women and to make them even more vulnerable in an already oppressive situation. Women's organizations ceased to function as Amin's network of spies and killers spread terror throughout the country. Women, therefore, developed a particularly passionate hatred for fascism.

The effect of Amin's policies on the economy was catastrophic. The prices of agricultural products and manufactured goods and the cost of services kept going up, while the government paid peasants less and less of what their cash crops earned on the international market; inflation peaked. The result was that peasants shifted back to production of food crops which were sold individually on the local market for better prices. Peasant women, who had remained in the production of subsistence crops while men had monopolized cash crops, found themselves in the more difficult situation of having to increase their food production in order to compensate for the lost family income from cash crops.

Ironically, the worsening economy strengthened many peasant wives relative to their husbands. Peasant women came out of their homes to market their food and to look for paid work. In the process, many became permanent workers or traders in the markets and towns. They learned how to earn money and how to spend it, became decision-makers, developed confidence and authority in their homes (Obbo, 1980). Widows and other female heads-of-households struggled, some for the first time, to support their families alone. They were exploited economically and very often sexually as well, but gained experience in working outside the family environment. The wives of rich men, too, realizing that one day they may not have a husband to depend on, went out to look for work.

The economic crisis, therefore, enhanced the position of many Ugandan women, especially poor and peasant women, and weakened the basis for men's domination. Social insecurity, widowhood, and exile pushed more women into paid work. At the same time, the brutalities meted out to women intensified their hatred and loathing of dictatorships. This period prepared women for future political action. When nationalist forces finally declared the beginning of an armed struggle against dictatorships, many women were ready to participate.

### The Guerrilla War, 1981–1985

The two years after Amin's fall were marked by a growing power struggle between the old politicians (heavily backed by their foreign sponsors) and the young and relatively unknown leadership of the nationalist and anti-fascist movement. These wrangles eventually culminated in a five-year guerrilla war. In 1981, after a massively rigged election, the National Resistance Army (NRA), the armed wing of the National Resistance Movement (NRM), declared a protracted people's war on the new, foreign-backed government led by Obote.

To understand women's overwhelming support for the resistance struggle, it is important to appreciate that at this stage war was not seen as one of several alternatives to solve Uganda's problems. It was the last resort of women and men who had suffered for nineteen years the excesses and atrocities of three violent dictatorships. The people had tried to resist nonviolently but without success. Parliamentarians who had spoken out in the 1960s against the first regime had been imprisoned without trial under emergency laws, and demonstrators had been shot. In the 1970s, peasants cut down their coffee trees in an attempt to stifle Amin's coffee-for-arms deals, but Amin borrowed money from keen lenders and bought more guns. Politicians, journalists, academics, preachers, lawyers, judges, and others protested and were killed openly or disappeared forever. Exiled Ugandans urged governments and international organizations to ostracize Amin's regime, they campaigned for an economic blockade, but received no response. Only Tanzania rejected Amin's government and consistently opposed it.[3]

## Women's Involvement in the Armed Struggle

Through a very painful process, women and men of all classes and backgrounds acknowledged the fact that peaceful means had failed to end the aggression of dictators and to bring the country to democratic rule. Instead, violence had escalated to horrendous levels. The situation left women with one option: to join men in armed struggle to defend their families and homes. It became clear that there was nothing to lose.

For women in the war zones, involvement in the resistance also became their most important strategy for empowerment. Of the NRM's main issues for mobilization and politicization, democracy, nationalism, and human rights had special appeal for women. Democracy was explained and understood as the opposite of dictatorship, and peasant women's anti-dictatorship sentiment was already very strong. But democracy was not merely promised by the NRM; it was established in the war zones through cells with Resistance Committees (RC's or *Bukiiko*). To be able to choose leaders and to participate in decision-making in their communities was a completely new and liberating experience for the people, especially so for women. The Bukiiko thus constituted the alternative to dictatorship. The initial motivation to join the NRM to fight dictatorships was transformed into a strong commitment to defend the Bukiiko. The Bukiiko was a personal structure similar to the old clan councils. For women, the personal was becoming political. They could sit on the Bukiiko and choose their representatives as well as dismiss them if they failed in their duties, were corrupt or unfair. Coming from a weaker and more disadvantaged position, women had more to gain from, and therefore more reasons to defend, grass-roots democracy.

The NRM explained nationalism as a "pro-Uganda" line, opposing every type of discrimination, including ethnic, religious, class, sex, and the distinction between the educated and those without formal schooling. In all its structures, and especially in the RC's and in the armed wing, the Movement insisted on practicing this principle. The worst victims of discrimination, illiterate peasant women, were particularly motivated to support the NRM due to its firm anti-discrimination commitment.

Although religious, ethnic, and class discrimination were crushed effectively within the Movement, there existed ambivalence about dealing with male domination of women. Some of NRM's leaders as well as rank-and-file members did not want to challenge male supremacy in order not to antagonize male peasants. Others seemed to think that focusing on "the women's question" would delay or divert the nationalist struggle. This stance on the part of the leadership postponed and impeded women's equal participation in the Movement.

Brutalization of women, children, and men by government troops made human rights the central issue for the guerrilla war. The NRA's humane record made the Movement a legitimate champion of human rights. As rape, killing of children, and abduction of women by government soldiers became the order of the day, more and more women sought and found refuge in and help from the Movement.

Generally, women and men were motivated to support and/or participate in the guerrilla war for similar reasons. However, many people observed that the NRM enjoyed more support from women then from men. I remember well that on the day of the final offensive for Kampala, mainly women and children lined the Masaka-Kampala road and waved us on with banana leaves and clenched fists. My impression has been that some men had sided with and benefited from the dictatorships, while very few women had done so. Thus more women than men supported the guerrilla resistance.

The reasons women gave for joining the armed struggle reflected the awareness that their interests—safety, better material conditions, equality, and just survival—could be served by allying themselves with the Movement. Some women joined the NRA because the men they depended on (husbands, brothers, or fathers) had been killed by government troops. Desperate and insecure, they found refuge in the Movement. A young girl guerrilla fighter told me how she had run away from her mother who was a nurse-midwife after her father was killed because she realized that they were unsafe. Her mother stayed behind, not wanting to abandon her clinic. Another woman, a guerrilla leader, often reminded me that she came to the bush seeking revenge on the vice-president who had personally ordered her husband's imprisonment without trial. When I met her, she had been involved in the struggle long enough to link her own experience with the oppression of others, and she talked about overthrowing "the whole system."

Some young urban women followed their boyfriends into the bush. The case of D is interesting, because it illustrates the complexity of women's motivation to join the NRA. D's brother was one of the first victims of Obote's dictatorship. D was doing well in school but realized that she stood little chance of occupational success within the corrupt and male-dominated system. She also had fallen in love with a young guerrilla fighter. Since most people in the area where D lived were known supporters of the man who had declared the guerrilla war, they were openly harassed, imprisoned, and killed by government agents. All these reasons combined to make D insecure, resentful, frustrated, and bitter. However, she managed to turn these negative feelings into positive contributions to the resistance war by making sacrifices and taking risks that were of great importance to the success of the Movement. D developed an egalitarian relationship with her boyfriend (who later became her husband), which is not surprising as she became a political activist in her own right. The war completely transformed D's life; had she not joined the struggle, the best she could have hoped for was to be a submissive wife of a rich, perhaps also educated, man. D is now a national hero, an equal to her husband, and continues to participate in the political process in Uganda.

Some single women, separated women, prostitutes, and others who were frowned upon by the traditional society, joined the resistance to gain respectability. One very beautiful woman who had many cows (an important economic asset in Uganda) remained unmarried because she could not have children. Since she had had many relationships with men, she was known as a "malaya" (prostitute) in her village and the surrounding area. She joined the Movement to escape condemnation and to be appreciated as an activist. While the NRM respected traditional values, it did not subscribe to them, but only stressed the importance of discipline and contribution to the war.

In Uganda, arranged marriages have been and continue to be common among some cultural groups (the Bahima and the Banyarwanda especially). Some young women ran to the NRM to escape such marriages.

Some women followed their relatives into the battle, others left unhappy marriages, and still others joined the Movement because they had lost their means of livelihood to the war. Many simply had nowhere else to turn, as government troops inflicted vengeance on the entire population for supporting the guerrilla resistance.

As the war swept through the countryside and the guerrillas captured town after town, women's support became overwhelming. Several young women admitted to me that among the reasons they joined the Movement was to find a husband. They had decided that they would not marry anyone except a hero of the resistance. Discipline, a just cause, and success made the struggle appealing to women looking for husbands, because on the one hand, they admired strength and heroism (traditional values), and on the other, they wanted disciplined and egalitarian men to live with. From numerous discussions with younger women who joined the struggle I concluded that they were not only angry at the dictatorships and their effects on their own lives and those of others, but were also seeking ways of resolving the unsatisfactory power relationship between men and women.

Older women articulated still other reasons for taking part in the resistance. One evening during the war, I listened to several elderly women telling of the repression since the 1960s. They talked of killings, rape, imprisonments, states of emergency, corruption, discrimination, inflation, and poverty. They agreed that restoring peace was the most important objective and that democracy was a prerequisite for peace. They were prepared to die to achieve these goals. "After all," one of them said, "Obote's soldiers will still kill me even if I did not support the resistance." This woman clearly recognized that she had nothing to lose but everything to gain by participating in the struggle. Older women, too, were able to achieve dignity and equality through the Movement. They could acquire decision-making authority through the Bukiiko and as elders were much respected by the guerrillas.

The majority of women who participated in the resistance struggle were peasants, although there were a number of women from the towns and cities who played important roles. In the first stages of the war, some urban women were involved in the sensitive tasks of gathering intelligence and the collection and transportation of arms, ammunition, and other supplies. They also carried information between the guerrillas in the bush and their supporters in cities and towns. They encouraged sympathetic soldiers in the national army to defect and then guided them to the guerrilla camps.

During the first year of the armed struggle, the view of the NRM leadership was that the situation in the bush was too difficult for women to bear. When pressed, leaders would say that when the situation would improve women would be allowed to join the guerrilla army. Although this was well-intentioned and can be understood as stemming from the traditional idolization of mothers, it inhibited and delayed women's participation in the war. As the war progressed, however, women pleaded and insisted and were eventually allowed to join the guerrilla camps.

The presence of women in the camps, however, did not automatically lead to their equality with men. Training as guerrilla fighters was not compulsory for all young women as it was for all young men. Many women in the camps became involved in such traditional tasks as cooking and health care as well as activities outside of combat, e.g., intelligence, courier, and administrative work. Others were involved in politicization and organization of people in areas taken over by the guerrillas.

When RC's or Bukiiko were set up within the war zones, peasant women often became active through them. They supplied food to guerrilla fighters, provided safe houses, passed on vital information about the enemy's location, and cared for very ill guerrillas. They were encouraged to attend their village Bukiiko meetings, and some were elected onto the RC's. However, the NRM did not attack the barriers (the shouldering of all domestic work and childcare, most of food production, and patriarchal attitudes) to peasant women's participation in the struggle. As long as such barriers existed, women's full political participation could not be achieved.

As the war intensified, it became necessary to evacuate the entire civilian population from the war zones. Only women who were, or wanted to be, guerrilla fighters and those with special skills, such as the grandmother traditional (herbal) healer, were allowed to stay in the camps. After a heated debate, the leadership of the NRA decided to establish the Women's Wing of the guerrilla army and to make a separate women's camp. The main reasons for the establishment of the Women's Wing were to maintain discipline, to prevent promiscuity, and to stop the spread of venereal diseases (as medicines were very scarce).

Although many women in the NRA opposed the establishment of a separate camp for women, the Women's Wing did a great deal to enhance guerrilla women's contributions. By being together, the women were able to support each other. They were able to overcome their shyness and feelings of inferiority vis-a-vis men. Had they remained in the men's camps, many of the women would have come out of the war as merely the wives of guerrillas and not the able, competent, and responsible freedom fighters they turned out to be. In the Wing, they concentrated on their training and took on more responsibilities in running the affairs of their own unit. As a separate, independent unit, the women fighters were better able to contribute to the struggle. Some of the women who were part of the Women's Wing eventually undertook important operations in the final offensive for Kampala. Today, many are still officers of the NRA, serving as unit commanders, trainers, administrators, and in other positions.

It is important to note that while the NRM/NRA leadership saw the need to establish a Women's Wing, it did not take the view that women should always be organized separately from men in the resistance. Later, when the NRA was expanding rapidly, the Women's Wing was disbanded and many of the women were deployed into positions of training, administration, and commanding new units (of men and women). I spoke with many members of the Women's Wing after the Wing ceased to exist, and they were pleased with their new positions. They saw the Women's Wing as a step taken out of necessity that helped them to develop as leaders and fighters. While many were deployed in noncombat roles, those who preferred to be on the front lines were able to be there.

Apart from becoming aware that they were valued as equal freedom fighters to their male colleagues and that they had equal opportunities to contribute to the struggle, the women guerrillas were not exposed to any explicit feminist consciousness-raising. The issue of male domination did not unite them. Some of the older women held strongly the view that a woman should submit to a man, whereas some of the younger women, while not openly challenging this view, were clearly seeking options that would liberate them from this tradition. Yet, a sisterhood did develop. Whenever they could be together, the women talked about their personal relationships and the struggle, they chatted freely about their sexuality, and their plans for the future (after the war). They talked little about women's subordination in general, tending to discuss their own and others' specific situations. Some wanted to marry and have children, others wanted to be single mothers. (Camp rules forbade pregnancies.) They kept up with each others' lives and got together as often as they could to chat, laugh, exchange news, and advise and encourage each other. The women rallied around any one of them with a problem, especially those who worked together.

All the women I knew admitted that they had developed a strong commitment to the resistance. They sometimes warned each other, laughingly, yet seriously, "never to betray the struggle" *(otaripinga)*. When their contributions were acknowledged and more responsibilities were assigned to them, the women found that the Movement was their greatest ally in asserting themselves in new roles as participants in national affairs. Hard work, discipline, sacrifice, and perseverance brought more influence and improved their status. The struggle provided a unique opportunity for Ugandan women to engage in self-governance. But without saying so, the women were also challenging the tradition of male domination.

By the fourth year, the war had advanced into the mobile stage. When the first big towns were taken over by the NRA, many secondary school girls left school to join the guerrillas. Single working women also joined the resistance in large numbers, as did many illiterate urban women.

On January 25th, 1985, the NRA took over Kampala, and during the next two months captured all the towns in Uganda and most of the countryside.

The success of the struggle would not have been possible without the important part that women played in the national resistance war, the overwhelming support they gave the guerrillas, and the women's loyalty and total commitment to the cause of national liberation from dictatorship and neo-colonialism. Ugandan women's involvement in the guerrilla war constituted an important stage in their history of struggle for their country, their families, and for their own equality.

## Conclusions

Seeking empowerment through participation in the NRM was far from easy for Ugandan women. The NRM leadership was fully aware of the extent of women's oppression, and in principle, it opposed sex discrimination. However, in practice, the leadership did not openly speak out against male domination of women. Some of the leaders of the resistance took the view that it was dangerous to highlight women's particular oppression within the larger, imperialist system because this could divert and divide the struggle. Some leaders believed, therefore, that in order to avoid the mistake of obscurantism it was necessary, at least for some time, to subordinate women's problems to the larger struggle for national liberation. Others believed that the exploitation of women by men would end once neo-colonialism was abolished and a national, self-sustaining economy established. Since men more than women were required on the battlefield, the leadership did not want to alienate men by directly attacking their domination of women. Also, as the leadership was predominantly male, neither could it be particularly sensitive to women's desire for equal participation in the struggle and beyond, nor could it fully appreciate the problems that limited women's involvement.

Yet, there is no doubt that the guerrilla war provided women the best opportunity, since Uganda's borders were first drawn, to be politically active. Within the guerrilla army, the Movement was firm about equality of women and men fighters. Women, who generally had less formal education than men, had advantage in the NRM's insistence on useful contribution rather than formal skills and education in promoting fighters. Criticizing and neutralizing elitist tendencies boosted the confidence and commitment of especially peasant women and men guerrillas.

The Bukiiko or RC's were as accessible as the old clan councils, but this time they were more democratic. The style of leadership was personal and consistent with the peasants' holistic approach to life. The Movement's very firm defense of human rights, opposition to discrimination, and promotion of democratic principles were an indirect attack on male domination. The climate was therefore favorable for women to take part in discussions and decision-making. The Movement's methods of clear analysis and explanation of problems of oppression, and its struggle to end dictatorships, were very effective. Illiterate peasants and urban intellectuals alike were able to participate in decision-making, because at all times the main issues were well understood.

The war is over now,[4] and Uganda is in a period of reconstruction. The government, which was formed by the National Resistance Army under the leadership of Yoweri Musevani, has been broad-based from the beginning, and achieved widespread legitimacy in a first national election held in 1989. However, the country is struggling with a slow revival of the economy, high inflation, and a determination to stay clear of foreign loans and investments to avoid domination by outside powers.

The most noticeable achievements of the resistance movement for women include the position of a women's representative on every village RC of the post-liberation government. The NRM recognized the importance of reserving seats for women at all levels of governance in order to break with the tradition of exclusion of women from formal decision-making bodies (Directorate of Women's Affairs, 1990). The RC's, especially at the lowest levels, play a significant role because they help to cope with local problems and to distribute scarce foodstuffs and other resources more equitably among the population. While there are still relatively few women in these local councils (about 15 percent), women have been elected to other positions besides the designated "secretary for women's affairs," and in one council in Kampala there are more women than men (Directorate of Women's Affairs, 1990: 5).

At the parliamentary level, 34 of the 278 seats are reserved for women (one for every district). In the 1989 election, 40 women attained parliamentary seats, and out of a 48-member cabinet, 9 were female appointees. While the relatively low female representation is still of minimal influence, it is significant that women occupy some of the most important cabinet positions; most notably, Betty Bogombe is Minister of State for pacification of the North, Victoria Sekitoleko, Minister of Agriculture, and Wandira Kazibwe, Deputy Minister of Industry and Technology (Directorate of Women's Affairs, 1990: 2).

The government has also established a Directorate of Women's Affairs which has been active in promoting the involvement of women in public life. In 1989, the Directorate proposed the formation of a national women's organization that would follow the structure of the RC's from the local (village) to national level. The secretary for women's affairs in the existing RC system would become the chairperson of the women's council at each level. The Directorate felt that this would provide more opportunity for women's views and concerns to influence the decision-making process. The Ugandan Parliament passed a bill authorizing the formation of women's councils, and the Directorate is now implementing their organization.

While the gains women have made in Uganda since the revolution may appear relatively modest, it is important to realize that for the first time since colonialism women are represented at all levels of governance, and new structures are being created to advance and strengthen the participation of women in the affairs of the country.

Since the revolution, women clearly have chosen to remain in the new political structures. Many are active through their village committees, many have remained in the army, and some have begun to organize themselves as women to achieve common objectives. Now that the Movement is in power, it cannot afford to be silent about the problems women face in political participation. There is a growing realization that it will not be possible to harness women's full potential in the urgent work of reconstruction and development unless they are well represented and are active at all levels in the RC system—the vehicle of democratic rule.

Ugandan women were not invited to take part in the national resistance war, they forced their way in. There was no women's movement in Uganda to encourage them, no leaders' speeches about women's emancipation, no consciousness-raising groups. The objectives of the struggle—human rights, democracy, nationalism—were clear and close to women's hearts. Through involvement in this struggle, they were able to address and resolve some of the problems of their own oppression as women. It was not possible, then, for these women to deal with their inequality outside the context of a nationalist, anti-imperialist movement. Women saw themselves as united with men in one resistance. The enemy were those forces which held power over all the people.

However, the problem of men's exploitation of women remains. If it continues to be subordinated to the ongoing struggle to end neo-colonialism in Uganda, the strategy will be self-defeating and contradictory. The further empowerment of women will be greatly impeded unless full recognition is given to both types of domination.

# Notes

1. Editor's Note: W. Karagwa Byanyima joined the National Resistance Movement in Uganda in 1982. She spent over a year fighting in the bush with a guerrilla batallion. This chapter is based largely on her personal experience as well as extensive informal interviews she conducted during and after the guerrilla war.

2. The first period of dictatorship took place between 1966 and 1971 under Milton Obote. Idi Amin established a military dictatorship in 1971 which was overthrown in 1979. In 1980, Obote came to power once more, and his second dictatorship ended in 1985 when the National Resistance Army took over the capital of Kampala.

3. It was Tanzania which in 1979 helped Ugandans to overthrow the dictator, Idi Amin.

4. Pockets of resistance still exist in the north and northeast. Although under a general amnesty of 1987 most dissident guerrillas, such as ex-Amin followers and ex-Obote army members, joined the NRM, some have remained outside the Movement and opposed to the new government.

C H A P T E R

10

# BETWEEN NATIONALISM AND FEMINISM

The Palestinian Answer

## *Orayb Aref Najjar*

"Teach me how to part the ocean without drowning."
Commando leader Dalal el-Mughrabi
to her trainer.[1]

Despite the well-publicized stories about Palestinian female commandos confronting Israelis or hijacking planes (Khaled, 1973), women's involvement in the Palestinian national struggle was and continues to be nonmilitary. During the 1970s, Palestinian guerrilla organizations based in Lebanon, Syria, and Jordan made military training available to women, and a few pioneers took advantage of it. Israelis imprisoned some women for resistance,[2] but an overview of women's contribution to Palestinian society shows that women have spent more time caring for victims of war and protracted conflict and on nationalist activity than on agitation for women's rights. Commando el-Mughrabi's statement is important, however, because it reveals her yearning for legitimacy and her feeling that she can attain it, not by demonstrating for women's rights, and not by asking for legal guarantees against sex discrimination, as Western women have, but by parting the ocean: or being willing to physically fight for the Palestinian cause.

The feeling that equality for Palestinian women can be attained through involvement in the national struggle in all its forms is widely shared. Hence, the phrase "the Palestinian women's movement" is a misnomer because it gives the impression that there was/is a Palestinian women's movement agitating for their rights, when in fact there are women's organizations and committees deeply involved in the national struggle; women who see their fate and rights as organically tied to the attainment of a Palestinian state.

Issam Abdul Hadi, active in Palestinian politics since the 1940s, has no doubts about where the stress should be:

> The Palestinian woman has been convinced since the 1920s that the cause of feminine development and liberation is closely linked to the cause of liberating her country from colonialism and various forms of oppression and exploitation. . . . She had therefore placed the general rule of protecting the homeland against Zionist and colonial aggression above any other consideration. The Palestinian woman, just as any other woman in Arab society, suffers certain problems . . . but she willingly places national issues above other issues. (Talhami, 1985: 9)

The much younger Mai Sayegh, poet and Palestine Liberation Organization (PLO) activist explains,

> . . . The problem of the condition of women in the context . . . of dispersion of all . . . and the questions people pose: "How to live, to eat, to find shelter? How many martyrs, how many orphaned children who are hungry, how many to educate?" . . . the condition of women seems of little weight. (Sayigh, 1984: 23–24)

Rosemary Sayigh comments that even if one disagrees with Sayegh's position that women's problems are of lesser importance than the problems shared by the oppressed, stateless Palestinians as a whole, it remains true that national crisis suppresses consciousness of class and gender oppression and accentuates women's reproductive role. Women are also conscripted on the symbolic level "into representing traditions and an authenticity threatened by a more powerful, alien culture" (Sayigh, 1984: 24). Sometimes the traditions that are celebrated and thus strengthened are not necessarily good for women. This tension between women's needs and rights and perceived national needs has led some to wonder whether the national struggle is retarding the efforts for women's equality (Peteet, 1986). On the other hand, the strain has led others to dismiss women's emancipation as a "secondary contradiction" (quoted in Sayigh, 1983), one that is not important enough to distract from the all-consuming struggle for national self-determination.

In this chapter, I describe the tension between Palestinian national rights and women's rights and discuss how women have dealt with its complications over time. I suggest that the old operating methods of women's charitable organizations, as well as historical realities between 1919 and 1977 would *not* have led to substantial gains in women's status in the long run, but that the strategies the new women's committees have been using since 1978 to empower women have been beneficial to women. At the same time, I argue that while the strategies I identify are important and effective, the inability of the four women's committees to unite behind a program based on gender-related issues places women's committees at the mercy of alliances between different political factions. It also leaves women exposed to restrictions imposed by the

Islamic movement that is now gaining strength on the West Bank, as it has in Gaza during the last few years.

## Is There a Palestinian Women's Problem?

There is no doubt that there is a Palestinian women's problem independent of the national problem. Palestinian researchers estimate that the average infant mortality rate in the West Bank is in the range of 50 to 100 per 1,000 live births (Said, 1985: 7). A study conducted on 600 families in five villages and five refugee camps revealed that 34 percent gave birth by themselves. Out of the 3,849 births in these families, 324 children died in the first year, and 16 more in the next two years, making the infant mortality rate 84 per 1,000. The study showed that women in refugee camps would not consider birth control until the tenth child (PFWAC Newsletter, 1988). Dr. Rita Giacaman notes that there is more malnourishment and infant mortality among baby girls than boys in the villages she has studied.[3]

Because of the expectation that females will marry in their teens, or because parents are reluctant to allow girls to travel to high schools in nearby towns, after a few years of schooling, many rural parents keep their daughters home to help with household chores. Whenever resources are scarce, males are given preference over females, starting as early as kindergarten (for which parents have to pay). Female illiteracy, which has improved dramatically since 1961, is still high among women over forty (Khader, 1988: 51–74). In legal matters—marriage, divorce, child custody, and inheritance—laws favor males.

While the PLO has employed women in its factories and various enterprises (in Lebanon), especially in care-giving jobs, few women hold leading positions in the organization. In 1986, the Palestine National Council (PNC), the Palestinian Parliament in exile, had 33 women out of a total of 428, and no women in the 15-member executive council.[4]

Despite discrimination women face because of their gender, the dimensions of the national problem, the total disruption of Palestinian agrarian society and the turning of Palestinian farmers into refugees in 1948 when Israel was established, have obscured women's concerns. Yet the exile of Palestinians from their homeland has accelerated women's education as well as their involvement in public affairs. However, even with all the changes that have taken place in women's role, women's interest in women's rights (as opposed to national rights) is a recent phenomenon that dates back only to the late 1970s, and is more pronounced in the West Bank than in other areas where Palestinians live. Feminist consciousness has stirred in the West Bank and Gaza, but has not yet developed into a full-blown program on gender relations. Women's demands are still couched in nationalist rather than feminist terms and have not yet been forcefully articulated on an inter-Palestinian level.

Because the condition of Palestinian women living in extended families is different from those of women in the West, the feminism that has developed does not consider "male chauvinism" as the issue, but blames gender inequalities on

> the underdeveloped and deformed social-economic structure which has in the past stood in the way of the woman taking part extensively in the community production processes as a necessary condition for her freedom . . . and on traditions which take their power from . . . concepts full of superstitions . . . which deprive women of their rights to education and to work. . . . (PFWAC, 1987b)

Three out of four of the Palestinian women's committees stress class over gender issues and so concentrate on *empowering* rural and refugee women through education, leadership training, employment, and the provision of childcare. At this stage, sex role differentiation is not the issue, but respect for the traditional role of women as nurturers is. Women's groups do not use the Western feminist argument that women should not be regarded *only* as wives and mothers, but argue instead that women should be respected *because* many *are* wives and mothers who are responsible for the upbringing of young Palestinians. Until now, the women's movement has not tackled sex-role stereotyping, believing that structural changes in Palestinian society will provide disadvantaged women with the educational opportunities well-to-do and/or educated women already have.

Palestinian women do not have the luxury of asking for immediate changes in their legal status because they are stateless (despite the declaration of a Palestinian state in November 1988). Instead, women are concentrating on action they believe will be conducive to ending Israeli occupation and to the establishment of statehood.

As members of a conservative society, Palestinian women were thought to function mostly in the private sphere, which was seen as one which precludes involvement in public affairs. Western feminists have questioned the utility of the "public/private" dichotomy often used to study the participation of women because "it has constructed an inaccurate account of the lives, feelings, and thoughts of women and men" (Andersen, 1988: 19). Without "rethinking the dichotomy," many of the political activities of Palestinian women would remain unrecorded. Neglecting them would constitute a serious omission, because grass-roots women's organizations are helping a society under siege keep its threads from unraveling. It is no exaggeration to say that preserving the cohesiveness of a society is the ultimate political act.

Suad Joseph, for instance, finds that the public and private roles of women and men change "as the state expands and retreats, kin and communal groups gain and lose control over members. Women's locations and the definition of their activities shift as the boundaries move" (Joseph, 1986: 4). Blurring between the public and private spheres occurs as communities draw on all their resources for survival. Throughout history, women's role has been more elastic than scholarly research, with its neat categories, cares to admit.

An examination of Palestinian daily life reveals that the conceptual dichotomy of public and private roles is sorely inadequate when attempts are made to apply it there. Consider, for instance, the provision of food: In normal times, cooking is "women's work" in the so-called private or domestic sphere. In times of crisis, women still obtain and cook the food, but do so also for public purposes. The first major act of Palestinian solidarity that helped the occupied deal with the shock of the 1967 defeat was undertaken by a women's organization which called for food donations to villages razed by Israeli troops.[5] In'ash el-Usrae Society in el-Bireh conducted tours to the villages of Yalu, Emmaus, and Beit Nuba to make volunteers understand the extent of the disruption. The donations that poured in, the collective cooking, and the logistics of getting the food to the refugees pulled the community together and showed Palestinians that they were not as helpless as they had imagined.

In normal times, embroidery may be used by women as a frill and as an art form; in times of crisis, traditionally female skills such as sewing, knitting and embroidery are done at home (in the private sphere) to further collective (public) ends. The folklore revival fostered by women's organizations not only provided women with work but also affirmed Palestinian identity. The new stitches created by the village women also provided a running commentary on formal political decisions affecting the Palestinian people. For instance, the dead-end-road stitch was introduced as a comment on the Camp David Accords and as an expression of women's rejection of an agreement that did not grant Palestinians self-determination. The two-snakes stitch mirrored women's feelings about Begin and Sadat.[6] Other examples include the knitting of five thousand sweaters in the winter of 1988 to show solidarity with prisoners of the Intifada, the uprising which started in 1987, and the sewing of thousands of Palestinian flags as symbols of the Palestinian struggle (PWWC, 1989: 27).

*Refusing to sew or cook* has also been used by Palestinian women for public purposes. In the Israeli prison of Neve Terza, Palestinian women declared a hunger strike in 1977 and refused to sew camouflage nets and uniforms for the Israeli army. In 1983, Palestinian female prisoners refused to cook for their Israeli guards (Palestine/Israel Bulletin, 1986: 5).

It follows then that while public and private spheres are heuristic devices to delineate the areas where action takes place, in real life it is often impossible to tell when a private action begins and a public one ends. When Palestinian mothers stage one of their frequent hunger strikes and sit-ins in front of the International Red Cross, is theirs a private or a public act? When Amnesty International responds to those women, do their actions still belong to the private sphere? When Palestinian mothers, despite their grief about losing their sons and daughters, refuse to wear black because their children are martyrs, is their role in encouraging personal sacrifice for the collective good personal or political? In the experience of Palestinian women, the two are interdependent in the same way as their emancipation as women is closely related to the liberation of the entire Palestinian people.

Because leaders of women's organizations believe that the personal is intertwined with the national, they argue that when women organize to bring about social reform within their communities (rather than in the corridors of power), women are engaged in politics.

But even after we redefine our terms, and even after we erase the public/ private dichotomy that obscures the contributions of women, we still need to ask: Is struggling for women's rights through the nationalist route the shortest path to the emancipation of Palestinian women? Many have criticized the strategy. Julie Peteet writes that in Lebanon

> Palestinian women's entry into the domain of formal, national politics did not necessarily marginalize the women's movement. But the process of formal integration into the national political body diluted their movement's potential commitment to women's issues and autonomy over their policies, positions, and development. (Peteet, 1986: 21)

Nawal Saadawi says that in Algeria, women were the first to die and the last to be liberated (Graham-Brown, 1987: 27). Some fear the same fate will befall Palestinian women, but others argue that there are important differences between the Palestinian and Algerian situations. Juliette Minces writes, for instance, that the majority of Algerian militants *had no goal other than independence,* and that "it was implicitly understood that it was only for lack of men and under abnormal conditions that men turned to women, there was rarely any connection made between women's actions and their value" (Minces, 1980: 159–60).

In the Palestinian situation, while traditional women's organizations had no feminist agenda, the four new women's committees started out with a few women's concerns but are slowly and cautiously making more demands on behalf of women. The question is, will this women's agenda be developed in time to withstand the creeping Islamization of the West Bank or will women be too busy resisting Israeli repression to notice that their personal rights are under threat from a strict interpretation of Muslim religious law?

## The Women's Movement 1900–1978

A brief history of women's activism since 1900 in what was once called Palestine shows that the national issue has always taken precedence over the emancipation of women. The first women's organization "The Arab Women's Union" was founded in 1919. While other women's unions in the Arab world asked for raising the marriage age, abolishing polygamy and summary divorce, and improving educational opportunities for women, Palestinian women adopted a set of nationalist demands instead. The Zionist threat to the Arab character of Palestine was at the time, and has continued to be, such an overriding issue that no other issue could be considered of equal importance (Talhami, 1985: 5).

Palestinian women organized a demonstration in Jerusalem in 1929 to protest British immigration policies. A female speaker explained why women got involved: 'This action, the first of its kind by Arab women for the first time in the history of Palestine was undertaken *to help their men save the homeland from its disasters and to rid it of its pains*" (my emphasis) (Khalifah, 1974: 39).

On October 26, 1929, the first women's conference held in Jerusalem and attended by three hundred women was also nationalist in nature, as were women's actions during the 1936 to 1939 revolt in Palestine.

After the Arab-Israeli war of 1948, when Palestinians were dispersed to refugee camps in countries surrounding the newly created state of Israel, a number of women's organizations, old and new, dispensed services to the refugee population. Since host Arab governments in Jordan, Lebanon, and Syria forbade nationalist activity within women's organizations licensed as charitable societies, Palestinian women joined the mostly underground existing Arab political parties. While these political parties had progressive rhetoric on women's issues, the parties were not willing to risk their other programs for women.

The PLO, too, was ambivalent about tackling the "woman's question." Since its establishment in 1964, the PLO made it a point to include women in its ranks, to recruit and involve women, but not to deal specifically with women's issues. The formation of the General Union of Palestinian Women (GUPW) in 1965 reflected the PLO's emphasis on the "liberation of Palestine." The GUPW constitution was even based on the PLO national charter (Antonius, 1980). While it could be argued that because the PLO represents Palestinians, its interests and the interests of women are synonymous, often the interests of women were and still are subordinated to the interests of preserving harmony within the different streams of the Palestinian movement.

The PLO consists of a number of factions and not all have taken the view that women's issues should be subordinated to the national struggle. The literature of the leftist groups, such as the Popular Front for the Liberation of Palestine (PFLP) and the Democratic Front for the Liberation of Palestine (DFLP), calls for a more progressive position on women and often criticizes Fateh, the largest commando group, because it provides services "the way an independent state provides them . . . without involving the masses in the confrontation to solve problems by themselves" (Khorsheid, 1972: 119). The DFLP, for instance, stresses the creation of cooperatives over the provision of charity and calls for involving women in the planning and implementation of decisions affecting them (Khorsheid 1972: 119, 120).

While the leftist streams within the PLO outside the occupied territories have more progressive views on women than Fateh, they have not made women's rights an issue for tactical and practical reasons. The leftist philosophy of organizing women and the leftist progressive attitude to social work can be seen more clearly in women's organizations on the West Bank and Gaza, organizations that are allied with the PLO, but that have flourished perhaps because of their distance from the official PLO male leadership outside the occupied territories.

## Women's Organizations in the West Bank: 1978–Present

Until 1978, two types of organizations served women in the occupied territories: charitable societies and several branches of the pre-1948 Arab Women's Union. The GUPW, founded by the PLO in 1965, is forbidden in the occupied territories, although several of its former members remain active in various charitable societies. The oldest of these organizations, which are now grouped under the General Federation of Charitable Societies, were founded by women and have always been traditionally female, but the federation that unites them is now headed by a male. All of these societies dispense social services, run kindergartens, and are active in the literacy movement.

In the early 1970s, the PLO started to pursue political struggle and called on activists to organize the masses and strengthen Palestinian-run institutions in the occupied territories. Voluntary work was encouraged and adopted by various institutions and organizations.[7] A number of young women activists in these volunteer groups at first tried to work within traditional societies but became dissatisfied with their top-down leadership style that did not allow rank-and-file women to take part in the decision-making process.

Activist women doing volunteer work in refugee camps and rural areas quickly realized that they would not be successful in recruiting local women without paying attention to social constraints to which women were subjected. Before women could work in their communities to help in the national struggle, *they had to be allowed to leave their homes.* Conservative customs observed closely in rural areas restricted the movement of women. Thus, the activists found that they could not separate the rights of women from nationalist activity. It became clear to women that they needed to change their strategy, to form an all-female organization (to absorb women of conservative backgrounds), and work for the empowerment of disadvantaged women.

In 1978 the Palestinian Union of Working Women's Committees (PUWWC) was established. The group chose to work as a "committee" rather than a "society" to avoid obtaining a permit from the Israeli authorities for its activities. Initially, the union consisted of women with loyalties to different resistance groups as well as independent women. Ideological differences emerged between members, leading some women to split from PUWWC and form other organizations. By 1982, the occupied territories had four groups or committees, of which PUWWC was one, representing ideological divisions within the Palestinian movement. The four groups agreed on the need for self-determination for Palestinians, had similar programs for women, but no common women's agenda they could present to the national Palestinian movement as a blueprint for action to improve the overall condition of women.

The Palestinian Working Women's Committee (PWWC) was established in March 1981 and is affiliated with the Communist Party. The PWWC was founded because some women felt that other groups did not pay enough attention to working women and to union matters. The committee believes that "the establishment of the PWWC is a qualitative leap in the direction of the movement because of its adoption of the cause of working women" (PWWC, 1985: 17).

The Palestinian Women's Committee (PWC) was established in March 1981 by women who sympathized with the PFLP. The PWC assigns relatively greater weight to the struggle against women's present status than other groups. As one activist explained,

> We place the women's question before the national question. We focus all our activities on bringing the women out of their homes to make them more self-confident and independent. Once they believe in themselves, they will know that they can become leaders in any field they choose, including the military field. A woman cannot fight the occupation if she is not even convinced that she has rights, for example the right to leave her house, for whatever reason. (Hiltermann, 1988: 445–46)

Hiltermann also finds that the percentage of uneducated and poor women in the PWC remains low (Hiltermann, 1988: 486–87).

The Union of Women's Committee for Social Work (WCSW) was established in June 1982. The group does not organize around a program but "those sympathetic to Fateh are drawn to us," notes one activist (WCSW, 1987: 7).

In contrast to the top-down structure of charitable societies, and to a certain extent, to the structure of the GUPW outside the occupied territories, the first three (leftist) committees have organizational strategies that are conscious of empowering women especially in rural areas and in refugee camps. The fourth group, WCSW, has branches in those areas as well, and offers similar services, but its rhetoric is much like that of charitable societies (WCSW 1987: 7). The WCSW has looser guidelines than the other three committees about organizing women in ways that would empower them, but activists note that they are working on a new structure. In contrast, an examination of the PUWWC whose name was changed to the Palestinian Federation of the Women's Action Committees (PFWAC) in June 1987, reveals well laid out guidelines for organizing.

## Strategies Women's Committees Use to Empower Women

### MASS RECRUITMENT

One of the most effective strategies for empowerment of Palestinian women has been through *inclusion*. Without inclusion in the national and the women's struggles, Palestinian women can not change their conditions. Zahira Kamal, executive committee member of PFWAC, estimates that in 1989, the number of women organized by all four committees and other organizations reached twenty five thousand. Kamal believes that while this figure is a great improvement on the past, it constitutes only 3 percent of the number of available women and, thus, much remains to be done (PFWAC, 1987a: 9). The PFWAC advises its different base committees to attract women members by avoiding rigid meetings and introducing instead activities such as lectures, films, poetry readings, and songs, and suggests distributing women's publications. (PFWAC, September 1987)

### PARTICIPATION IN THE DECISION-MAKING PROCESS

The structure of all committees and their locations in rural areas encourages participation in the decision-making process at the local level. The building blocks of PFWAC, for instance, are its "base units." Each unit is expected to have fifteen to thirty members. The purposes of this structure are to localize decision-making at the neighborhood level and to train women to take charge of their communities.

Participation is the key word in the work of PFWAC, and it takes place at every level. Members of the base unit decide on the type of committees they want to set up (prisoners' committee, literacy committee, production committee, etc.). The PFWAC, for instance, had 1,504 children in its kindergartens because women in base committees thought childcare was a priority (PFWAC, 1987c). The PFWAC aids in the establishment of *elected* mothers' committees in its kindergartens. The involvement of rural and refugee parents in the education of their children is a new and revolutionary step in Palestinian society. The value of such forms of participation is that they provide models for institutions in a future Palestinian state. While the committees are grass-roots organizations and thus assume that all Palestinian women are potential leaders, the committees realize that many women lack organizational skills that could make them more effective participants. Thus, leadership training sessions are provided where women are encouraged to take a more active part in the movement.

### EMPOWERMENT OF WOMEN THROUGH EDUCATION

The education of women has helped Palestinian society cope with their refugee status in different countries after the 1948 diaspora. Yet economic need as well as conservative traditions force a large number of women in rural areas to leave school. Members of committees sometimes convince families not to pull their daughters out of school. In a few cases, PFWAC members have organized villagers and petitioned the local bus company to provide better transportation to schools. Although these efforts have not been undertaken on a large scale, the fact that women's groups are tackling women's education is encouraging. The PUWWC has also procured scholarships for some women to study in the Soviet Union.

Women's committees have also taken advantage of the fact that the Higher Committee for Literacy pays the salary for a teacher and donates furniture to villages interested in opening literacy classes. The PFWAC's policy is "Wherever there is a base unit, there should be a literacy center" (PFWAC, 1986: 33). In 1987, PFWAC supervised thirty-two classes which enrolled 318 women. Statistics of the Higher Committee for Literacy show that the number of people who registered for classes in 1986 was 2,451, of whom 95.4 percent were women between the ages of fourteen and fifty. Of that number, only 258 women "graduated" fully literate. While this is an improvement over 1980 where only 150 learners graduated out of a total of 5,475, the number of women who drop out is still high (Khader 1988: 71, 74).

What is remarkable about PFWAC is not that it is providing literacy classes, but that it is trying to develop strategies that will reduce the drop-out rate. While charitable societies operate classes only when at least ten students are interested, PFWAC believes that women from small villages should not be penalized if only four or five illiterate women express interest in studying. The committee is also less strict about attendance, realizing that in villages and refugee camps, women are responsible for all kinds of social obligations that take them away from classes. Women are encouraged to make up for the absences rather than to drop out. The PFWAC finds that to keep women from dropping out, they have to tailor the classes to women's specific needs (PUWWC, 1987).

## FINANCIAL EMPOWERMENT THROUGH VOCATIONAL TRAINING AND EMPLOYMENT

Both traditional societies and the new committees teach women skills that allow them to gain a small measure of financial independence. Some women raise poultry on a cooperative basis, others pickle vegetables or bottle fruit juice. The PFWAC women in the Issawiyyeh village near Jerusalem have an enamel and a brass frame workshop. Most of the projects women are engaged in have sprung from women's attempts to respond to local needs and Israeli restrictions. In the fall of 1988, for instance, the Hebron branch of PFWAC initiated a pilot project for the production of raisins and molasses. The project is designed to help grape farmers hurt by Israeli restrictions on the export of grapes, the main crop of that region (PFWAC, March 1989: 5) Cooperatives have also been established in different villages in an attempt to find work for women where they live, rather than to leave them no option but to work for Israeli contractors. Most of the projects undertaken by women are in traditional women's occupations—embroidery, secretarial work, canning—but the committees have expanded women's skills by training them to manage all aspects of work. For instance, it was the case in the past that women only sewed; now they buy the material, distribute and collect it from women in different villages, and advertise and sell the finished items.

In two successful cooperatives that the Palestinian Women's Committee (PWC) set up with the help of Norwegian development funds, eighteen women of the village of Beitello in the north of the West Bank, and sixteen women of the village of Saeer in the south were trained by a team of women (a sociologist, a nurse, a nutritionist, and an economist) to run all aspects of the cooperative. The idea behind the cooperative is to enable women to develop independence by training them to control administration, marketing and production, and to place them into a direct relationship with the market. The most positive aspect of the experience lies in the essence and philosophy of cooperatives which foster relations that are built on planning, taking the initiative, being creative and independent, experiences that carry within them great responsibilities for rural women (Kuttab and Al-Ratrout, 1988: 24–26).

### EMPOWERMENT THROUGH "REALISTIC SOLUTIONS": THE PROVISION OF CHILDCARE AND HEALTH SERVICES

To neutralize objections of women working or volunteering outside the home, committees provide badly needed daycare for children of active members and others. Committees also hold summer camps. All of the women's committees and some of the charitable societies are heavily involved in helping medical groups in the West Bank provide health care to rural areas. In 1986, for instance, PFWAC, in cooperation with the Health Care Committee in the occupied territories, participated in sixty-five medical work days, in which the voluntary medical personnel made health care visits and examined people in various villages and refugee camps. PFWAC held 350 lectures focusing on preventative health care issues for women and children and screened fifty-five videotapes to 3,700 women all over the occupied territories (PFWAC, June 1987: 3).

### EMPOWERMENT THROUGH COMMUNITY SOLIDARITY

Another strategy used by the women's committees to empower women is to build community solidarity. Israelis use collective punishment to cow the population and to pressure the families of those who resist. Women's organizations perform support services to cancel the effect of the absence of a male due to Israeli measures. For instance, when Israelis close off some villages during the olive-picking season, women volunteers sneak into the villages through the hills and help the families of martyrs, of the imprisoned, or of those in hiding pick olives. Activists also visit the families of prisoners during the Muslim feast and take presents to the children; committees hold "consumer markets," which sell local products at reduced prices, and they raise funds to aid families during periods of curfews.

### EMPOWERMENT THROUGH CONTACTS WITH INTERNATIONAL AND ISRAELI WOMEN'S GROUPS

Another way that the women's committees have been increasing solidarity is through contacts with international women's groups. International female visitors help remind Palestinian men that women are part of a worldwide movement for liberation, and that women involved in this movement can be an important source of solidarity for Palestinians. This building of world solidarity has recently extended to include those Israeli women who accept the concept of self-determination for Palestinians and believe that Israelis should negotiate with the PLO. While contacts with Israeli women remain controversial, a number of Palestinian women's groups maintain such contacts by holding peace conferences with some recently founded peace groups, such as Women in Black, Women Against the Occupation, The 21st Year, and Women's Organization for Women Political Prisoners.

EMPOWERMENT THROUGH THE USE OF WOMEN'S PUBLICATIONS

Women's publications are slowly becoming important vehicles for empowerment because they encourage discussion, instruction, and participation. The PFWAC stresses the importance of discussion in all its literature to the base units. Women's magazines raise consciousness by reporting how women in the occupied territories and in the diaspora cope with the scarcity of resources, how families scale down their expectations of dowries in marriage and avoid ostentatious weddings during the Intifada. The PWWC publications encouraged women to write about their own contributions on the walls of West Bank towns and villages, and its members have written slogans saluting women for their participation in the uprising. Swedenberg noted that the important activities of women during the 1936 revolt were not recognized as political both because some of them took place in the "private" sphere, and because women themselves did not find their actions significant (Swedenberg 1985/86: 33). In contrast to 1936, women now have a voice, in the form of their own publications, and through them stress that women's contributions inside and outside the home are important for political struggle and for nation-building.

On December 14, 1990, the Higher Council of Women sponsored a conference on "The Intifada and Women's Social Issues." Participants criticized the lack of in-depth coverage of women's issues in the press and in literature, and recommended encouraging women writers with the help of the Arab Journalists' Union. This is the *first* time women's committees (as opposed to academic women) tackled the subject of women in the media and literature in an open forum (Tawfeeq, 1990: 9).

EMPOWERMENT OF WOMEN THROUGH UNITY

Of the strategies for improving the status of women, unity among women's committees and charitable societies remains the most problematic. Although the four women's committees have similar and sometimes identical programs for women, divisions over national policy have, until recently, kept them apart. On March 4, 1987, the four committees held their first unified celebration for International Women's Day. The four speakers representing the different committees called for unity "on an anti-reactionary and anti-imperialist basis," yet there was no joint action on women's problems.[8] Although the four committees have come to appreciate the need for unity "to extract women's rights" (PFWAC, 1987c), they have not yet drawn a nationwide program to tackle women's problems. Until they do, they remain an easy prey for conservatives who could wipe out all the committees' gains by calling on all "good women" to cover up and stay home and let the men do it all (Hammami, 1990).

Finally, the most important strategy has been to empower women through participation in the national struggle. In addition to taking part in supportive activities without which the struggle could not have survived, women have organized and participated in demonstrations and generally taken a strong resistance stance against Israeli actions. Thus women were responsible for 84 percent of the demonstrations held in 1968, a year after the Israeli occupation, and 71 percent in 1976. Women were responsible for 55 percent of the sit-ins in 1969 and 100 percent of those in 1974 and 1985 (PFWAC 1987b). Palestinian girls and adult women frequently stand up to Israeli soldiers and refuse to be intimidated by threats to their lives (Halabi, 1981: 106, 280).

Being included and recognized in the national struggle has led Palestinian women to expect that they shall be included in formal Palestinian government structures. There is reason to believe that this expectation is realistic.

In August 1988, a document found by the Israeli authorities among the papers of the head of the Arab Studies Society, Faisal Husseini, proposed forming a Palestinian legislative body in the occupied territories made of persons who will be considered automatically members of the Palestine National Council (PNC). Eighteen women were included in the list of 152, which contained mayors, heads of trade unions and professional societies, educators, doctors, artists, and community leaders. While this number is still inadequate by the standards of, for instance, Scandinavian countries, it is a good start for a society with a relatively weak women's movement.[9] Women are expected to be included in the government of the new Palestinian state because many female leaders now have a history of political struggle.

A five-member Palestinian delegation which met in 1989 with the head of the U.S. State Department's policy planning staff, Dennis Ross, as part of the Palestinian-U.S. dialogue, included Zahira Kamal, one of the founding members of the largest women's organization, PFWAC. Kamal was also a member of a delegation of thirteen who met with U.S. Assistant Secretary of State John Kelly, August 3, 1989.[10] Kamal, along with Dr. Mikhail Ashrawi, also met with Secretary of State James Baker in April 1991. At all three meetings Kamal was not there to represent women, but to represent her political stream. The difference between her and Abdul Hadi of the GUPW, however, is that Kamal's group is slowly developing a feminist agenda and realizes that women have specific problems that have to be addressed in the new Palestinian state. Should she hold an important position in that state (a very likely possibility), she is expected to join the state with a strong women's agenda.

## Conclusion

As Rosemary Sayigh pointed out, crisis accentuates women's reproductive role (Sayigh, 1983), and the Intifada has had both positive and negative effects on the status of women. On the other hand, the ordeal has proved that women can function well in every aspect of Palestinian life. Women's committees showed that the grass-roots organizing they had been engaged in since 1978 was extremely useful to combat Israeli "iron fist" policies. Neighborhood committees were so effective that Israelis banned them. On the other hand, statistics indicate that the crisis has set back women's efforts to discourage early marriages— up to 90 percent of brides in some villages and refugee camps have been under eighteen years of age (Manasrah, 1989).

Although Palestinian women have come a long way since they first marched for national independence, a great number of problems remain. Palestinian academics complain that the image of women in literature has not changed since 1967. Women appear in literature not as themselves "but as the embodiment of the unattained, the perfect goal: fertility, lush land, the womb of society, Palestine itself," says Hanan Ashrawi, who also adds that "very few writers deal with women as conscious beings who handle their own problems" (Pesa, 1985: 11). Ilham Abu-Ghazaleh, who analyzed the poetry written during the Intifada, writes that even though women actively resist the occupation on a daily basis, women in poetry are depicted as passive. Women are told what is happening on the street, and are even told what the events men relate to them mean (Abu-Ghazaleh, 1989).

Najah Manasrah (1988) writes that even though we can feel optimistic about the increase in women's participation, we ought to differentiate between change in the role of women, and change in their status within the general population. Although role changes will eventually lead to improved status, that improvement will take place slowly because of a number of factors, such as the environment, social customs, and education (Manasrah, 1988). Many wonder whether Palestinian women will suffer the same fate as Iranian women. Suad Joseph does not think so and argues that the Iranian revolution obtained its legitimacy from the clergy, who defined appropriate political behavior for women after the success of the revolution. Because the source of Palestinian women's mobilization has been a secular nationalist movement, it is highly unlikely for that revolution to follow the Iranian example (Joseph, 1986: 6–7).

But events in Gaza and the West Bank in 1989 and 1990 appear to suggest that, unless women are careful, they will have to put up with a number of Iranian-type restrictions. A movement aimed at forcing women to wear Islamic dress appears to be getting stronger by the day. Even though Hamas, an Islamic group in the occupied territories, is a relative newcomer to the Palestinian scene, its growing influence and its proven ability to force women (including women who belong to committees) to cover their heads suggests that perhaps the influence of the four women's committees is not as strong as they believe it to be.[11]

An examination of the history of the Palestinian women's movement as well as of the continuing attempts of women to balance the national struggle with women's rights lead to the following observations:

*The political mobilization of women and nationalist movements are strongly associated.* In fact, the emergence of the Arab women's movement in many cases is linked to the emergence of nationalist movements. In Egypt, Algeria, Sudan, and Iraq women were first mobilized to demonstrate against colonial rule and in support of nationalist forces. In all these and other cases, women's organizations were established by these same mobilized women (Smith, 1980: 238– 42). Taking part in the national struggle, however, will not automatically be translated into gains in women's rights and status, but the experience women gain in the national struggle serves them well in their fight for equality during and after liberation if they choose to adopt women's issues.

*The involvement of women in nationalist politics is a necessary but not sufficient condition for women's emancipation at a later stage.* What counts is not the mere presence of women but the type of agenda they bring with them to the nationalist movement. Women's groups who are able to incorporate the rights of women into the nationalist struggle *before* liberation are more likely to succeed than groups which depend on the good will or "progressiveness" of male revolutionaries.

*A certain degree of organizational and financial independence is required if women are to assert their demands.* Women need well-run organizations of their own and access to independent sources of funding. The women of the General Union of Palestinian Women (GUPW) depend on funding from the PLO, and so the mostly male leadership determines the organization's priorities. The new women's organizations are also allied with the PLO but have a more diversified base for funding, and thus have more freedom in determining their programs.

*A united women's movement will carry more weight than a number of organizations allied with men's political parties.* Like any mass-based "party," women's organizations need members that can be mobilized as pressure groups for specific causes, and for making alliances in return for a larger share of the political pie. Traditional women's organizations had many leaders but few members, or at least few empowered members. In contrast, the new grass-roots organizations have activated many rank-and-file women and are working on building solid structures that promise to make grass-roots mobilization easier. However, since groups are difficult to unite ideologically, their common denominator may turn out to be a few gender issues they can agree on. Each group needs to retain whatever makes it distinctive on the national scene (e.g., communists should not be expected to turn into Muslim sisters), but there must be common goals liberals and conservatives can accept, especially in questions such as maternal health, education, and childcare. Without unity the collective weight of women will be diminished.

*Legal changes in women's status, while important, are no cure-all.* Legal status changes are more enforceable in Western societies with weaker family and community ties than in societies where families have always taken on the welfare role of the state. The family, with its strong sense of obligation, has helped Palestinians withstand repeated onslaughts, refugee status, and poverty. While legal issues need to be tackled eventually, taking away some of families' rights over its members has to be handled carefully. Before any state "legally" emancipates women, a good legal system and a support system need to be in place to allow women to benefit from their new legal status. Because the new Palestinian state is bound to be poor, changing consciousness through long-term nonsexist education for men and women may be the most lasting and realistic road to change.

*Palestinian women must not take the gains they have made for granted,* but need to cement them in various ways. Because each of the four committees is allied to one of the four most important Palestinian factions, women should demand more support from the males of their respective organizations and should ask the different groups to take the Muslim fundamentalist tide more seriously. Although women's committees have formed a group to tackle the issue of rising fundamentalism, they were slow to react to the danger the fundamentalist threat posed to women's freedom of dress and movement, with the result that women have lost the battle in Gaza.

Even while recognizing the achievement of the women's committees since 1978, one is still tempted to ask: After the establishment of a Palestinian state, will the new forms of organizing women leave an imprint on Palestinian society or will gains for women wither under the shadow of a patriarchal Palestinian state and the growing strength of fundamentalists? Zahira Kamal thinks that change is here to stay. To illustrate, she recalls an incident that occurred during the Intifada. One of the elected members of the PFWAC was arrested, the West Bank was in turmoil, and Kamal asked another woman to take over without consulting with the women of the area. Two weeks later, Kamal received an urgent note asking for a meeting. During the meeting, women wanted to know who had the authority to appoint their representatives for them. "With due respect," they told Kamal, "we have been electing our representative democratically for ten years now" and added that they should have been asked to hold elections. "New circumstances do not mean extraordinary powers," they told Kamal, who adds, "My initial reaction was that of hurt because I have always prided myself on the democratic nature of our base units . . . but my unease was momentary. I felt very proud of the women because they had something no one can take away from them: consciousness of the importance of determining their own future. I do not think it will be easy for anyone to deprive them of that."[12]

Women's freedom of dress and of movement has already been circumscribed in Gaza and is under threat in the West Bank. Suppressing women's rights might not be "easy," but unless women's committees take the threat the conservatives pose to women's self-determination as seriously as they take the Israeli threat to Palestinian self-determination, Palestinian women's groups will lose most of the gains women have made since the founding of the first women's committee in 1978.

One favorable sign is that the Higher Council of Women publicly attacked fundamentalist attempts to restrict women's dress and public action in a December 1990 East Jerusalem conference attended by five hundred people. Women and their male supporters admitted that they have lost the fight over women's freedom of dress in Gaza, but called for action to stop the fundamentalist coercion in the West Bank. The most encouraging part of the conference was that many in the audience criticized both the women's movement and the national movement for abandoning women in their fight with conservatives. Asked one woman, "Do we have a real women's movement? I say no; our women's movement is really a nationalist movement . . . and they [the nationalist leadership] use us as a media front" (Tawfeeq, 1990: 9). The conference also called for the preparation of a first draft of a personal status law. This call demonstrates that women's committees finally have realized that unless they tackle women's issues, their movement will become irrelevant, as different Palestinian factions, and the fundamentalists, struggle for power.

# Notes

1. See Bendt and Downing (1980: 98–102). On March 11, 1978, Dalal el-Mughrabi and ten male guerrillas under her command landed in Tel Aviv in a rubber boat they boarded in Lebanon. The group was killed when the bus they had hijacked burst into flames during a shootout with the Israeli police. One policeman was killed, and nine were wounded. Thirty-two Israeli civilians were killed and seventy-two were wounded.

2. For a listing of the names and occupations of the 1,229 women arrested between 1967 and 1979, see Antonius (1980).

3. Interview with Dr. Rita Giacaman, Ramallah, July 19, 1986.

4. Statistics obtained in October 1989 by Nuha Ismael from Maysoon Sh'ath, PNC member.

5. Between June and July 1967, the Israeli government seized twenty thousand dunums of cultivated land belonging to the Palestinian villages of Beit Nuba, Yalu, and Imwas. The Israeli military destroyed over six thousand houses in order to prevent villagers from returning to their homes in that border area. The demolition left about ten thousand villagers homeless (see Halabi 1981: 51–53).

6. Interview with Mrs. Sameeha Khalil, Head of In'ash el-Usra Society, summer 1985.

7. For example, in 1985, The Voluntary Work Committee (VWC) said it cultivated nineteen thousand dununs of land as part of a program to assist local farmers and planted thirty seven thousand seedlings in 118 lots to benefit six hundred farmers. Members also picked olives from ninety villages, 474 tons of watermelons from the Jordan Valley area, and citrus from two districts (Al-Fajr, March 8, 1985: 3).

8. Al-Fajr, March 6, 1988: 5.

9. Asked abut the percentage of women in the PNC, Dr. Hanan Mikhael-Ashrawi, then dean of the College of Arts and Sciences at Birzeit University in the West Bank, said that it is higher than the percentage of women in the U.S. Congress and added "but that is not saying much" (Lewis, 1989: 7).

10. Al-Fajr, May 22, 1989: 13 and August 8, 1989: 4.

11. Palestinian women make up the following percentages in occupational union

membership: 22.92 percent of pharmacists, 12.45 percent of dentists, 8.06 percent of doctors, 7.89 percent of agricultural engineers, 6.27 percent of lawyers, 6.85 percent of journalists, 3.67 percent of engineers (Kuttab and Al-Ratrout, 1988: 21). If the activities of Hamas in Gaza are any indication of what is to come, women will be encouraged to go only into traditionally "female" fields, and university education will no longer be coeducational.

12. Interview with Zahira Kamal, August 1, 1989.

C H A P T E R

11

# FROM HOME TO STREET
## WOMEN AND REVOLUTION IN NICARAGUA

*Barbara J. Seitz*

Presently the poorest nation in the hemisphere, Nicaragua spent the 1980s struggling to achieve stability after a decade of rebellion, characterized by nationwide strikes, clandestine activities, and guerrilla warfare which eventually involved every segment of the population. On July 19, 1979, the popular Revolution led by the Frente Sandinista de Liberación Nacional (FSLN)[1] defeated and expelled Anastasio Somoza Debayle (1967–1979),[2] a repressive dictator who diverted wealth to his own pocket while perpetuating the poverty of the masses who lacked educational opportunities, medical care, and a political voice.

With Somoza's removal and the institution of a new government in 1979, freedom from oppression and potential for personal growth became new possibilities. However, after such impressive accomplishments as a national literacy campaign, which reduced the illiteracy rate from 50 percent to 13 percent in twelve months (Ruchwarger, 1987: 110),[3] a malaria reduction effort that dramatically curtailed the disease's incidence (Garfield and Vermund, 1986), and the establishment of a national health care system, which vastly improved the general level of health (Braveman and Siegel, 1987), the nation ran headlong into political conflict with the United States. Made anxious by Soviet-Nicaraguan military relations, the United States attacked the port of Corinto on October 10, 1983, put in place an economic blockade, and began to fund an army of counter-revolutionaries known as the "Contra" to undermine the nation's economic, social, and political welfare (Edelman, 1988). Contra attacks concentrating on small communities, schools, health personnel and facilities (Braveman and Siegel, 1986), forced diversion of attention from reconstruction to defense. The 1980s became a decade of radical change, of social transformation, and of progress mixed with recession and the psychological and physical devastations of war.

In a context of extreme economic and political-military pressure, elections were held in February 1990. Observed by hundreds of representatives from around the world, these elections were universally judged a model for all democratic nations. The outcome awarded victory to Violeta Chamorro, widow of the revolutionary hero, Joaquin Chamorro, internationally honored journalist and editor of the opposition paper *La Prensa*, who was murdered by Somoza's National Guard. Chamorro and the UNO (Unión Nacional de Oposición, or National Union for Opposition) coalition of fourteen political parties, united only by their opposition to the Sandinista party, won by a narrow margin over the incumbent FSLN. In this election many Nicaraguans voted for an end to U.S. economic and military aggression, in other words, against the status quo of hunger and war. Many, especially women, voted for an end to the military draft and continued deaths of their children.

Integrally woven into the fabric of these developments has been the struggle of women for emancipation and empowerment. In this chapter I describe the heritage of Nicaraguan women and the course of their movement for equality. The information contained herein derives from personal observations and numerous interviews I conducted during six visits to Nicaragua over the past four years, supported and complemented by documentation from published sources.

I examine the struggle of Nicaraguan women in the context of the restrictions and responsibilities placed upon women by their culture and the long-standing contradiction between the ideal "vision" and the reality of most women's lives. In the first part of the chapter I recount the traditional ideal of women as domestic caregivers and of their subordinate role in decision-making and in family and couple relationships: I contrast this with their critical role as wage-earners and examine changing attitudes toward women's participation in the labor market. The second part follows the emancipation movement from its identification with the revolution to its present dilemma in the face of government policies favoring a return to tradition.

## The Historic Contradiction

Traditionally in Nicaragua, the identity of the Nicaraguan woman has been tied to her relationship with other people (her children and especially her husband) whom she nurtures. This is especially obvious in her work activities according to the traditional division of labor, which assigns women ideally to operations in the private domain *en la casa* (in the house) and men to the public domain, popularly referred to in Nicaragua as *en la calle* (in the street). For generations women's self-image depended upon this vision. A young female medical doctor described her grandmother's objections to her daughters' holding jobs and granddaughters' picking coffee, activities which she described as *andando en la calle* (walking in the streets) when a woman's place, she said, is *en la casa* (in the home).[4] This "ideal" system ties women to their home and family in a subservient position, while men are to occupy positions of leadership in all spheres, particularly the public political one.

Prior to the Revolution, men actually held decision-making authority in both private and public domains, with limited female participation. Women's authority resided principally with home and children. But even here, officially, according to Somoza's Family Code and the law of *patria potestad,* the father had sole rights over his children, and his wife was regarded largely as his property. Men were to work at jobs for pay; women were to stay at home, be loyal and loving spouses, bear children and nurture them out of love for the family. One woman described it this way:

> Before the triumph, women were marginal. Women didn't have the power to develop themselves in their labors equally as men in their work, because it was understood that women were only for the home, for being in the home, nothing more. For the kitchen, for caring for the children, for marrying. From early childhood they taught us this.[5]

Except for the very rich who were cared for by female servants, all young girls learned to help and perform household chores. In a developing nation these can easily consume the greater portion of the day, especially when combined with childcare. Boys, and especially men, were not expected to participate in these tasks.

In historically Catholic Nicaragua, centuries of tradition have associated women with the figure of the madonna, the pure and virtuous mother. Adopting this ideal of woman, called *marianismo,* Nicaraguan women identify strongly with the image of the devoted mother. In fact, they often think that giving a man children will gain or hold his affection.[6]

In the Nicaraguan countryside nearly every woman I saw who was between eighteen and forty-five years of age was either pregnant, had a babe in arms, or both. Many have ten children or more, and 21 percent of mothers are under the age of twenty. These Nicaraguan women belong to the set of mothers described by UNICEF as a target group needing assistance for their own and their children's sake:

> A significant improvement in the state of the world's children . . . depends most of all on the state of the world's mothers . . . the everyday hardship and discrimination which women face—in food, in education, in health care, in work, and in rewards—is the single most important barrier to the improvement of their own and their children's health.
>
> With less education and status, less access to technology or training, and few resources of either cash or credit, women in almost all communities are expected to be not only wives and mothers but . . . income-earners, homemakers and health workers, fuel-gatherers and animal-feeders, food-providers and water carriers. It is too much. . . . (UNICEF, 1988: 55)

The plight of these mothers is extreme in a country ravaged by economic scarcities, war, and a whole range of problems shared by developing nations.

Because Nicaraguan women identify so closely with their roles as wives and mothers, living to a large degree through others, the war held especially excruciating consequences for them. Mothers lost sons and daughters, wives lost husbands, some of whom remain missing-in-action. Women lived in a constant state of anxiety for loved ones, fathers, husbands, brothers, sons and daughters, currently serving or soon-to-be-called to service, then mobilized to the mountains where they might not be heard from for months.

Most Nicaraguan couples live in common-law marriages, registered neither with church nor state. Nicaraguan Catholics are not the orthodox variety found in the United States, bound by the letter of the law. Like other Latins in Europe and the Americas, Nicaraguans seek the "spirit" of the law and feel excused from certain "rules," for example, a church wedding, by virtue of circumstance. For most Nicaraguans, church weddings are considered unaffordable, as they entail the purchase of a wedding dress, ring, and making a contribution to the church. "Wedding rings," I was told, "are only necessary for church weddings."[7] And though civil marriage is cheap and required by law in addition to any church ceremony, most couples opt to live without formal contract. Perhaps Catholic tradition has influenced couples' decisions not to enter a civil contract since the church does not recognize a civil marriage. An opinion expressed by a young man in Managua maintains that it is a truer sign of love that people stay together without force of legal contract. He, therefore, thought it best not to formalize his relationship with his partner, mother of their two children.[8]

In any case, relationships in Nicaragua operate under a set of assumptions about appropriate behavior founded on the female and male concepts of marianismo and machismo. *Marianismo,* which requires women to be virtuous and humble, serves to support the male regime of machismo. *Machismo,* a system of male superiority and dual standards, exists in traditional Nicaragua in an extreme form. Dual standards greatly restrict women's freedom and make them highly accountable to men, who, in turn, enjoy freedom of movement and action with virtually no accountability.

The vast majority of women with whom I spoke agreed that it is to be expected that husbands will have a certain number of affairs each year, and they see this as inevitable: "One accustoms herself that the man has that freedom, and one sees it as natural. That the man leaves, and yourself, no."[9] In contrast, Nicaraguan women have no interest in obtaining the sexual freedoms cultivated by their men. They see such behavior by women as not only outrageous but in strict violation of their duty as women to be at home waiting for their husbands. A young woman medical doctor put it quite bluntly,

> It has not gotten to the point where one says, 'I am a man,' and then [the woman responds] 'Because you are free, I want to be, too.' No, the woman knows well what is her place. She must be waiting for the man. She has to be in her house.[10]

If they cannot control their husbands, the wives at least hold themselves strictly accountable.

That women were held more accountable by the society was substantiated by the divorce laws[11] on the books from the days of Somoza until 1988. These old laws blatantly discriminated against women. A man's saying that his wife committed adultery was sufficient proof for obtaining a divorce; but in order for a woman to obtain a divorce she had to establish that her husband was living in residence with another woman or that the relationship was public knowledge (Ruchwarger, 1987: 193).

Women, especially before the Revolution, were expected to stay close to home with their children and even to ask permission to go out in the evenings. A campesina (peasant) woman told me that before the Revolution, if a woman wanted to attend a meeting in the evening, her husband might say no and then she could not go.[12] On the other hand, if a man does not feel like informing his wife about his activities away from home, he feels justified in maintaining silence. The wife should assume trust and not question him. Women learned at an early age about the female side of machismo, that women's place is in the home. Only if economic pressures make it impossible to stay home are women to work outside the home, and then only to supplement the family income.

Thus it came to pass that despite the traditional ideal that the woman's place is in the home, Nicaraguan women entered the labor market. Even before the Revolution more women in Nicaragua worked outside the home than in most other Latin American nations, providing an important condition for a women's liberation movement. To understand how the Sandinista government would take the unprecedented steps it had to empower women and accept the cause of women's emancipation, we must look to the nation's exceptional history.

Somoza maintained control for his elitist power structure through brutal repression of the masses, carried out by his corrupt and violent National Guard forces. The resulting mass poverty caused family disintegration. Men without work, unable to fulfill their traditional responsibilities to wife and children, frequently abandoned their families, going off to search for jobs. Women found themselves alone, with responsibility for home and children. Consequently, larger numbers of women in Nicaragua came to participate in the labor force than in other Latin American countries where repression was less acute. Forced self-reliance, independence, and participation in the labor sector ripened Nicaragua for a strong women's movement.

Under Somoza, in 1963 according to census statistics, 20 percent of all households nationally, and 25 percent in Managua, were headed by women. Similarly in groups, not families, living together, 20 percent nationally, and 25 percent in Managua, were headed by women (República de Nicaragua, 1964: 93,100). In 1979 labor force statistics from the Organization of American States reporting economically active population (1950–1965) and projections (1970–1980) by country and sex for all of Central America showed Nicaragua leading the rest of Central America in the percentage of females in the total work force (Buttari, 1979: 38).

These working women were not, however, voluntarily electing a career; rather, there has been a consistent and direct correlation between civil status (women heads of households) and employment, and economic necessity and employment. Women heading households have constituted the largest portion of working women, and this is a large percentage of all Nicaraguan women. In 1978 women headed roughly a third of all households (Lobao, 1987: 14). More recent figures indicated that in 1983 in Managua 49 percent of all households were headed by women and in 1981 that 83 percent of all women who worked headed households (Ruchwarger, 1987: 53; also Maier, 1985: 32). Surely, a majority of the remaining 17 percent of working women were compelled to supplement their husband's income, leaving a scanty few who worked for satisfaction rather than economic necessity. Given the continuously deteriorating national economy, from comments made to me by women and my observations of changing lifestyles, it is apparent that today more women are working or seeking employment in the face of layoffs and massive unemployment than ever before, and that the primary motivation remains economic necessity.

Attitudes toward women working, however, have changed radically. A growing number of women are choosing to be single professionals,[13] others to be single-parenting professionals,[14] and still others to be married career professionals.[15] When asked about their commitment to their careers, these women confirm that they would elect to continue working even if there were no necessity. Women and young girls agreed that Nicaraguan women will continue to work and in greater numbers regardless of what happens to the economic state of the nation in the future.[16] Many young girls talk about working when they grow up and are making educational plans for realizing their choice of career.

In summary, women in Nicaragua traditionally defined themselves in terms of motherhood and those whom they nurture. Their primary sphere of activity and limited authority was the home, especially homemaking and childrearing. They have lived in a context of machismo, which idealizes women but places them in subservient positions, restricted in freedom of movement and held accountable to men in virtually every aspect of their lives. Despite the ideal of woman as domestic nurturer, for generations Nicaraguan women have worked outside their homes out of economic necessity, often as heads of households.

The official and societal view of women in Nicaragua changed markedly with women's full participation in the Revolution and under the Sandinista government, which supported the women's movement and recognized the need to address and respond to women's issues. To understand these events and envision the future direction of the women's movement, the role of women in the process of the Revolution and in the context of the new government must be explored.

## The Movement for Emancipation

The commencement and growth of the women's movement in Nicaragua paralleled the course of the Revolution. Linda Lobao (1987) compared the involvement of women in guerrilla movements in Cuba, Colombia, Uruguay, El Salvador, and Nicaragua in terms of the extent of female participation, women's social class origins, and functional roles. She found that in Cuba a small number of women (about 5 percent of troops) served essentially support and relief roles, being actively mobilized only after the insurgency with the establishment in 1960 of the Federation of Cuban Women. In Colombia in the mid-1960s women did not take part to any significant degree in the EPL (People's Liberation Army), founded supposedly by educated middle-class people. In the Tupamaros Uruguayan movement women from primarily the middle class constituted 25 percent of the membership by 1972 and served in support and combat capacities. In El Salvador, women make up 40 percent of the FPL (Popular Forces of Liberation) and Revolutionary Council, and hold positions as high-ranking commanders. There women came primarily from the middle class (in the late 1960s), joined by rural working women and then by urban working women (in the late 1970s) to participate in support and combat activities on a seemingly equal status with men (Lobao, 1987: 20–35).

In Nicaragua, women took part in every phase of the Revolution to overthrow Somoza and made up 30 percent of the FSLN guerrilla membership at the time of the final offensive. Women of all classes were encouraged to take part. Despite cultural norms which reserved the realm of politics for men only, "women of all ages broke the taboo . . . to take up their spot in the combat trenches" (FSLN, 1987: 17). As early as 1965, women (e.g., Gladys Baez in Randall, 1981: 171–72) were imprisoned for political activities, and from 1967 onward women functioned as an integral part of the FSLN, including fighting in the mountains as guerrillas. They participated in strikes, demonstrated in the streets, and helped hide undercover combatants and weaponry. Numerous names of female heroes of the Revolution are well known: for example, Luisa Amanda Espinoza, Arlen Siú, Doris Tijerino, Gladys Baez, and the women of Cuá. Women like Dora María Téllez, leader of the extremely important western front, commanded units and led major offensives, such as in León where four of seven commanders were women.

The Frente Sandinista de Liberación Nacional, or FSLN, appealed to women and recognized their immediate and long-term needs. Already in 1969, the FSLN declared itself committed to upholding the rights of women: "The Sandinista Popular Revolution will abolish the discrimination that women have suffered with respect to men; it will establish economic, political, and cultural equality between women and men" (FSLN, 1987: 12). The program went on to outline at least seven means by which the FSLN would accomplish this, including guaranteed maternity leave and guaranteed rights for illegitimate children, special services for mothers and children, the elimination of prostitution and of women's servitude in general, the institution of childcare centers to assist working mothers, and the elevation of the "political, cultural and vocational level of women via their participation in the revolutionary process" (FSLN, 1987: 12–13). Widespread participation by lower-class women in the Revolution attests to its identification with their needs.

The experience of women in the Revolution has influenced heavily both men's and women's attitudes toward women, especially regarding women's work and leadership capacities. Women look back upon the Revolution as a time of awakening:

> When the Frente Sandinista began . . . women also within the lines . . . fought in the role of men; that is when the women realized that we can work the same as a man, that we can develop equally as a man. . . . They were heroines. They showed us, they gave us really an idea that the woman in the world, in life, can work, can be equal to a man in work. . . .[17]

Today many women argue they could never return to the repressive pre-Revolutionary lifestyle because they are now "awake" and could never again be fooled into tolerating such injustice.

The participation of women in the Revolution became both a means and a rationale for their emancipation. Many men saw it as a justification for change, pointing out that women had "earned" the right to equality through their heroism, for they had proven themselves capable of any task performed by a man. Men voiced a duality of perspectives on women's relationship to the Revolution. On one side, they idealized women as pure virgins and devoted mothers and saw themselves as their defenders. At the same time, life experience taught them to expect women to be strong and self-reliant in difficult times.

This combination of respect, concern, and protectiveness is heard in the singer's voice in "Venancia," a song by Luis Enrique Mejía Godoy (Enigrac, 1989) wherein the singer warns Venancia, who is risking her life running messages for the Frente, to "be careful." The composer describes Venancia in terms of her humble peasant origins, her relationship to a brother killed for his affiliation with the Revolution, and her courage. The singer tells her, "your smile, Venancia, is the banner in our struggle." For male combatants the image of the committed woman, plus the macho sense of duty to defend, added purpose to the struggle.

Respect for women blends with love in the song, *"Mujer, mujer"* by the Grupo Pancasan (1985), which describes women *hecho de amor y besos* (made of love and kisses) and courageous in combat:

> Vos asistes para alcanzar la gloria
> (You help to achieve the glory)
> Vos ganastes tu lugar en la historia
> (You [have] earned your place in history)

Yet even in the setting of the battlefield the association between women and new life is suggested.

> Dulce combativa guerrillera
> (Sweet guerrilla fighter)
> Al frente del combate . . .
> (To the battle front) . . .

. . . sembrar la Primavera
(. . . to plant the Spring)
Propiendo con su sangre . . .
(Propogating with your blood . . .)

Based in a tradition of respect for women's strength of character and dedication to family, today's male image of women derives more from an extension of qualities formerly attributed to women than from a complete transformation of men's view of women. One encounters the commonly heard comment that women have "earned" their new rights, something quite different from saying that women have intrinsic rights. In this same context a former combatant, a vigorous supporter of women's rights, can describe the Revolution as a woman whom one can never completely conquer.[18]

With the customary Latin American respect for motherhood, the Nicaraguan government has shown appreciation for women who lost children in the Revolution. These *Madres de Héroes y Mártires* (Mothers of Heroes and Martyrs) are the recipients of many social welfare and recreational programs. These women fulfilled their social and patriotic duty to the highest degree, propagating, rearing, and sacrificing children who otherwise might have provided them with companionship and material assistance during the rest of their lives. How indicative of the close identification of women with children and family that no similar programs of recognition honor the fathers of those killed in combat!

In Nicaragua, the first organizations of women with political-social objectives were based on the common concerns of mothers. In neighborhoods women formed Mothers Clubs to pursue responses to the situation (Maier, 1985: 75). Mothers of political prisoners staged strikes. During the 1960s, with the support of the FSLN, the Patriotic Alliance of Nicaraguan Women helped prepare women to join with men in the struggle to confront Somoza. Gladys Baez, who worked with this group in the late 1960s, described their activities: "We organized peasant and working women. We worked to set up safehouses, raised money and agitated for better conditions in the prisons" (Randall, 1981: 179). Thus women became involved first out of familial concern as mothers, and later in a formal network for the cause of the Revolution.

In 1977, under the direction of the FSLN, the Association of Nicaraguan Women to Confront the National Problem (*Asociación de Mujeres Ante el Problematic Nacional*, AMPRONAC) was founded by mainly upper- and middle-class women in concert with men. Like the Louisa Amanda Espinoza Association of Nicaraguan Women (AMNLAE) today, it was concerned with achieving a society which offers full participation to women and men equally.

### The Role of AMPRONAC

In 1978, AMPRONAC called, among other things, for the repeal of all laws that discriminated against women, equal pay for equal work, and an end to the commercialization of women (Ruchwarger, 1987: 49). The organization was also instrumental on a national scale in demanding freedom of association. Its members visited ministers, passed out leaflets, and held public meetings. During a demonstration associated with a hunger strike, in which women of various political-party affiliations participated (Enriquez, 1985: 258), one woman was killed by Somoza's National Guard. Later many women suffered arrest and torture.

This dynamic group raised women's consciousness and was instrumental in the formation of the Sandinista government, which recognized many of their demands. Because of their forcefulness in projecting their perspective, the struggle became cooperative. Instead of women merely acting as supporters in the traditional nurturing role, they actively forged their nation's future and promoted solutions to women's problems, assuming parallel roles with men.

## The Role of AMNLAE

The Luisa Amanda Espinoza Association of Nicaraguan Women, AMNLAE, was founded with the establishment of the new revolutionary government and was named for the first woman FSLN militant to die in combat against the National Guard in 1970 (AMNLAE, 1983). Initially, this organization, closely aligned with the FSLN, strove principally to integrate women into the work of the Revolution. Gradually, after surviving near disbandment in 1981, when the need for its existence was questioned, the organization became more assertive in addressing specific women's issues and in the formation of the new Nicaraguan Constitution. In 1988 its name was changed to Movement, rather than Association, of Nicaraguan Women.

An important aspect of the women's movement in Nicaragua has been its consistently integrative rather than separatist approach. For women, the initial and long-range objective remained the emancipation of society, the integration of men and women as equal partners in every facet of life. Hence the tenth anniversary slogan, "Together in everything!" The AMNLAE seeks for the Nicaraguan woman "the full development of her human potential" (AMNLAE, 1989a: 3), an objective which it proposes can only be achieved by defending and deepening the revolutionary process which would emancipate society from exploitation and oppression (AMNLAE, 1989b: 3).

The AMNLAE operates principally in three areas: education, integration-participation, and legislation. Before women could be emancipated they needed to acquire an education, which under Somoza typically was unavailable to them. They needed to learn about their rights, their bodies, ways to improve their health and to be offered a medium through which to develop themselves personally and in their common interests with other women.

The AMNLAE has worked for "the promotion of the political, professional, cultural and technical advancement of Nicaraguan women, and their integration into grassroots and labor organizations" (Centro de Comunicación Internacional, 1987: 25). Serving as a coordinating body, AMNLAE facilitates the work of women in various sectors and mass organizations, such as trade unions and the Mothers of Heroes and Martyrs.

The AMNLAE has enjoyed remarkable success in achieving legislative reforms. With regard to division of labor, AMNLAE has helped to influence gradual changes in attitudes concerning women's role. The government in 1981 and 1982 enacted new laws, the "Law Regulating Relations between Mothers, Fathers, and Children" and the "Law of Nurturing." Both parents are assigned equal responsibility for childrearing, and all members of the household, including adult men and young boys, are to assist in the performance of household tasks. It is not unheard of today for a husband or son to help the wife/mother with jobs that formerly were considered exclusively hers. Shaping future generations, women active in AMNLAE today teach their sons to participate equally in domestic labor.

Under the Sandinista government, alimony and child support became newly legislated rights. Common-law marriages, the most typical kind, and "illegitimate" children, the majority of all children, were now recognized, giving many times more women and their children protection under the law. In Managua, AMNLAE opened a Legal Office for Women where women can seek the services of legal advisors concerning their rights, including the right to seek child support, a newly legislated obligation of parents who leave children with a former spouse. Legal counsel is also available at most of the *Casas de la Mujer* (Women's Homes).

The Women's Homes serve the needs of mothers, teaching women about their reproductive health, family planning, and prenatal, infant and child care. Recognizing that abortion is the second main cause of maternal deaths (AMNLAE, 1989b: 1), AMNLAE made family planning and contraceptive education a high priority and worked to counsel young women against the common notion that having children is a means to capture and/or hold a man's affections. Parents are urged to limit their families to the number of children they can clothe, feed, and educate.[19]

## Conclusion

Women in Nicaragua have successfully challenged the age-old tradition of machismo and have won, to varying degrees, individuals rights, which should be awarded to women as birthrights. By means of their valiant and indispensible role in the Revolution, women discovered and affirmed their capacity to function equally with men. Experience gained during decades of forced labor in the job market and organizational skills forged and refined during the revolutionary struggle served to empower a strong and vocal women's movement. The most powerful expression of this movement, AMNLAE, came to represent Nicaragua's women to the legislature and to coordinate the activities of many other grass-roots women's groups. Women's vision in Nicaragua has been integration on equal terms with men. Significant progress toward fulfillment of the vision has been made in the public domain and also in the private sphere, where macho values and behaviors are most difficult to confront. The prospects for continued progress in the emancipation of women depends largely on women's ability to control their reproductive lives. Recent reports from Nicaragua indicate that the new government's policy will be to ban contraception, except the rhythm method, and to eliminate sex education from the schools (DeSantis, 1990), serious blows to the work of women over the past eleven years. Official government policy seems allied with the Nicaraguan Catholic church's view, which was expressed in a sermon I heard in August 1990. The theme was that women's place is in the home, caring for children and performing the traditional domestic chores. The future role of AMNLAE remains unclear, but the resiliency of its members is indisputable. If not able to continue to function in an official capacity, they will certainly continue to exert influence and work for reforms through mass organizations. In the words of the campesina AMNLAE volunteer Elba Aguilera Nervaez, mother of ten and local community leader, and echoed by Orbelina Soza Mairena and the spirits of thousands of Nicaraguan women, whatever else happens, "Seguimos adelante. No cansamos." "We keep moving forward. We do not tire."[20]

# Notes

1. The FSLN, the Frente Sandinista de Liberación Nacional or Sandino Front of National Liberation, is named for a popular hero, César Augusto Sandino (1893–1934), a peasant who led a guerrilla movement which forced the eventual withdrawal of U.S. Marines from Nicaragua in 1933 and who was subsequently assassinated by Anastasio Somoza Garcia (1896–1956).

2. Anastasio Somoza Garcia, who had studied at the Pierce School of Business Administration in Philadelphia, set up a military dictatorship in Nicaragua in 1936. His eldest son, Luis Somoza Debayle, took over in 1957 after his father's assassination and governed until 1967, when a younger brother, Anastasio Somoza Debayle, succeeded him. Educated at West Point and more violent in personality, Anastasio relied on military power and a deliberately corrupted National Guard for strength.

3. In all, over 80,000 teachers and over 100,000 individuals participated in the process which taught approximately 400,000 formerly illiterate Nicaraguans the basic skills of reading and writing. The volunteer instructors were 60 percent women, supported by outreach groups of the national women's organization, AMNLAE. Middle- and upper-class urban volunteers worked in rural areas where they learned to appreciate the hardships and culture of the peasants, or campesinos (Ruchwarger, 1987: 110–11).

4. Interview with Ivette Amor Quiñonez Cruz of Region II, Nicaragua, August 3, 1989.

5. Interview with Orbelina Soza Meirena, Region II, Nicaragua, August 9, 1989.

6. An objective of the women's movement today is to rid women of this belief. This was pointed out to me by the Director of AMNLAE, Region II, Nicaragua, on August 9, 1989.

7. Conversation with Auxiliadora Alvarado, witness for a civil marriage which she said required no new dress or wedding ring.

8. Conversation with Ismael Gonzalez, Managua, August 1, 1989.

9. Ivette Amor Quiñonez Cruz, Region II, August 7, 1989.

10. Interview with Ivette Amor Quiñonez Cruz.

11. Undoubtedly soon to be completely revised through the efforts of the women's organization, AMNLAE.

12. Interview with Elba Aguilera Nervaez, Region II, Chinandega, Nicaragua, August 2, 1989.

13. For example, Antonica Alvarado Puente, Associate Director, Ricardo Morales School, and ex-Director, School of Heroes and Martyrs, Region II, Nicaragua.

14. For example, Angela Guardado Bravo, teacher and mother of an adopted child.

15. For example, Ivette Amor Quiñonez Cruz, mother of two young children and sole medical doctor serving a population of eighteen thousand rural Nicaraguans.

16. Interviews with women and children during July and August 1989.

17. Interview with Orbelina Soza Meirena, Region II, Nicaragua, August 9, 1989.

18. Interview with Ignacio Delgado, August 1990.

19. Interviews with Ivette Amor Quiñonez Cruz, medical doctor, and Orbelina Soza Meirena, of AMNLAE, Region II, August 1989.

20. Interview with Elba Aguilera Nervaez, Region II, Nicaragua, July 31, 1989.

# WOMEN AND POWER IN POLAND

Hopes or Reality?

## *Joanna Regulska*

*With the assistance of Agnieszka Gerwel*

The socialist political system introduced in Poland in 1945 provided women with constitutional guarantees of equal rights. Since then, women in Poland have made considerable progress by achieving higher educational status and greater participation in both the labor force and in public life. Nonetheless, in order to cope realistically with a patriarchal socio-economic system, Polish women have remained subordinated in both public and private life, and the traditional notion of woman as wife and mother has continued to persist throughout the society. Consequently, constitutional law guaranteeing equality for both men and women was successful in theory but not in practice.

This chapter attempts to answer the question of why women in Poland have not achieved equal status with men in the family, the work place, or in public life. First, I look at how the Polish cultural heritage persists in preserving society's traditional values and attitudes. I then focus on the Communist era as well as examine the divergence between theory, implementation and practice of the political tenets provided in the Constitution. In the last part of the chapter, I discuss how political developments during the eighties have influenced the prospective emergence of a feminist movement. Throughout I stress the absence of women's views and demands from the political process. Neither under Communist rule nor in the Solidarity movement did Polish women participate in leadership roles or as representatives of their sex. Thus under the new Solidarity-allied government women's concerns are not only absent from the agenda but women are experiencing serious threats to the rights they gained after 1945.

Polish scholarship on women is scant and scattered. No curricula have been developed in women's studies. Furthermore, it is only recently that feminist groups have begun to organize. The weak status of research on women reflects on the part of academics and activists a lack of consciousness of, and interest in, the role and position of women in Polish society. It also represents a traditional assumption of what women's role is, that is, that it does not even merit attention. As a result, the data which could be used to explore the position of Polish women in the changing politico-economic context are incomplete and lack a historical perspective. What is available are the standard demographic and socio-economic indicators routinely gathered by the government, and sporadic research conducted primarily by sociologists. Consequently, the research data for this chapter are based on various sources, including official statistics, individual research, and informal interviews with Polish women.

## Tradition Dies Hard

Throughout Polish history women have played an important role as protectors of the family and the country's cultural heritage. Until the eighteenth century, education, the most important predictor of social advancement, was strongly desired by Polish women but impossible for them to attain. The existing laws barred women from achieving educational progress. The Commission for National Education, established in the mid-1800s and the first of its kind in Europe, introduced an elementary school reform which enabled both girls and boys to attend schools. In 1808 the Supreme Supervisory Council, also the first of its kind, was created to establish a program for girls' education. Along with it, the first official women's group of volunteer workers came into existence. Feminist circles emerging at that time fought primarily for the educational rights of women. It was not until the partitioning of Poland and the armed uprisings of the 1830s and 1860s, during which there was a massive imprisonment and emigration of many eminent male intellectuals, that women started to play a more important role in the intellectual elite (Sokolowska, 1977). A "spiritual matriarchate" ruled, lead by Narcyza Zmichowska (1819–1876) who, as a writer and champion of women's emancipation, demanded legal, economic, and social independence for women. Education remained the most important goal of this early feminist movement, as it was believed to be the only way to secure women's independence.

During the years of struggle for freedom (1830–1918), Polish cultural traditions and the country's heritage survived primarily because of women who became volunteer organizers, educators, and at the same time preserved family life. It is not by accident that women have often been referred to as "Polish Mothers," a term implying their multiple roles. Women worked mostly at home, taking care of the entire household, or in agriculture. In both cases, however, they were rarely paid wages or received any kind of compensation.

The restoration of independence in 1918 brought major success for women: in 1918 the Sejm (the Polish Parliament) accepted equal voting rights for persons over the age of twenty-one (Regent Lechowicz, 1990). This event marked the first legal acknowledgement of sex equality.

While women's concerns were put aside during both World Wars as the country struggled for independence, the interwar period brought some advancement. The number of women students increased significantly, and by 1920 laws were passed permitting the unrestricted admission of women to schools. Nevertheless women still had great difficulty in attaining equal educational and professional status. Some organizations (e.g., physicians and lawyers) fought to maintain the "male orientation" of their professions (Sokolowska, 1977).

Women's participation as elected officials had also been low. After obtaining the right to vote and to be elected (1918), women constituted only 2 percent of the elected deputies in the Sejm. Between 1920 and 1935, women's rate of participation actually declined, and by 1935 there were only two female deputies. In 1938 only one woman held a seat in the Sejm. In the Senate (upper house) the proportion of women senators was slightly higher, oscillating between 2.7 percent and 5.2 percent from 1922 to 1938 (Regent Lechowicz, 1990). During the Nazi occupation as well as the post World War II period, the family again took on the important task of raising its children in the Polish tradition, with women playing the most important role in this effort. The Catholic church persistently fought to maintain the leading role of the family in society, a deeply rooted tradition in Poland. Church teachings have made it clear that women should be passive, patient, and have forbearance toward suffering. Indeed over the centuries Polish women have frequently displayed these tendencies, often putting their own health at risk while overprotecting their husbands and children. Similarly, women's problems were put aside as national and political and economic debates took place. Women were always told to wait and bide their time.

## The Communist Era

The end of the Second World War brought drastic changes in Poland, including the restructuring of the socio-political order in what later came to be known as the "Soviet Bloc." The establishment of the socialist state, with its roots in the Marxist-Leninist ideology, created fundamental changes in the country. The new constitution, approved in 1952, provided equal rights, irrespective of sex, for all citizens of Poland in public, political, economic, and social life (Article 67 and 68, Constitution of 1952) (Bureau for Women's Affairs, 1988). A woman had the same right as a man to work for the same pay, according to the constitutional provision of "equal pay for equal work." Discrimination against women was abolished in civil, family, and criminal law: a new Communist vision of woman was rapidly imposed on traditional Poland.

The Constitution of 1952 reaffirmed the right to education for all citizens (Article 71). The public school system was expanded, with the government establishing evening schools and preparatory courses for less-advantaged people (workers and farmers were especially encouraged to attend). The increasing number of women in schools was notably prominent and promising. Many women took advantage of the new educational opportunities, and currently most women have at least a primary level of education. However, about 40 percent terminate their education at this point and, compared with men, end their educational experience early in life. This is especially common in rural areas.

While at the high school level women, who have had a higher proportion of graduates than men since the 1950s, have been recently surpassed by men, at the college level women have consistently constituted a majority in several fields of study. In the eighties they represented the larger portion of students in the humanities (78.9 percent), medicine (66.0 percent) and economics (62.0 percent) (GUS Statistical Yearbook, 1988). By 1985 women were more likely than men to become university graduates. This shift should not, however, be interpreted as a sudden opening of new opportunities for women. It reflects, rather, a reinforcement of the traditional attitude exhibited by Poles: women can be educated, but they will not necessarily need to apply their skills. Therefore women, as persons with less earning power and responsibility for household income than men, can continue their "educational advancement." Male students, on the other hand, need to think about avenues other than academic ones in order to secure their families' economic stability.

Despite the fact that women have been well represented as students, they have continued to confront discrimination in many areas. For example, in one of the more prestigious medical sectors, that is, surgery, women have been accepted reluctantly. The explanation offered for this discrimination is that women are physically weaker than men and would not be able to stand at the operating table for long periods of time. In contrast, the physical condition of the textile workers standing eight hours a day at weaving machines has been of little or no concern to the traditional male establishment (Polish Feminist Association, 1987).

Similar situations occur in other fields of study. In schools of art, admission committees annually specify the proportion of women and men to be accepted; in film schools, only two out of ten available places are for women. The typical arguments offered in support of such practices are that, compared to their male counterparts, women are weaker, not as good, not as creative in exceptional art, do not strive hard enough, and after graduating, tend to become housewives rather than practicing professionals. Hence the argument that money spent on women's education is wasted has been perpetuated.

The situation of women in post-graduate study programs has been equally, if not more, discriminatory. Although one out of every three doctorate degrees has been awarded to a woman (31.3 percent in 1983), the relative proportion of women gaining assistant professorships in the academy is low (GUS Woman in Poland, 1985). Women have been rarely granted the title of associate professor and, during the period from 1975 to 1983, the proportion of women holding this title actually declined sharply (from 22.7 percent to 17.8 percent). The decrease in the number of women promoted in the physical, mathematical, and biological sciences has primarily contributed to this decline. At the highest professorial level women have made some progress. While in 1960, 3.5 percent received the title of Professor I, by 1983 18.2 percent were promoted. Women were, however, far more excluded from receiving the title of Professor II, and by 1983 only 9.0 percent held this distinction (GUS Women in Poland, 1985).

Despite limited advancement, it is not accidental that special attention was given to the educational progress of women: education is essential for women to achieve not only economic, but also social and political independence. The Communist regime offered equal education rights to Polish women, many of whom took advantage of these new opportunities. But it is clear that these opportunities were not translated into more favorable conditions at work, at home, and in public life. The above discussion implies that, while changes in the institutional and legal framework were essential to creating advantages for women, the reforms were at the same time inadequate in the context of Polish culture. It would appear that legislation and education could not suffice to overcome the traditional attitudes toward women. Moreover, it can be argued that, while an overall increase in the population's level of education was determined desirable by the Communist leaders, the primary goal was to advance Poland's industrialization. This presented two conflicting needs: on the one hand, to increase the work force, but, on the other, to rely heavily on the unpaid labor of women in the home. This created a duality of women's role—women as homemakers and workers—in Polish society.

### WOMEN AS WORKERS

The aftermath of World War II, and the subsequent establishment of the Communist state, brought drastic economic change to Poland. The rapid forced industrialization required a new and larger supply of workers. As the urban areas were assigned the leading role in establishing a planned economy, postwar Poland showed significant increases in the number of city dwellers. There was a desperate need for employees.

The importance of women as a part of the emerging working class was growing. The new model of an ideal woman was presented: she was a worker. The country had been devastated, and women were needed in the effort to stabilize and rebuild the economy. The literature, songs, and paintings of that period focused on the portrayal of young, healthy women and men as the major work force and future leaders of Poland. The essence of the spirit of those days was captured in the slogan, "We are building our socialist homeland together!" The equal right to work was supposed to be a cornerstone of the socialist ideology, to enhance the equality between men and women, and give women financial independence and freedom of career choice.

Aware of the conflicts stemming from the duality of woman's role as mother and worker, the Communists attempted to mediate these tensions and, in the fifties, introduced several pieces of legislation to protect working women. Legal protection was granted to mother and child and to pregnant women. Women were provided with free health care, job and wage protection during pregnancy, and sixteen weeks of maternity leave with salary (Uscinska, 1990). In 1971, a new law went even further by allowing a woman with a child four years old or younger a three-year unpaid leave. She was still eligible for free health care, and if she wished, she could return to work before the end of her leave.

During the post-war years the female employment rate increased more rapidly than the male employment rate. In subsequent years, women began to hold a wider variety of jobs. Ultimately they were represented in all sectors of the economy. The employment of women increased from 32.9 percent in 1950 to 39.3 percent in 1970, and to 44.3 percent in 1983 (GUS, Statistical Yearbook 1970, 1985). By the end of the eighties, 86 percent of women were working full time.

Yet, under closer scrutiny, this picture of women's advancement in the labor force looks far more questionable. In the mid-1970s women's salaries still tended to be 30 percent lower than those of men (Sokolowska, 1977). In the 1980s the majority of Polish women with higher education worked in three occupations regarded as "traditionally female": dentists (80.9 percent were women), pharmacists (80.3 percent), and medical doctors (47.9 percent). About 70 percent of women with higher or secondary education degrees were hired by the health service or educational institutions. However, most men with similar qualifications were employed by industry, where salaries were substantially higher. Such patterns of employment indicate job segregation where women were pushed into occupational ghettos.

What then contributed to the situation of women being mostly confined to low salaried, low-status jobs? The interpretations are diverse and reflect a collaboration of the Communist regime's thought and societal belief that woman's role as mother and wife is the more appropriate one for Polish women. Despite the attribution that women and men are equal, the Communist leaders believed that this concept of equality should not be realistically entertained in the realms of education and employment. The Communists, and Poles in general, assumed that men should be directors and managers; women were perceived to be absorbed by household responsibilities, therefore unable to dedicate sufficient time and energy to such high level jobs.

The importance of the productive sector in building a socialist economy resulted in the creation of an occupational hierarchy. The jobs directly contributing to the fulfillment of these goals paid better and carried more benefits. Thus, for example, since medicine was seen as a service rather than a productive profession, it paid less than engineering. In addition, the job of medical doctor was not thought to be a "masculine" profession, and thus was not deserving of high pay. By the same token women's income was not considered as essential to the economic stability of the household, therefore justifiably could be lower. However, even women who were employed in "men's jobs" such as engineering, continued to be discriminated against ". . . women engineers are graded lower when they start working, are more rarely promoted, and earn less on the same post . . ." (Lobodzinska, 1970: 167).

Theoretically, the Communist era provided women with greater opportunities for individual fulfillment and advancement. But did Polish women perceive these opportunities as such? A survey conducted among rural and urban residents reflecting women's views of their jobs revealed a large degree of dissatisfaction, feelings of inadequacy, and a general perception of discrimination (Antoniewicz and Kazimierski, 1988). Most of the women interviewed felt overworked, overtired, and too worried about their domestic responsibilities to take their jobs seriously. Additional contributing factors to their attitudes included inadequate transportation to the workplace, lower wages for women holding the same positions as men, quality of jobs, boredom, and little to no prospects for advancement.

The above findings, however, contrast greatly with the government report "On the Application of the Convention of 1979 on the Elimination of All Forms of Discrimination Against Women for the Period from 1983 to 1988" which optimistically noted:

> The principle of full employment observed for 40 years as well as the constitutional guarantees of equality of rights without distinction to sex in all spheres of life . . . created conditions for the change of the socio-professional position of women in the working environment, in family and society. (Bureau for Women's Affairs, 1988a: 3)

The report further claimed that these changes have contributed to "a change in the image of women" as well as to a change in "consciousness of women themselves" (Bureau for Womens' Affairs 1988a: 3). Subsequently, the Bureau for Women's Affairs confirmed these conclusions by asserting that: ". . . in the Polish legal system there is no sign of . . . discrimination" (Bureau for Women's Affairs 1990a: 1).

The report goes on, however, to explain what is meant by this statement and it is at that point that one may see the deeper meaning of the term *equality*

> It [the Polish legal system] primarily includes all norms of treating men and women equally, and if in specific cases it introduces differentiation according to sex, it stems from giving women special rights of protectionist character, because of their psycho-physical and biological functions (childbearing) which are of significant social character. (Bureau for Women's Affairs 1990a: 1)

Indeed, Polish law devotes special attention to this differentiation according to biological function, emphasizing the need to "protect women's labor." Women are not permitted to carry, to lift, and to transport materials beyond the established norms (Uscinska, 1990). Women are also precluded from employment in ninety specified jobs (e.g., in mining or other jobs requiring physical strength, especially in heavy industry and construction jobs, where a person can be exposed to chemicals and radiation, work involving explosives, and exposure to constant vibration). Beyond those restricted areas approved by the Council of Ministries, individual enterprises can also establish their own protectionist practices (Uscinska, 1990).

Both in the law, as exemplified above, and in the professional legal literature, there is a widespread belief that women should be protected. The message is clear: women represent a reproductive resource of great social importance, and as such it requires special attention. At the same time women's role in the production process has been of crucial importance. The question, then, was how to negotiate the balance between the two. The Communist regime's answer was to maintain paternalistic attitudes toward working women.

## WOMEN AS WIVES AND MOTHERS

The role of wife and mother is common among Polish women: the majority (77 percent) of women are married and only 13 percent have no children (Bureau for Women's Affairs, 1988a). Only 5 percent remain single throughout their entire life. On the average, women have 2.3 children, with urban women having fewer children (1.9) than rural women (2.8). Women increasingly experience divorce, and as most of them retain the custody of their children, they become single mothers (5 percent of all women). It is estimated that almost one million children live in female-headed households. Women in urban areas are, more often than their counterparts in rural areas, single or divorced, work outside the home, and are the sole breadwinners for their families.

According to 1987 data published by the Polish Main Statistical Office, basic household duties are performed mostly by women, and the time dedicated by women to such work is three times that contributed by men.

Time budget analyses have been persistent in pointing out the unequal distribution of household tasks. While women spend four hours and fifty-six minutes daily on household duties, men devote on the average one hour and twenty-one minutes to those tasks. Indeed, men have two hours more leisure time than do women (GUS Woman in Poland, 1985).

The already strained situation has been worsened by the lack of childcare facilities. Only 4 percent of the youngest children have a place in the nurseries, and 45 percent of children aged three to six are in childcare facilities (Heinen, 1988).

Polish mass media have played a significant role in supporting the notion of "good mother" and thus making it more difficult for women to become professional and political figures. They have often portrayed women confronted by conflicting economic and daily life problems, the solution to which could only be found if women returned to their traditional role as wives and mothers. The issue for society, then, is not that there is a need for radical change in the institutional structures; rather the emphasis is placed on the inability of women to combine the many roles that they are forced to perform. Little attention is given to the fact that the problem may lie with the existing occupational structure or with the way in which services are delivered, and that indeed both address far better the needs of men than those of women.

## WOMEN AS ACTIVISTS AND POLITICIANS

Prior to the Second World War, women's participation as elected officials was low. However, under the Communist regime, with its formal emphasis on sexual equality, women's participation was encouraged: the first term of the Lower House of Parliament included 17 percent women deputies. By the mid-1980s representation rose to 23 percent and remained at this level until June 1989.

At the subnational level, the system of provincial and local authority provided two additional avenues for women's formal political participation. Until 1958, women were rather poorly represented at the provincial and local levels. Since the 1960s, a steady increase occurred in the number of elected female officials, and by the late 1970s almost 30 percent of officials at the provincial level and 26 percent at the local level were women.

Not all environments, however, were equally conducive to women's political activism. A closer analysis of the data indicates that women were more likely to be politically active in urban areas, especially at the neighborhood level, and relatively few were elected from the rural areas. For example, in 1958 while 4.7 percent of rural council members were women, in the urban settings their participation was significantly higher (14.4 percent). By the mid-sixties, although overall women's political representation rose, nonetheless the dichotomy between urban and rural settings remained the same (23.5 percent for urban neighborhoods and 13.7 percent for rural areas) (GUS Woman in Poland, 1985). Further research done in the seventies confirmed the persistence of greater suppression of women's political activism in rural areas (Nelson, 1985). Rural areas, exposed to a much lesser degree of social and economic change than urban areas, served much longer as the bastions of tradition.

To evaluate women's political activism and the degree to which women have actually participated in the decision-making process, one needs to look beyond quantitative data and focus on the hierarchy of the positions occupied by women. Women as elected officials have tended to hold low-level positions. In the sixties, only 4.9 percent of council presidium members were women, although the provincial level had slightly more women holding these offices (5.4 percent) than the local (4.5 percent) (GUS Woman in Poland, 1985). The highest representation can be noticed at the district level in the large metropolitan areas (16.8 percent) and at the neighborhood level in the cities (11.5 percent). By the mid-eighties improvement was evident: the proportion of female presiding officers increased to 12.7 percent in provincial councils and at the local level to 15.1 percent (GUS Woman in Poland, 1985).

Why, however, have so few women held high-level positions in the provincial and local government hierarchy? As research has pointed out, women elected to these positions were well-educated and young: they did not differ drastically from men occupying the same posts (Nelson, 1985). However, as Nelson noticed: "Despite relatively high educational levels, women who enter local political life had not had the same degree of managerial and professional experience as have men" (Nelson 1985: 158). If we accept Nelson's findings that women have been less experienced than men as managers and that this professional knowledge is crucial to women obtaining access to power, then the question arises as to why women have been elected at all.

The answer seems to lie in the Communist ideology and its goal to achieve equality among all citizens. This, in practical terms, also meant representation in public life. The Communist leaders needed women's participation in politics in order to justify their achievements (Jasiewicz, 1979; Nelson, 1985). What counted most was not the quantity or the level of their participation but the fact that such representation was taking place. These findings parallel the earlier discussion in this chapter regarding the lack of women in high-level professional and managerial jobs, which often were reserved only for men. It suggests that Polish women fell victim to double discrimination: women could not hold high-level political positions because they did not possess appropriate professional experience, which in turn they could not easily obtain because they were women.

During the Communist era, a few state women's organizations came into existence. The most popular among them were the League of Polish Women and the Rural Housewives' Circles. By the beginning of the eighties, each had a membership of over a half million. While their official goal was to represent and discuss the problems of women's daily lives, it cannot be argued that these were feminist organizations truly concerned with equality and interested in empowerment of women. Althought their programs dealt with women's concerns, they focused mainly on addressing the effects rather than the causes of discrimination and subordination. To a large extent these organizations did not see the need for structural change, as their goal was to "facilitate women's adaptation to the economic and social policies implemented by the state" (Sieminska, 1987: 27).

Women were also represented in the three main political parties, at a rate of 26 percent to 30 percent in 1985 (GUS Statistical Yearbook, 1986). However, very few of them held high-level posts. For example, in the Polish United Workers Party, in 1980, only 10.5 percent of the central committee members were women and subsequently, in 1981, their representation dropped to a little over 7 percent. These organizations did not have women's committees or other groups representing women's interests. As a result they did not develop gender-specific agendas, and women's concerns were addressed only sporadically (e.g., legislation regarding protection of working women). Indeed, women's views and interests had no organized expression within the institutions of the Communist regime.

## A Bleak Encounter: Road to Transition

### EMERGENCE OF SOLIDARITY

The 1980s marked the beginning of an intense period of major transformation in Poland's political and economic life. The emergence of the Solidarity trade union movement, as a result of the Gdansk Agreements signed on August 31, 1980, manifested widespread opposition to the Communist regime. Although detailed data regarding women's participation in Solidarity are not available, it is estimated that the proportion of female members was equal to the overall participation of women in the labor force, or about 50 percent. Women were an important part of those historic moments: they participated in the demonstrations and strikes, distributed underground literature, and provided shelter for political activists hunted by the police. Nevertheless, as various studies and interviews have shown, most of the Polish women involved in the opposition movement did not assume positions of leadership (Jancar, 1985; Pomian, 1989). Only two women (Anna Walentynowicz and Joanna Duda Gwiazda) were members of the Interfactory Strike Committee Presidium in August 1980. Neither was the signer of the Gdansk Agreements. Women tended to provide "supportive services" such as typing, preparing tea and coffee, or answering the phone. When the time came to elect delegates to the Solidarity Congress, women's representation had shrunk to 7.8 percent. Only one woman was elected to Solidarity's National Executive Council.

During the 1980s, women involved in the Solidarity movement saw their interests as the same as men's in the struggle for democracy and national liberation. Even as Solidarity grew into a mass movement of opposition to the Communist regime, its critique of the order did not include patriarchy. With the Catholic church as the movement's staunchest ally, its leadership maintained social conservatism. Even though a feminist group did emerge at the University of Warsaw in 1980, "it found itself isolated and unable to grow," staying "together as a small discussion and support group" (Bishop, 1990: 18). Thus women's perspectives and interests were conspiciously absent from the Solidarity agenda.

The notion that women required special protection by the state returned during the summer of 1980, when the Gdansk and Szczecin agreements between the Communist regime and Solidarity were negotiated. A three-year paid maternity leave was the only provision directly concerning women. In addition, Solidarity pushed for the expansion of kindergarten and nursery facilities for working mothers. There is no doubt that Solidarity expected the state to play a protectionist role toward women, especially toward working women. In essence, they continued the view expressed by the Communists that women are equal, but some are weaker and have a different role to perform. What the shipyard workers wanted to see was women in their traditional role as wives and mothers, and they were not going to ask women to make their own choices. In practical terms such protection meant for many women the subordination of their values to those of the patriarchal system.

The implementation of martial law brought harsh repercussions for both men and women but affected each group differently. Men who were political leaders and activists were arrested and interned in disproportionately larger numbers and for longer periods than were women. But women who were imprisoned suffered special burdens. As primary caretakers of children they experienced the psychological trauma caused by the rapid and unexpected separation from their families. Often, at the time of the arrest of the parents, children were left alone at home without anyone to take care of them. They were frequently separated by force from their mothers and placed in foster care. Those women who avoided being interned were left with full responsibility for their families and their imprisoned partners. They were the ones who arranged visits to prison and sent food and medical parcels. They were the pillars of the families' psychological well-being, while at the same time they themselves remained uncertain about the future.

Throughout the eighties a more active involvement of women in political activities can be noticed. Women began to take part in protests because they wanted to see, for the sake of their children, an improvement in living conditions. The Chernobyl accident prompted women and the environmentalist movement to organize a demonstration in Cracow on June 1, 1986, to call for better environmental standards and improvement in health protection. Women were also initiators of strikes and work stoppages in the textile and clothing industries. However, at the same time very little initiative to establish feminist support groups took place. The effort initiated by students from the University of Warsaw met with reluctance and only partial interest. It was argued that women were already participating in other political activities, chiefly in Solidarity, and many women did not perceive a need for a feminist organization (Sieminska, 1986).

THE "NEW BEGINNING"?

When the Round-Table negotiations began in February 1989, women were again omitted from the main negotiating group. Furthermore, not even one woman was a chief negotiator for any of the eleven subgroups. Women participated only as members of the negotiating subteams and only a health subgroup could claim to have a reasonable representation of women (38.9 percent). For other groups, the participation rate was much lower and ranged from 0.0 percent in the subgroup on unions, to 8.7 percent in the group negotiating changes in law and in the judicial system. The overall women's representation was pathetic: women were not men's partners in the historical beginning of the collapse of the Communist regime.

The political and economic restructuring is regarded by many as progress toward a new democratic order. Poland is among those struggling to establish democratic institutions, to establish the rule of law, and in short, to replace a totalitarian way of governing. Progress has already been achieved by guaranteeing political rights, freedom of expression, securing democratic elections, and the rewriting of hundreds of pieces of legislation in the area of economic development, local government, and education. Nonetheless, not everyone participates equally in these events nor, does it seem, will share equally in the benefits of change. Polish women and the elderly (who are predominantly women) have become increasingly vulnerable and often become the first victims of "progress." Indeed, women are the majority of the new unemployed and have already lost their right to long-term parental leave. Womens' concerns seem to be left out, or as in the case of the right to abortion, the lawmakers are actively fighting against them.

From the perspective of political participation, women were drastically defeated in 1989, in the first open Parliamentary elections to the Sejm (Lower House) and to the resurrected Senate. While all seats were open for election in the Senate, based on the Round-Table agreements, only 35 percent of the seats were for a free competition in the Sejm. Two hundred women ran as candidates, but in the first round, only sixteen women, all members of the opposition, received a majority necessary for election. The rest of the winners (fifty-three) were elected in the runoff election. In the end, women won 6 of the 100 seats in the Senate (6 percent) and 62 of 460 seats in the Sejm (14.8 percent).

The election of women to the Parliament has, however, very little to do with a clear feminist stand. It was the political support of Solidarity and of Lech Walesa himself which got both men and women the seats. The lack of that support almost automatically precluded chances of winning. There were few attempts on the part of independent women to compete for parliamentary seats in order to advance womens' concerns. Unfortunately, the complete control of the campaign by Solidarity, the lack of financial support, and most importantly, a continued strong societal prejudice against women's ability to hold high-level political and managerial positions precluded many female candidates from winning.

Nineteen-ninety brought dramatic changes in local government—the reforms eliminated provincial councils, making the local councils the key decision-making bodies. On May 27, 1990 over 140,000 candidates competed for offices. New councilors were elected in the first free democratic elections. Women, however, did not fare well, gaining only 10.2 percent (5,813) of the seats on the local councils. In comparison to the past, it was a serious setback. On the other hand, such a statement is too simplistic. The fact that the election even took place and that the reform in itself is one of the most progressive elements of the current political transformation suggests that Poland is in the early stage of building a democratic nation in which, one hopes, women will gain equal political representation. Nonetheless, the results imply that this will neither be a short nor an easy process.

The current debate and struggle to preserve abortion rights probably best illustrates the difficulties confronting Polish women. In February 1989, a bill was introduced in the Sejm "protecting the unborn." If passed, the new bill automatically would have terminated the existing legislation. The 1956 abortion law was liberal, permitting abortion during the first twelve weeks of pregnancy when the woman's health was threatened, in case of rape, when fetal deformities existed, or more ambiguously, due to difficult living conditions. It has been estimated that over 600,000 abortions were performed annually—mostly due to "difficult living conditions."

The new proposal provided for severe penalties, for example, a three-year jail term for doctors and women who violated the prohibition. Furthermore, the bill provided for appointment of a legal guardian of the fetus and required financial support by the father. It did not permit, however, for legal procedures contesting fatherhood to be initiated during the pregnancy (Ciechomska and Plakwicz, 1989).

The bill was introduced by members of Parliament on behalf of the Catholic church and received immediate support of several prominent Solidarity leaders. Numerous demonstrations and picketing were organized in May 1989 by students at the University of Warsaw and a small number of newly emerging feminist groups. The strongest opposition came from the Communist media.[1]

The bill was quickly tabled due to open protests and in recognition of the pre-election political climate. Although it was deferred for future public consultation, several changes in the administrative procedures within the Ministry of Health were accomplished in May 1989. These required a woman seeking abortion to have written certification permitting abortion from two or three physicians. Furthermore, they demanded the woman see a psychologist, at which point the Church also would have input in the discussion. The Ministry began a special training and certification process for psychologists to follow. Women basically were denied any input in the final decision, which entirely rested with the doctors and state officials. The process of restricting women's freedom to decide had begun.

The issue returned to the Parliament a year later, in the spring of 1990, when the Senate's Commission on Legislative Initiatives began preparing a bill. At the end of September the Senate devoted two entire days to the debate. The main foci of the discussion were the question of conception as the beginning of human life, the necessity to protect the unborn child, the right of legislation to control freedom of choice, and the right of the courts to initiate criminal charges against women and medical personnel. It was a disturbing scene—a Senate room filled predominantly with men arguing what is right and what is wrong for women, when they should and when they should not have a child, and finally, how they should be penalized in case of misbehavior. In the section reserved for the public ten to fifteen men were agitating in favor of the new legislation, but not one woman was present. At the same time, outside the Parliament there was a drastically different scene—several hundred people demonstrated with speeches, slogans, and chanting. Here, however, predominantly women and children were the participants. Few men were present. One of the banners read: "Abortion—the most important anti-democratic legislation," another "Instead of computers—introduction of religion in school," making reference to the recent introduction of religion into the school curriculum.

These two worlds were far apart that day. In the name of change and establishment of a new democratic process, the traditional, religious, and male-dominated Poland was winning. At the end of the debate the Senate decided to initiate the new anti-abortion legislation (forty-two to twenty-six votes with seven abstentions). In the subsequent round of voting, the Senate rejected the establishment of penalties for women who had abortions, and it accepted the imposition of criminal charges against medical personnel who performed abortions. The bill then was sent to the Sejm (the Lower House). Within hours of publicizing the results a shock went through the society. People were talking with disbelief and outrage. They were questioning their future democracy and wondering if the Polish version would be a totalitarian one and dominated by the church and men.

Despite the anger, little organized protest has emerged. On the other hand, there is no doubt that the emergence of the anti-abortion debate has prompted women to begin to speak out. Since the spring of 1989, a number of small feminist and women's groups have emerged. A recent survey conducted by the Bureau for Women's Affairs identified over twenty-one groups, circles, clubs, and formal associations (Bureau for Women's Affairs, 1990b). This indicates a major increase since the early eighties when only four such organizations could be identified. The feminist groups seem to exist exclusively in large urban areas, and their membership varies from three to over two hundred members. They differ in terms of their legal status: seven have the status of association; three groups function within already existing organizations (League of Polish Women, Polish Episcopate, Polish Socialist Party) and others are in the process of institutionalizing their activities.

The analysis of their programs points to widespread differences in goals and types of activities. However, the major objectives of most of these groups include the protection of constitutional equality and of its implementation in political, social, and economic spheres; collective and individual consciousness-raising among women; revision of legal, political, moral, and cultural forms of discrimination against women; elimination of socially and culturally rooted discrimination against women; and protection of women's rights of free choice regarding motherhood.

Depending on the availability of human and financial resources that each of these groups has at its disposal, different forms of action or strategies have been identified as ways to accomplish goals. The most frequently cited strategies include: organization of meetings, discussion groups, seminars, workshops and conferences; support of feminist research; periodical reports on the status of women; translation of foreign feminist literature; organization of film and theater festivals; networking among women's groups; exchange of information and experiences; establishment of contacts with feminist groups and individuals abroad; and organization of protests, demonstrations, lobbying, and media publicity (Bureau for Women's Affairs, 1990b).

The results of the survey demonstrated clearly the emergence of a women's movement in Poland. This movement is young and struggling with similar problems to those faced by women in other countries. Women's groups often do not have adequate financial resources to carry out their activities, and they lack appropriate space. They experience difficulties with press coverage. Most importantly, they still lack wide support among Polish women, as frequently women do not perceive that discrimination persists. Nevertheless, Polish women are speaking out more frequently and loudly than ever before, as they begin to seek inclusion in the democratization process of their country.

## Conclusion

Even though, constitutionally, equality between men and women has existed since 1952 in Poland, the reality is different. The duality of women's role finds its discriminatory power in the fact that only a few women occupy high-level management, professional, or governmental positions. Consequently, they are also faced with lower wages and low-status jobs. The paradox of Polish life is that indeed women have often been forced to take such jobs in order to be able to take care of the family and their household. The chronic shortage of adequate infrastructural facilities has frequently prevented them from becoming more involved in their work and carrying it out more effectively. In the end, women have often been blamed for not being good workers. The inequalities at home have been carried into public life.

Clearly neither the Communist regime, nor the nationalist wave of Solidarity activities achieved gender equality. The Communist system, although presenting women with new opportunities, was not interested in permanently securing those opportunities through the restructuring of power relations between men and women. Women did not assume leadership positions nor were they able to propose a women's agenda under Solidarity, although they were taking part in the political struggle. And the Catholic church, with its tremendous influence over Poland's social and political life, has struggled to preserve the central role of the family and traditional position of women.

With the exception of a brief period in the nineteenth century, women in Poland did not speak out in the past. They have just begun to voice their concerns, and their agenda still needs to be agreed upon. A consensus also needs to be reached regarding the strategies to be used to improve the status of women. In electoral politics, as past experiences have shown, the issue is not so much how many women hold positions as elected officials, but which positions they do hold and whose interests they represent. Indeed, at this particular point in the dismantling of the Communist regime, the participation of women in the legislative process could be the most urgent need. It is now that the new institutional and legislative framework is being created, and thus it is the time to argue for nondiscriminatory legislation. It is not an accident that one of the most important pieces of legislation from the women's perspective, abortion rights, is being currently debated by the Polish Parliament. The outcome of this debate will be felt for years, not only by women but also by the entire society. This could be the first test of freedom and equality that women could have in the new Poland. The way it is currently proceeding could mean a serious setback for women.

Nevertheless, the process of change has begun. It is hopeful that the women's struggle will continue and that Polish women will achieve equality with men in real life.

# Note

1. This should not be interpreted, however, that the Communists were great supporters of women's rights in Poland. It simply was only one element of the pre-election strategy. The Communist regime recognized that, from a societal point of view, abortion is a decisive issue and that, with the increasingly controlling role of the church, women could expect little support from the opposition. Indeed, throughout the short debate Solidarity remained silent (Ciechomska and Plakwicz, 1989: 1).

C H A P T E R

13

# EMPOWERING WOMEN IN RURAL INDIA

A Model for Development

*Dorane L. Fredland*

Contradictions characterize women's rights in India. While the Constitution protects women, traditional social customs do not; while the pace of development and change in India is increasing, many of its citizens, and the majority of women, remain tied to the past. These contradictory forces are particularly noticeable in rural areas, where the social structure, based on a strong class or caste system, enforces old patterns of behavior that respond slowly to development schemes or legislative instructions. If the quality of life for women is to improve in these areas, attitudes and customs that reinforce inequality and discrimination must be altered.

This chapter explores traditional practices which persist in demeaning the status of women and examines in particular a project in southern India that is empowering women with skills to address these traditional attitudes and enabling women to improve their status and environment. It is not the purpose of this study to explore all aspects of development nor the entire span of issues related to the discrimination of women in India. It does, however, set forth a model for change.

## Rural Development

Development is an intangible concept: it is difficult to know when development has actually taken place, when it has been completed, if ever; nor can we be sure whether it is a political, economic, or social process. In Western terms, development has been defined as a process which moves a society toward "modernization" (see, for example, Palmer, 1989; Heeger, 1974). Despite this rather vague definition, modernization usually means technological and economic change that brings the less-developed countries closer to the material standard of the developed world and involves the establishment of new industry, extensive market economies, multinational corporations, and, usually, a build-up of armament. Development strategies at the national level in India (and in many other so-called Third World countries) have focused on catching up with the developed world and emerging on the world and regional scene as a strong state.

In recent years, however, development in the non-Western world has emerged as a movement outside the traditional arena of established political parties and governments. These grass-roots movements have sprung from a growing demand to cope with pressing, often desperate, needs of the poor (Kothari, 1983: 551). Development directed toward improving the quality of life for people in need can have substantial meaning for people who live in rural areas.

Charlton argues that understanding development in terms of Western rationality and scientific knowledge is not adequate in defining programs for agrarian societies today. When development is focused on human well-being, human desires "are the basis of legitimacy in public policy, including development policy" (Charlton, 1984: 8). It therefore follows that if development strategies are to improve the daily lives of the poor in India, they must bridge the gap between the goals of development and the realities of rural life.

This has been difficult to achieve since 80 percent of the Indian population lives in rural areas where approximately 65 percent are engaged in agriculture, and where at least 45 percent are far below the poverty level (Balasubramanian, 1989: 6). A large rural, poor population has remained, despite the fact that since independence India has built a strong, autonomous, and economically viable nation. India is now ranked among the fifteen largest economies in the world, yet the country remains one of the poorest in terms of per capita income.[1] People at the bottom of society, tied down by social traditions and isolated from decision-making positions, have benefitted the least from a growing economy. This is especially true for women who remain at the lowest economic level in rural society (Heeger, 1974: 4).

Growing industrialization has primarily benefitted the middle class, according to Palmer (1989), because they have been able to participate in the process. This growing middle class—managers, doctors, lawyers, upper-level bureaucrats, exporters, importers, and others with special skills and education— constitutes a "growing middle sector far removed from the poverty of the slum dwellers and the rural peasants. . . . In India, the poverty of the poor stands in sharp contrast to the new middle-class prosperity" (Palmer, 1989: 132).

Rural development was not a high priority of Indian government programs until the mid-1960s when efforts to stimulate agricultural production "only spotlighted the vast inequalities and intense degrees of human degradation still present in the Indian countryside" (Franda, 1979: 258). When Western economic development programs were adapted to rural environments, the basic character of society was often undermined. When rural workers, for example, produced goods needed for a market far removed from the needs of the rural population or went to urban locations to work, they became detached from the daily life of the rural population of which they were a part and were no longer able to contribute fully to the needs of their own communities. Women, who contribute substantially to agricultural chores, were also affected by new economic development. They not only had more labor as a result of men moving to the cities to work, but they were overlooked in the development process. New farm equipment, for example, was often provided to and operated solely by men. Traditionally women have worked harder in the fields, doing difficult manual labor, while men worked fields with power provided by animals or machines. Providing men with more opportunities and equipment continued to give women an inferior status in society.

Many government programs, including the National Integrated Rural Development program initiated to attack problems of poverty, have been increasingly criticized for their shortcomings and for "insufficient public involvement" (Balasubramanian, 1989: 6). Development planned without regard for social considerations, and without participation by those persons most affected by the proposed changes, has failed. This has been particularly true for women.

"Integrating women into development projects at once changes social and political structures, the distribution of wealth, and cultural mores. It is, in short, revolutionary in its implications" (Franda, 1979: 8). When women are involved at the decision-making and implementing stages of development, communities thrive, and roles and behavior patterns are redefined. Since life in the villages depends on the work of women in the home and family, in the fields, and at the market, it is important to give attention to the specific needs of women if constructive development is to occur. The model described in this chapter illustrates what dramatic changes are possible when women are actively involved in the total development process.

For purposes of evaluation, the project will be examined in terms of its effectiveness in empowering women as leaders in development. This involves determining whether women have become, as a result of improved conditions, full participants in community decision-making and enjoy improved physical and social well-being. The success of the project must also be measured in terms of the adaptability of the whole community to changes and whether mechanisms or methods for further development are well established in the community. While the observations and impressions of the project detailed below are admittedly subjective, they concur with the expectations defined in substantive research and analysis by scholars in evaluating effective development for women (see, e.g., Charlton, 1984; Franda, 1979; Sharma et al., 1984). The long-term and overall development of India depends on the success of these and similar projects dedicated to improving the quality of life for all, men and women, in the rural areas.

## Women's Status in Contemporary Rural India

The pace of change is quickening for India's 800-plus million people, but less dramatically so for the 80 percent who live in small villages. Resistance to change can be very strong in these areas.

Though the villages vary in size and character, they have many similarities. Every villager is a member of an extended family and is acquainted with most of the other members of the village. Each social organization represents a distinct entity, with its individual mores and beliefs. But different castes and communities inhabiting the village are integrated through economic and social ties, as well as ritual patterns of mutual and reciprocal obligations (Srinivas, 1960: 202).

Caste and family dominate and seriously undermine efforts to improve village conditions. All people in an Indian village live by an accepted code of behavior, not by formal law, and the negative patterns of those codes of behavior affecting women are particularly strong. Although women's work varies by culture, region, caste, and farm size, the daily life of most women is very difficult. Women, who represent about one-half of the agricultural labor force, serve multiple roles as wife, mother, and field-hand. These demands are exacerbated by the traditions of early marriages and large families.

The further one goes into the countryside, the more aware one becomes of the difficulties of life there. Small villages are isolated from each other by rough roads and the lack of public transportation; the walk to a neighboring village is often long and tedious. This isolation of the villages contributes to the continuation of traditional social patterns and stagnant social and economic relations.

Tied closely to the agrarian structure, women suffer, in comparison to males, poorer health and lower life expectancy. Still, there have been recent improvements. Life expectancy for all Indians rose from an average thirty-two years in 1951 to fifty-four in 1981, due primarily to a dramatic drop in infant mortality. Estimates and data vary from source to source, but the average life expectancy given for women in 1985 was fifty-three years, and men averaged about one year more. This is contrary to expectations in most countries where, on the average, women live longer than men (Sivard, 1985: 25).

The increasing number of males over females is causing Indians concern. In 1961, there were 13,351,631 more males than females. In 1981, there were 23,611,076 more males than females (Karkal and Pandey, 1989: 17). Many reasons have been given for this "masculinization of the population," but it is clearly linked to discrimination against women. In this culture of son preference, malnutrition and morbidity rates for females are higher than those for males from birth to age thirty-five. In some areas, the mortality rate among female children is estimated to be 50 percent higher than for males (Bouton and Oldenburg, 1989: 132). There are appreciably fewer girl births registered than boy births, leading some demographers to conclude that sickly females are given less care than male babies and are more readily permitted to die (Hazarika, 1981). There is also alarm over the increasing use of amniocentesis, followed by abortion of female fetuses. These are major obstacles to improving the status of women.

Although there has been a significant decline in the infant mortality rate, it remains 120 per 1,000 births compared to 12 in the United States (Karkal and Pandey, 1989: 39). Another study recently found that a woman in India with six surviving children over one year of age had typically been pregnant eight times over the thirty-year span of her reproductive life (Sivard, 1985: 26). Every pregnancy is a drain on a woman's health, and recent estimates show maternal mortality rates at 418 per 100,000 births (Bouton and Oldenburg, 1989: 132).

Although Indians may now live longer, the frequency of illness is only marginally less than it was for their ancestors. While the worst communicable diseases have been largely eliminated (e.g., tetanus), and clinics for treatment of acute illnesses and injuries proliferate in the countryside, nutritional and environmental problems continue to affect the health of millions.

Family-planning programs, crucial to improving life for women, have also failed. Since the mid-1960s, the birthrate of 41 per 1,000 has dropped only to 35, and still less than a quarter of the population practices any form of birth control. Many experts, including Dr. V. A. Panandiker, chairman of a government committee on population, believe that the key to controlling India's population is for the government to alter radically the entire approach, and "let local people shape and operate their own programs." He uses the Arole project (discussed in this chapter) as an example of a family-planning success (Marshall 1981: 3).

Although women are the ones with primary responsibility for the health of their families, government programs in the past have failed to recognize the importance of women's needs or their participation in development schemes. Programs have often "neglected this aspect [women in decision-making] and this has not always been to their benefit as they neither have reproductive rights nor do they have control over their own bodies" (Karkal and Pandey, 1989: 3). It is now clear that programs must be designed to include women as leaders, and as primary targets of development schemes.

India has one of the highest percentages of anemia cases in the world because of malnutrition. About 60 to 80 percent of pregnant women in South India suffer from iron deficiency (Karkal and Pandey, 1989: 7). Research by Safilios-Rothschild suggests that while malnutrition is often widespread among children in the rural areas of many developing countries, some evidence indicates that it is more widespread among pre-adolescent and adolescent girls than boys, regardless of their caste (Bernard, 1987: 216). A hospital in India recently reported that of those suffering from severe malnutrition, 71.43 percent were women and 28.57 percent were men; from mild malnutrition, 56.40 percent were men and 43.60 percent were women; and of those who were normal, 69.20 percent were male and 30.80 percent female (Karkal and Pandey, 1989: 39).

Other major causes of female ill health are inadequate food intake, lack of protected water supply, chronic infections, and the aftermath of chronic debilitating diseases. Health problems are compounded by the lack of education and availability of basic information to enable people to change their conditions.

Statistics also indicate that while more people are now receiving some education, women still lag behind men. In 1985, the adult literacy rate was approximately 33 percent for women, and 58 percent for men. This was up from 13 percent for women and 42 percent for men in 1960. Approximately 1 percent of the women and 5 percent of the men (twenty to twenty-four years old) were enrolled in higher education in 1960; this figure rose to 5 percent for women and 13 percent for men in 1985. This increase in the number of women students has not eliminated disparities between the sexes in education, especially in the rural areas. At all levels of education, boys still represent a majority of students (Sivard, 1985: 19,40).

Solving these problems in the rural areas is difficult, but if positive changes are to occur, attitudes about education and sex roles must conform to expectations which are quite different from the past. The very fabric and customs of society may be challenged by a general resistance to any new changes, especially those tied to religious traditions.

Religious teachings are often responsible for creating and reinforcing customs that contribute to the low status of women in society.[2] Hinduism, the dominant influential religion in India, teaches young girls to model themselves on Sita, the mythological wife of the legendary hero, Rama, who followed her husband into the wilderness and never failed to do his bidding. In a Hindu family the girl's role is clearly defined. She is taught early that she is responsible for winning over the family into which she marries and for making a place for herself in her new family.

Manu, the codifier of ancient Hindu Law, referred to the proper role of woman in society as one that in childhood is "subject to her father, in youth to her husband and when her lord is dead, to her sons. A woman must never be independent." No one can say whether, in the struggle over the role of women, the teachings of "Manu or the dictates of a modern nation state will predominate. . . . The laws of Manu have maintained Indian society for several thousands of years; independent, democratic India is just 31 years old" (Hazarika, 1981).

The caste system as defined by Hinduism influences what a person can and cannot do, as well as with whom one may do it. Untouchables, for example, are members of villages, but may not participate as others in village life. Caste members are linked by ties of kinship, but there are clear social and sex divisions. For example, water regulation, transplanting of crops, and weeding are tasks performed by women, but plowing is done by men. These practices of caste and sex discrimination continue to contradict the Indian Constitution's more contemporary tone against discrimination "on grounds of religion, race, caste, or sex."

Other customs harmful to women also continue in spite of efforts by the government to abolish them. Two of the most serious are: *sati*, burning a widow on her husband's funeral pyre, and dowry payments. Reports of *sati* events and construction of *chabutras*, or *sati* temples, and of dowry deaths and debt (caused by the failure of a family to fulfill its material obligations) are frequently reported in the Indian press. Although primarily a phenomenon of Hindu middle-class families in northern India, the dowry system has crossed boundaries of provinces and transcends education and religious differences.

Palaniappan Chjidambaram, Home Affairs Minister, gave the number of dowry deaths in 1985 as 999; in 1986, 1,329; and in 1987, 1,786 (Crossette, 1989: 4).

Pramla Dandavate, a pioneer in the women's rights movement, blames the lack of respect for women as the primary cause for these practices. "We are a feudal society. Basically, we don't believe that people are equal. Our education system does not teach respect for women. We have lost our sense of justice . . . and [we] are neither Westernized nor have remained Indian" (Crossette, 1989: 4).

The Indian government, international organizations, national organizations, and women's groups have had limited success in affecting changes for rural women for a number of reasons. One basic problem has been the inability of people from urban environments to communicate effectively with residents of rural areas. Professional women who have spearheaded the programs aimed at improving the lives of poor rural women often find it difficult to understand and identify with their problems. Furthermore, educated urban dwellers have notions of development which are borrowed from the Western world and typically are inappropriate to the situations of poor, rural residents. Since planning is mostly done by influential "and relatively rich urban dwellers, the government provides facilities for the urban elite to the neglect of the rural masses forming eighty percent of the total population" (Arole, 1987: 1).

## A Successful Development Program

Addressing these political and social issues of the poor is important for future development in India, and the project described below offers signs of hope. It reaches to the heart of village society, seeking to improve the environment and quality of life for people there by addressing the major problems of health care and other problems prevalent in rural India.

In 1971, physicians Rajnikant and Mabel Arole initiated the Comprehensive Rural Health Project. They began their work in Jamkhed, in Maharashtra state, a typical drought-prone and arid rural area in western India, where people live in small houses or huts grouped together and surrounded by the fields that provide their livelihood.

One major problem in serving the health needs of the poor in India, particularly those who live in isolated areas, is the lack of physicians. Medical training and practices tend to be geared toward urban and industrial communities, and rural health services experience great shortages of trained personnel.

In 1988, I visited one of the villages to determine if this project had made a difference for people there, and especially for women. It became immediately clear that significant changes were underway, and that problems of malnutrition, illiteracy, high infant mortality, unsafe water, and poor land were being addressed. Old practices were giving way to new ideas, and life was much better for those who only a short time before had experienced life as meager and brief. Women, working at the forefront of the project, had become both agents of as well as benefactors of the changes. An examination of the project gave a clearer understanding of the reasons for success.

The program had been designed from the beginning with consideration for local concerns and interests. An informal advisory committee, formed with representatives from the villages, provided a forum for constant dialogue about the endeavor. This was extremely important to its success, as involvement of local residents in the project from its beginning provided a sense of ownership and commitment necessary for accomplishment of change.

After deciding to open a clinic in an old veterinary dispensary to handle emergencies, the local community agreed to provide housing for the staff (the two doctors and several trained nurses). Since the physicians employed staff without regard to caste, it was a chore of great significance in this caste-ridden society and an important accomplishment with far-reaching implications (Arole, 1987: 4).

After securing adequate facilities, the staff went to the villages to introduce preventive health care, family planning, and the prevention of diseases by immunization, sanitation, safe drinking water, and good nutrition. Although efforts made by the trained nurses were well-meaning, progress was slow and it became clear that basic changes in lifestyle were not occurring as the planners had hoped and expected. Unsafe deliveries and high infant mortality rates, problems specifically addressed by the program, continued.

There were several reasons for this slow start. First, for the majority, health was not a priority (Arole, 1987). The basic needs—water, food, employment, shelter, and clothing—were more important. Second, the nurses' formal education, urban manner, and style of dress made them unacceptable agents of change in the village. Concluding that the current staff were the wrong persons to effectively dispel unsafe health practices and harmful social practices, the planners initiated a new strategy, which consisted of providing safe drinking water for everyone and nutritious food for young children.

Providing safe water presented several problems in this caste society. Drinking wells had to be strategically placed since the Harijana, or outcasts, were not allowed to drink water from wells placed in higher caste localities. Eventually, with the help of voluntary agencies specialized in digging tube wells and with donations from agencies concerned about drought, 156 tube wells for drinking water were drilled in the area. Almost all were located among the poor communities, so that those who needed them most would have the easiest access to water (Arole, 1987: 7).

As plans were developed for further work, the Farmers' Clubs (organized initially for men only but eventually also for women) played an important role. These clubs succeeded in breaking down social barriers, and played a significant role in determining strategy for carrying the Comprehensive Rural Health Project forward at a critical stage of development. Understanding the need to change tactics, an idea was born at one of the club meetings: a woman from the local village would be chosen as the village health worker and be trained in basic health skills at the clinic, with special attention to maternal and child health, including family planning. Eventually she would be trained as a birth-attendant (midwife).

As the program developed and expanded, guidelines were refined. Selection of the health worker was crucial. Basic education would not be emphasized, and she could in fact be illiterate; but she had to be middle-aged, married, and have roots in the village. The health workers were then trained at the clinic where they learned to recognize and treat a child with diarrhea in the early stages before the disease became serious; to administer a few useful, but not potentially harmful drugs; to serve as a mid-wife; and to deal with adult illnesses, such as leprosy and tuberculosis. They also learned the fundamentals of preventive health care, such as clean preparation of foods and proper diet. Carrots, for example, were important to decreasing the high incidence of eye diseases.

The effectiveness of the health worker in the community first became obvious when she was able to identify persons with leprosy more accurately than the professional staff had been able to do. In the village I visited the professional nurses had located only four cases of leprosy, but the health worker, because of trust among the villagers, had located twenty-five with early lesions. The ability of the health worker to identify so completely with the needs and feelings of those in her own village led to the gradual change in attitude and acceptance of new information. This included education about birth control methods and the importance of planning families.

Within the first ten years of the project, the village health workers had managed to persuade 70 percent of the district's married couples to use contraceptives, and this had reduced the fertility rate from 36 per 1,000 to 25. For the first time, families with only two children were not only accepted, but applauded. With family planning assured, the communities could focus on the larger social and economic issues.

By 1986 the project was serving seventy-five villages ranging in size from five hundred to thirty-five hundred persons in an area where approximately 60 percent of the population is extremely poor. There has been positive development in these villages, and there is every indication that progress will continue. The well-established Farmers' Clubs continue to meet and plan and have special projects. In the village I visited, the men's club measures the height of all children regularly to monitor their growth and note any appearance of health problems. The women's club, in addition to being involved in health programs, has now undertaken a reforestation project. The clubs also formed cooperatives to gather and distribute food and were involved in a variety of other community activities. The most important role of the clubs continues to be, however, to provide a forum where people can discuss and solve their own problems. Now united, they are "able to recognize their rights and find the courage to approach government officials, or functionaries at the village level, in order to avail themselves of all government schemes" (Arole, 1987: 16). The impact on women has been particularly encouraging. With new confidence and respect, they too feel, for the first time, "free to approach the banks for loans and to start self-employment schemes which will add to their incomes" (Arole, 1987: 16).

At the village meeting called during my visit, I realized how far the villagers had come in breaking down the old social barriers. Men *and* women eagerly and proudly spoke about how they plan their families, care for the health of children and mothers, and take care to drink only safe water. They explained the importance of treating diarrhea before serious problems developed, and of preparing clean surroundings for the delivery of a baby. They noted with satisfaction that they had had only one infant death in the last ten years, but before that only 50 percent of the newborns had survived. After the meeting, they insisted that we walk several miles to see the thousands of trees they had planted and cared for in an area badly in need of reforestation. This, too, is a shared activity. The women plant the trees, while the men guard the area from roaming animals.

## Conclusion

There have been many discussions about the meaning of, and methods needed for, successful development. John Kenneth Galbraith, after serving as U.S. Ambassador in Delhi, realized how urgent was the discussion of economic planning, village development, schemes for health and educational betterment, development of village crafts, and of course, family planning, and yet how slow would be the consequences. The discussion became, according to Galbraith, "an art form of the modern slice—or, at best, an expression of its conscience and concern. The reality was the absence of any levers for moving the great village mass—the absence, on occasion, even of means of communication with the India of the millions" (Moraes and Howe, 1974: 39). It has not been easy to find the right "levers" to move the masses. Projects organized by outside "experts" who understand world economics and can mobilize vast national resources have had serious shortcomings. Now, new methods are being explored with success.

The Comprehensive Health Project is an important model for development because it offers an effective "lever" for grass-roots change. Social patterns that have in the past contributed to poverty and disease in rural India are being replaced with ones which have improved people's lives. This has been accomplished by willing participants from within the communities, and by women who have become equal partners in all aspects of development. Now with the necessary groundwork in place, and a positive attitude toward change, there are strong expectations that progress toward an even better future will continue.

These developments have contributed significantly to improving the quality of life for the villagers. One woman told me that "we no longer get beaten when we don't have dinner on the table in time; we no longer have one child right after another; no longer expect our babies to die at birth; and no longer wait for others to make all our decisions." This firsthand account explains why the Rural Comprehensive Health Project has been a liberating process for women, and an effective avenue for their empowerment.

## Notes

1. In 1987, India's GNP was $241,305 million, approximately $300 per capita (*The Europa World Book 1989*, Vol. I: 1294).

2. According to the 1981 census, religious groups in India represent the following percentages of the population: Hindus, 83 percent; Muslims, 11 percent; Christians, 3 percent; Sikhs, 2 percent, and Buddhists, 7 percent.

# CONCLUSION

## Jill M. Bystydzienski

The chapters in this book focus on politics as redefined in feminist terms. Politics is taken to mean not only participation in the public sphere of governance but also in such less traditional activities as involvement in social movements, local development projects, networking and informal coalition building, protesting and demonstrating, as well as the use of conventionally "female" activities (e.g., cooking, sewing, and taking care of others) for the attainment of empowerment. It is within the realm of politics as seen in such broader terms that the authors of this book focus on strategies women have used successfully, and sometimes unsuccessfully, to become empowered or enabled to take charge of their own lives.

Huber (1990) pointed out that to understand how human beings make choices and organize themselves, we need to formulate links between macro (societal) and micro (personal) levels. Ecological, technological, historical, structural, and cultural factors may limit or facilitate the ways in which women and men respond to their conditions and transform them in turn (Huber, 1990: 3). The contributors to this book have shown that, in different countries and under varying societal conditions, women have developed a number of different strategies for empowerment. The preceding chapters cover many different parts of the world, deal with countries that possess varying degrees of modern technology, focus on diverse government structures, societal values, and ideologies. It is important to consider under which of these macro-conditions specific strategies developed and used by women have empowered them. The strategies considered effective are those which increase the quality of women's lives by enabling them to contribute to the decision-making processes in their communities and societies, to achieve a more equal status with men, and to participate in changing their environments in the direction of greater social justice and democracy.

Under what conditions can effective strategies emerge? What types of strategies are appropriate to different societal conditions? I will attempt to answer such questions in these concluding pages.

As the chapters in the first section indicate, one major source of strategies for women's empowerment is a "women's culture," a set of values and activities which arise from the division of labor by sex and the consequent devel-

opment of ways of thinking and acting which are specifically "female." While
a women's culture exists to some degree in all societies where women's activities have been separate historically from those of men, it is allowed different
forms of expression in different societies. Thus in countries such as Norway,
Japan, Canada, and to some extent the United States, issues and concerns which
are specifically women's have been brought by women politicians into the public sphere of party agendas and government debates, usually aided and encouraged by women's groups outside government. In other countries, such as Spain,
for instance, women developed their own demands and forms of participation
but were relatively absent from traditional political institutions. Still another
possibility, exemplified by the cases of Palestine, Uganda, and India, is that
women may draw on their traditional activities, such as cooking and caretak-
ing, in contributing to nationalist or economic development struggles which
are seen to benefit them in the long run.

An important strategy derived from the women's culture involves getting
more women into the formal political system. As in Norway and Japan, the
strategy is based on the belief that women can make a difference because they
bring into politics a specific set of values, experiences, and behaviors which
will eventually transform the agendas and structures, taking them in a democratic direction. However, societies vary in the degree to which they pose barriers to this strategy. It appears that countries which have a parliamentary,
multiparty system of government and, in addition, proportional representation
have higher rates of women in public office (Norris, 1987; Rule, 1981). Thus,
as the table below indicates, Norway and Canada have relatively high levels of
female representation at the national level as compared to, for instance, the
United States and Great Britain.[1] On the other hand, the relatively high female
representation at the state level in the United States can be accounted for by
multimember electoral districts (Darcy, Welch, and Clark, 1987). A steady
increase in the percentage of women in Japan's Upper House of the Diet has
occurred since a proportional representation system was introduced in 1980
(Kubo, 1990).[2]

However, the voting system is but one factor which can promote or impede
the entry of women into elected offices. The existence of left-wing parties in a
multiparty system tends to faciliate women's entry (see, e.g., Norris, 1987:
126). Thus in Norway, Mexico, Canada, and recently Japan, women have been
more strongly represented in Socialist and Social Democratic parties than in
any of the parties in other countries under comparison. The higher percentages
of women at the national level in Nicaragua, Uganda, and Poland are due at
least in part to having left-wing governments.

Finally, an important factor that facilitates the entry of women into existing
political institutions is a cultural ethos that places strong value on equality and
group rights. Norway, which by far has the highest female representation in
our group of countries (see table), in addition to a multiparty/proportional
representation system and a prominent labor party, has a long history of beliefs
in social justice for the collectivity and in the role of government as equalizer
of economic and social inequities.[3] Thus women's claims to participation, es-

## Women in Legislatures as Percentage of all Elected Officials

| Country | Date | National Level | Intermediate Level | Local Level | Source |
|---|---|---|---|---|---|
| Canada | 1990 | 13.7 | 11.5 | — | Status of Women Canada (1990) |
| Great Britain | 1990 | 6.3 | — | — | British Embassy |
| Greece | 1990 | 5.3 | — | 8.2 (municipal) | Ministry of Internal Affairs |
| India | 1990 | 5.8 | — | — | Embassy of India |
| Japan | 1990 | 5.9 | 4 (prefectural) | 2.3 (municipal) | Kubo (1990) |
| Mexico | 1989 | 12 | 3.2 (state) | 4.5 (municipal) | Embassy of Mexico |
| Nicaragua | 1987 | 13.5 | — | — | U.N. Economic Commission for Latin America (1989) |
| Norway | 1990 | 35 | 40 (county) | 31 (municipal) | Royal Norwegian Embassy (1990) |
| Poland | 1989/90 | 14.8 | — | 10.2 (local authorities) | Official Election Results (1989 & 1990) |
| Palestine | 1986 | 7.7* | — | — | PLO (1989) |
| Spain | 1989 | 7 | — | — | El País (1989) |
| U.S. | 1990 | 5.4 | 16.9 (state) | 14 (county and municipal) | Center for the American Woman in Politics (1990) |
| Uganda | 1990 | 14.4 | — | 15 (local councils) | Directorate for Women's Affairs (1990) |

*Palestine National Council in exile.

pecially in extant political structures, are more acceptable than in countries where the cultural emphasis is more on individual rights and equality of opportunity (e.g., in the United States and Great Britain) rather than equality of results.

It is clear that just getting more women into elected offices will not bring about effective change. The women entering the realm of formal politics need to have training in grass-roots women's movements and to have a feminist agenda to bring with them. While in office, they need to form coalitions with other women politicians, and women's groups and organizations outside the system. The cases of Japan and Norway clearly show the importance of women politicians' grass-roots training, and as Melissa A. Haussman indicates in her comparative chapter on Canadian and U.S. feminists' struggles to obtain constitutional equality guarantees, the alliances between women seeking legislative change and those in political parties and governmental structures are invaluable.

Where access to official governance structures is particularly difficult and cultural ethos does not support women's equality, women develop other strategies for empowerment derived from the women's culture. As Judith Astelarra indicates in her chapter on Spain, women's organizations, even though officially "invisible," developed their own, specific demands and forms of participation that enabled women to voice their concerns and to become involved in actions and campaigns. Although women's groups were not directly involved in shaping political agendas and institutions during the period of democratization after Franco's death, they nevertheless influenced public opinion to such an extent that the government passed a number of laws favorable to women.

Whether or not women succeed in altering political institutions to reflect their numbers or views and demands, they can still achieve a significant degree of empowerment by organizing themselves into groups which articulate the realities of their oppression and help them transform personal relationships and local conditions. The small consciousness-raising group, characteristic of the early stages of the second wave of the feminist movement in many countries and discussed in the chapters on Norway, Spain, Greece, and Mexico, gave many women the strength and support they needed to gain control of their lives. Such collectivities come into being when well-organized mass organizations are not yet in place or when societal conditions do not permit women's movements of greater scope, as in Poland of the 1980s. Frequently, these small groups have served as stepping stones for many women's involvement and participation in a larger, more encompassing women's movement.

Women's movements constitute another important source of strategies for women's empowerment. While such movements have existed in many parts of the world, and not, as has been assumed until recently, only in Western countries, the success of their strategies has depended to a great extent on the societal context within which they have developed and operated. Strong women's movements have come into being in societies which have had both relatively open governmental structures and an ethos of equality (e.g., Norway, Canada) and in those where access to official politics has been denied historically to women and cultural norms have stressed inequality between women and men (e.g., the United States, Japan, and Mexico).

Chafetz and Dworkin (1989) found that urbanization, economic expansion, and the growth of the middle class have been directly related to the development of women's movements all over the world. As increasing numbers of women gained access to education and either found their way to paid employment blocked (as in the first wave of the movements) or gained access to the labor force but encountered inequality of treatment (as in the second wave), women mobilized to change their conditions (Chafetz and Dworkin, 1989: 336–41). Women's movements emerge at times of change and ferment when there are diverse avenues for participation and politicization. Thus, both the first and second waves of the women's movement in the United States came during periods of significant change and development of other social movements (the abolitionist movement in mid-nineteenth century and the civil rights, student, and anti-war movements in the 1960s). This was also the case in Japan, as the early stage of the women's movement coincided with the liberalization period of the 1880s and the more recent phase with the student and union movements of the 1970s. Mexico's golden period of the women's movement took place during the 1930s when a strong workers' movement also flourished. It revived during the 1970s, another period of great social change which spewed forth many social movements. Both waves of the Greek women's movement occurred during times of economic and political change and social unrest.

A strategy used by women's movements in many countries has been consolidation of diverse women's groups and coalition building with women and organizations outside the movement. In order that a women's movement have the ability to present its demands clearly and forcefully it must have a considerable degree of unity, at least on a few major issues, and many women and groups willing and able to work toward getting their demands accepted. In some countries such as Norway and Japan, women's movements have been able to present a rather unified front and have had little trouble agreeing on the most important goals. These societies seem to have relatively homogeneous populations as well as a high degree of acceptance of a separate women's culture. In most countries, however, activists have experienced great difficulty getting women mobilized as a cohesive group. Important divisions among women separate them into interest blocks and identity groups. In the United States, national heritage, race/ethnicity, social class, and sexual orientation constitute sometimes insurmountable barriers between women. In Greece and in Great Britain, ideological differences related to social class and political party affiliation weaken the women's movement.

Nevertheless, as the chapters in the section on women's movements indicate, despite the tendency toward fragmentation, activists frequently are able to mobilize disparate groups behind issues and demands of great importance to many women. Reproductive rights, the election of more women into public offices, equal pay, childcare, as well as environmental and peace issues have the force to unite many women from different backgrounds and ideologies. An effective strategy here is one that recognizes the timeliness of a given issue and does not sacrifice women's diversity in the sole interest of obtaining legislative or other change. It is indeed a precarious balance that needs to be struck between preservation of women's multiple voices and consolidation of interests for a women's movement to be truly successful.

In addition to uniting various women's groups under the auspices of a larger movement, an important strategy used by women's movements is the building of coalitions with groups and organizations outside the movement. Coalition partners include political parties, labor unions, professional organizations, and many others which are perceived as possible allies in women's struggles. Such alliances, however, usually are not conducive to a unified expression of women's demands. As the chapters on Greece and Great Britain indicate, political parties, local authorities, and ideological factions help to diffuse women's issues by subordinating them to more general concerns. On the other hand, Mexico's recent popular women's movement seems to have arrived at a more comfortable alliance between women's groups and political organizations, preserving the movement's autonomy and yet being able to infuse the agendas of the allies with feminist views.

Under what conditions can women's movements be relatively successful in developing alliances without compromising their independence? It seems that a broad-based movement with a strong sense of the few important demands that the general membership can agree on is an important element. Another is the existence of an openness toward change, which is usually substantial at times of social ferment and with the emergence of many new groups and organizations. Finally, as several chapters in this collection indicate, alliances between groups can be strengthened and women's views preserved through linkages between women within the women's movement and those in political parties and other organizations.

Another important strategy used by women's movements in many countries is to increase public awareness of women's issues and concerns and to influence public opinion in favor of women's demands. In societies where mass media technologies are well developed, activists have used printed materials, radio, and television to disseminate feminist messages. Women in Greece, Mexico, Spain, Norway, the United States, and elsewhere have found that while it is not easy to get access to the media, once it is obtained, it can be a powerful mechanism for changing public opinion. As Astelarra has shown, while feminists in Spain had little access to formal political channels, they nevertheless managed to influence public views to such an extent that the government eventually passed legislation favorable to women.

And finally, a strategy frequently used by women activists to change public policy is that of lobbying legislators. Feminists in Greece, Mexico, and Canada have utilized this strategy quite effectively. As Vicky Randall shows in her chapter on Great Britain, lobbying has been the most important strategy for the women's movement in that country during the 1980s in its struggles to hold back the conservative backlash. Lobbying seems to be most effective where activists have control over the definition of the issue which legislators are debating and where they have a vocal, well-organized group which can mobilize quickly a substantial mass of people to write letters, make phone calls, sign petitions, and turn out for demonstrations. As Melissa Haussman indicates, Canadian feminists were much more effective in their use of lobbying for a constitutional equal rights clause than their U.S. counterparts because they defined equal rights in a way that was acceptable within the societal value system (group rights) and sought a substantial backing of women's groups and organizations which could mobilize Canadian women. Canadian feminists were also able to draw on the ties they had established between women's movement organizations and female officeholders as well as on their movement's more institutionalized character.

The comparative chapter on the United States and Canada shows that in order to be able to develop effective strategies to change social policy, women's movement members need to be very much aware of the timing, the political structures with which they have to deal, and the cultural norms and values within which they operate. While it is not possible to predict how successful particular strategies will be, a heightened awareness of the context within which strategies are developed and tried, as well as knowledge of what has been attempted before by movements in other countries, can go a long way toward increasing the chances of success.

While women's movements have flourished in many parts of the world, they have not been a viable avenue for the empowerment of women in a number of societies. The chapters in the last section of this book focus on countries where access to official governance has been long denied to women as well as to the majority of men. In these societies the masses of people have been poor, oppressed, and without a viable voice. To become empowered under such conditions, women have had no choice but to join with men in national liberation movements as in Uganda, Nicaragua, Poland, and Palestine, or in grassroots development movements as in India.

Nationalism has empowered millions of women. It has created pride in indigenous cultures, a demystification of innate superiority of foreign oppressors, and a recognition of community. The development of a national consciousness has allowed many women to feel confident to take part in public debate and in organizing across barriers of social class and political party. As Cynthia Enloe pointed out, however,

> Women do not benefit automatically every time the international system is reordered by a successful nationalist movement. It has taken awareness, questioning and organizing by women inside the nationalist movements to turn nationalism into something good for women. (Enloe, 1989: 13)

As the last five chapters of this book illustrate, nationalist and economic development movements can become important avenues for women's empowerment when women bring their awareness of specific issues and demands into these movements, develop their own organizations, and participate side-by-side with men, and thus are included and recognized in the struggles.

In Nicaragua, where women took part in the Sandinista revolution from the very beginning and where their needs and demands were acknowledged by the leadership (which included women), rather extraordinary public policies were developed, including the recognition that sex roles within the private (family) sphere would need to be altered in order that women may achieve equality. In Uganda, while women had a more difficult time gaining acceptance for their demands within the revolutionary movement, they insisted that equality be extended to all groups, including women, and thus made sure that they took part in all aspects of the revolution and the creation of institutions in the post-revolutionary society. Palestinian women, through their recent committees, have had a substantial effect on the Palestinian nationalist movement, which increasingly has recognized their contributions and recently began to support their struggle against Islamic fundamentalism. And in local villages in India, the inclusion of women in development projects has empowered them to bring about change in the quality of everyday life.

In contrast, the chapter on Poland indicates what happens when women's views and demands are not inserted into a nationalist movement agenda. Women's absence from leadership roles and their lack of participation as representatives of women's interests in Solidarity has resulted in the neglect of women's issues within the new, post-Communist order. Indeed, only the threat of losing the rights attained under the previous regime, especially the right to abortion, has mobilized Polish women to defend their interests and to begin to formulate their own goals and demands.

What strategies have been effective for gaining empowerment through nationalist movements? First and foremost, women involved in nationalist struggles which have recognized women's interests have had to establish their own groups and organizations within the larger movements. Such structures have enabled women to promote the view that, while they share the basic goals of democracy, freedom, and equality with men, they also have specific needs and demands which the movements must address if they are to combat all forms of oppression: foreign domination, class inequality, racism, *and patriarchy*. Thus if women are to be free along with men in the "new" societies that the nationalist movements want to bring about, these movements cannot neglect women's oppression; rather they have to struggle to eradicate it within the revolutionary process itself, and women's liberation must be a vital component of people's liberation in post-revolutionary societies. However, unless women themselves question and organize and press for change within nationalist movements, they are not likely to achieve recognition. Thus the development of women's committees, fronts, and even informal groups within nationalist or revolutionary people's movements are essential for placing women's issues on their agendas and for ensuring the inclusion of women's interests later, when the struggle is won.

Under some conditions it is more difficult for women to confront inequities between the sexes within nationalist movements. The case of Poland is instructive here, since it raises the problem of a false consciousness shaped, on the one hand, by Communist ideology, which in theory gave women equal rights but in practice "protected" them from filling many roles, and, on the other hand, by a longstanding cultural belief that women are weaker than (i.e., inferior to) men. Under such conditions the general perception was that women had the opportunity to be engaged in the same activities as men but because of their "natural" weakness or lack of interest stayed away from traditional male positions. Such views and beliefs carried over into the Solidarity movement, and subsequently into the newly emerging order, and only now are starting to be questioned and discarded by a growing number of Polish women. It is likely that with increased consciousness and mass organization women in Poland will take on their rightful role in shaping a new society.

In summary, it appears that certain strategies in combination with particular societal conditions result in especially successful empowerment of women. The strategy of getting more women into political bodies where they can make a difference seems to work best where governmental voting structures are relatively open, left-wing parties exist, and where cultural values of equality and group rights are firmly embedded. Once in public office, women can be especially effective if they have support of other female elected officials and of women's groups outside government. Nevertheless, when access to formal governance is restricted by the political opportunity structure, it is possible for women's movements to transform official agendas and policies by changing public opinion, particularly through the use of the mass media where such technologies are available.

Women's movements are most effective when they are unified but also able to preserve women's diversity. The strategy of coalition building among women's groups and organizations works best when an issue emerges on which many women can agree (e.g., abortion rights) and when the time is ripe for mobilization of support. Building alliances with groups and organizations outside the women's movement is a particularly viable strategy in times of social ferment, when many new social movements are emerging and there are numerous groups working to bring about social change. However, in order not to become swallowed up by other movements and organizations, the women's movement needs to keep its identity separate and focus on specific goals and agendas.

At times of conservative backlash and lack of public receptivity to women's interests and concerns, an effective strategy for the women's movement has been the lobbying of legislators. The strategy is traditional and therefore not threatening and can be used to keep women's gains from being eroded by new legislation. The success of the strategy depends on women activists seizing the definition of the issue being debated and building coalitions among diverse women's groups and organizations.

Small consciousness-raising groups can empower women to change their personal and immediate circumstances and thus are an important strategy. Such groups can come into being when larger, more encompassing organizations are impossible, for example, when the social climate is such that it will not support mass feminist organizations, and in the early, formative stages of a women's movement.

Finally, joining with men in nationalist and economic development movements becomes a viable strategy for women when they bring into these movements their own interests and agendas. Only then can they be ensured of a meaningful role in the structures which emerge out of such movements. Certain conditions facilitate women's participation as representatives of their group interests in nationalist movements—ideologies which stress equality and participatory democracy, and members' willingness to have women in all positions, including leadership roles. The establishment of women's own organizations within the movements helps women achieve their goals.

The authors of this book offer a number of strategies women have used, and can use in the future, in their struggles to empower themselves. Specific strategies are effective under particular conditions, and I have attempted to point out the circumstances under which given strategies may work. While the basis for the analysis are thirteen countries in different parts of the world, this volume cannot claim to have exhausted the possibilities. Indeed, I view this work as a beginning, and I challenge others to conduct research and to write more about how women have sought effective ways to transform politics all over the world.

# Notes

1. Although Britain has a parliamentary system of government, as Randall points out in her chapter, its highly centralized character is not conducive to the entry of new groups.

2. Under a multiparty, proportional representation system, each geographically defined election unit sends several representatives to the governing body, typically from more than one party, and normally more than one from each of the largest parties. When several persons can represent a party in one constituency, women candidates have a better chance of being nominated and elected.

3. Other Scandinavian countries have this tradition as well. Sweden, Finland, and Iceland also have over one-third women legislators at all governmental levels.

# R E F E R E N C E S

Abu-Ghazaleh, Ilham (1989). "Women in the Poetry of the Intifada," *Al-Katib* (The writer) 110 (June): 65–76.

Agerholt, Anna Caspari (1973) [1937]. *Den Norske Kvinnebevegelses Historie* (History of the Norwegian women's movement). Oslo: Gyldendal.

*Al-Fajr* (The dawn) (1989). August 8, p. 4.

——— (1989). May 22, p. 13.

——— (1988). March 6, p. 5.

——— (1985). March 8, p. 3.

AMNLAE (Luisa Amanda Espinoza Association of Nicaraguan Women) (1989a). *Boletín Quincenal* (Fifteenth bulletin) March 8, Managua.

——— (1989b). *La Mujer en Datos* (Data on women). Managua (pamphlet).

——— (1983). "No Quiero los Colores Sicodelicos de las Ciudades, Amo la Sencillez del Campesino" (I do not like the psychedelic colors of the city, I love the simplicity of the country). Managua.

Andersen, Margaret (1988). *Thinking about Women: Sociological Perspectives on Sex and Gender*. New York: Macmillan.

Anderson, Bonnie S., and Judith P. Zinsser (1987). *A History of Their Own*. New York: Harper and Row.

Andreas, Carol (1985). *When Women Rebel: The Rise of Popular Feminism in Peru*. Westport, CT: Lawrence & Hill.

Antoniewicz, Piotr, and Jan Kazimierski (1988). "Praca Zawodowa w Swiadomosci Zatrudnionych" (Professional work in the consciousness of workers), *Kobieta Lat Osiemdziesiatych* (Women of the eighties). Warsaw: Niezalezna Oficyna Wydawnicza, 129–163.

Antonius, Soraya (1980). "Prisoners for Palestine: A List of Women Political Prisoners," *Journal of Palestine Studies* 9/3(35) (Spring): 25–32.

——— (1979). "Fighting on Two Fronts: Conversations with Palestinian Women," *Journal of Palestine Studies* 7/3(31) (Spring): 38–49.

Arole, R. S. (1987). "Role of Community Participation in Population Programme" (unpublished).

Arthur, Marilyn, et al. (1976). *Conceptual Frameworks for Studying Women's History: Four Papers*. Bronxville, NY: Sarah Lawrence College.

Aruri, Naseer (ed.) (1983). *Occupation: Israel Over Palestine*. Belmont, MA: Association of Arab-American University Graduates.

Ås, Berit (1979). " 'Stå På' Utrettelig Gjennom 20 År: Fra Stortingets Saksarkiv 1947–1966" ("Stand up" enduring relentlessly for 20 years: from parliamentary case records 1947–1966), *Kvinnepolitisk Tiskrift* (Women's political journal) 18 (February ): 45–48.

——— (1975). "On Female Culture: An Attempt to Formulate a Theory of Women's Solidarity and Action," *Acta Sociologica* 18(2/3): 142–161.

Astelarra, Judith (1989). "The Transition to Democracy in Spain," in Yolande Cohen (ed.), *Women and Counter Power*. Montreal: Black Rose Books.

——— (1986). *Las Mujeres Podemos* (We women can do it). Barcelona: Icaria.

Atkinson, Ti-Grace (1970). "Radical Feminism and Love" (mimeographed).

Aubert, Vilhelm (1974). "Stratification," in Natalie Rogoff Ramsøy (ed.), *Norwegian Society*. Oslo: Universitetsforlaget, 108–57.

Avdela, Efi, and Angelika Psarra (1985). *Feminism in the Interwar Period*. Athens: Gnosi (in Greek).

Bakker, Isabella (1988). "Women's Employment in Comparative Perspective," in Jane Jenson et al. (eds.), *Feminization of the Labour Force*. London: Polity Press.

Balasubramanian, Jaishree (1989). "Rural Development in India," *India News* Delhi (August): 18–23.

Banks, Olive (1981). *The Faces of Feminism: A Study of Feminism as a Social Movement.* New York: St. Martin's Press.

Bashevkin, Sylvia (1985). *Toeing the Lines: Women and Party Politics in English Canada.* Toronto: University of Toronto Press.

Baxter, Sandra and Marjorie Lansing (1980). *Women and Politics: The Invisible Majority.* Ann Arbor, Mich: University of Michigan Press.

Belenky, Mary, et al. (1987). *Women's Ways of Knowing.* New York: Basic Books.

Bendt, Ingela, and James Downing (1980). *We Shall Return: Women of Palestine.* London: Zed Books.

Berer, Marge (1988). "Whatever Happened to 'A Women's right to Choose'?" *Feminist Review* 29 (Spring): 62–76.

Berger, Michael (1976). "Japanese Women—Old Images and New Realities," *The Japan Interpreter* 2 (Spring): 51–67.

Bernard, Jessie (1987). *The Female World From a Global Perspective.* Bloomington, IN: Indiana University Press.

Bhasin, Kamla, and Nighat Said Khan (1986). "Some Questions on Feminism and Its Relevance in South Asia." New Delhi: Indraprastha Press (booklet).

Bingham, Marjorie Wall, and Susan Hill Gross (1987). *Women in Japan.* St. Louis Park, MN: Glennhurst.

Bishop, Brenda (1990). "From Women's Rights to Feminist Politics: The Developing Struggle for Women's Liberation in Poland," *Monthly Review* (November ): 15–34.

Black, Naomi (1989). *Social Feminism.* Ithaca, NY: Cornell University Press.

Boles, Janet (1982). "Building Support for the ERA: A Case of 'Too Much, Too Late,' " *PS* 15(4) (Fall): 572–77

———— (1979). *The Politics of the Equal Rights Amendment.* New York: Longman.

Bookman, Ann, and Sandra Morgen (eds.) (1988). *Women and the Politics of Empowerment.* Philadelphia, PA: Temple University Press.

Boserup, Ester (1970). *Women's Role in Economic Development.* London: Allen and Unwin.

Bottorff, David (1990). "Takako Doi: Leading Lady of Political Scene," *The Japan Times Weekly International Edition* February 12–18, sec. A, pp. 1, 4.

Bouton, Marshall M., and Philip Oldenburg (eds.) (1989). *India Briefing, 1989.* Boulder, CO: Westview.

Braveman, Paula, and David Siegel (1986). "Nicaragua: A Health System Developing under Conditions of War," *International Journal of Health Services* 17: 169–178.

Brock-Utne, Birgit (1985). *Educating for Peace: A Feminist Perspective.* New York: Pergamon.

Brodsky, Gwen, and Shelagh Day (1989). *Canadian Charter Equality Rights for Women: One Step Forward or Two Steps Back?* Ottawa: Canadian Advisory Council on the Status of Women.

Bunch-Weeks, Charlotte (1970). "A Broom of One's Own: Notes on the Women's Liberation Program," in Joanne Cooke, Charlotte Bunch-Weeks, and Robin Morgan (eds.), *The New Women.* New York: Bobbs-Merrill, 164–87.

Burack, Cynthia (1988/89). "Bringing Women's Studies to Political Science: The Handmaid in the Classroom," *NWSA Journal* 1(2) (Winter): 274–83.

Bureau for Women's Affairs (1990a). *Sytuacja Prawna Kobiety w Polsce* (Legal situation of woman in Poland). Warsaw.

———— (1990b). *Stan i Cele Programowe Nowych Ruchów Feministycznych w Polsce: Analiza Informacyjnych Ankiet Luty 1990* (Status and program objectives of new feminist movements in Poland: informational analysis survey—February 1990). Warsaw.

———— (1988) *Report of the Government of the Polish People's Republic on the Application of the Convention of 1978 on the Elimination of All Forms of Discrimination Against Women for the Period from 1983 to 1988.* Warsaw.

Burris, Barbara (1973). "The Fourth World Manifesto," in Anne Koedt, Ellen Levine, and Anita Rapone (eds.), *Radical Feminism.* New York: Quadrangle Books.

Burt, Sandra (1988). "The Charter of Rights and the Ad Hoc Lobby: The Limits of Success," *Atlantis* 14(1) (Fall): 74–81.

Buttari, Juan J. (1979). *Employment and Labor Force in Latin America: A Review at National and Regional Levels.* Santiago: Organization of American States.

Bystydzienski, Jill M. (1989). "Women's Political Culture as a Source of Peace." Paper presented at the International Conference on Women and Peace, University of Illinois, Champaign-Urbana (March).

—— (1988). "Women in Politics in Norway," *Women and Politics* 8(3/4): 73–95.

—— (1987). "Women in Politics in Norway." Paper presented at the Third International Interdisciplinary Congress on Women, Dublin, Ireland (July).

Cacoullos, Ann R. (1988). "Women in the Political Life of Greece Today: Notes on Issues and Non-issues." Paper presented at the 14th World Congress of the International Political Science Association, August 28–September 1, Washington, D.C.

Caldecott, Leonie (1983). "At the Foot of the Mountain: The Shibokusa Women of Kitas Fuji," in Lynne Jones (ed.), *Keeping the Peace.* London: The Women's Press.

Carroll, Berenice (1972). "Peace Research: The Cult of Power," *Journal of Conflict Resolution* 6(4): 585–616.

Carroll, Susan J. (1985). *Women as Candidates in American Politics.* Bloomington, IN: Indiana University Press.

—— (1975). "Women's Rights and Political Parties: Issue Development, the 1972 Conventions, and the National Women's Political Caucus." Master's thesis, Indiana University.

—— and Ella Taylor (1989). "Gender Differences in Policy Priorities of U.S. State Legislators." Paper presented at the Annual Meeting of the American Political Science Association, Atlanta, Georgia (Aug. 31–Sept. 3).

Center for the American Woman in Politics (1990). "Women in Elective Office 1990," New Brunswick, NJ: CAWP (fact sheet).

—— (1989). "News and Notes" (Winter) New Brunswick, NJ: CAWP.

—— (1989). "News and Notes" (Spring) New Brunswick, NJ: CAWP.

—— (1984). "Women Make a Difference." Report in the series Bringing More Women Into Public Office. New Brunswick, NJ: CAWP.

Centro de Comunicación Internacional (1987). *How Do You Do, Nicaragua?* Managua.

Chafetz, Janet Saltzman, and Anthony Gary Dworkin (1989). "Action and Reaction: An Integrated, Comparative Perspective on Feminist and Antifeminist Movements," in Melvin A. Kohn (ed.), *Cross-National Research in Sociology.* Newbury Park, CA: Sage, 329–50.

Chaki-Sirear, Manjusri (1984). *Feminism in a Traditional Society: Women of the Manipar Valley.* New Delhi: Shakti Books.

Charlton, Sue Ellen M. (1984). *Women in Third World Development.* Boulder, CO: Westview Press.

Chodorow, Nancy (1978). *The Reproduction of Mothering, Psychoanalysis and the Sociology of Gender.* Berkeley: University of California Press.

Christian, William and Colin Campbell (1989). "Political Parties and Ideologies in Canada," in Alain G. Gagnon and A. Brian Tanguay (eds.), *Canadian Parties in Transition.* Scarborough, Ont.: Nelson Canada, 45–63.

Ciechomska, Maria, and Jolanta Plakwicz (1989) (unpublished manuscript).

Cohen, Yolande (1989). *Women and Counter Power.* Montreal: Black Rose Books.

Cook, Blanch Wiesen (1977). "Female Support Networks and Political Activism: Lillian Wald, Crystal Eastman, Emma Goldman," *Chrysalis* 3: 43–61.

Cott, Nancy F. (1977). *The Bonds of Womanhood: 'Women's Sphere' in New England, 1780–1835*. New Haven, CT: Yale University Press.

Croll, Elisabeth (1980). *Feminism and Socialism in China*. New York: Schocken Books.

Crossette, Barbara (1989). "India Studying 'Accidental' Deaths of Hindu Wives," *The New York Times International*, January 15: 2.

Dagash, Jamilah (1989). "This is the Palestinian Woman," *Al Ghadd* (The tomorrow) (March): 24.

Dahlerup, Drude (ed.) (1986). *The New Women's Movement*. London: Sage.

Darcy, R., Susan Welch, and Janet Clark (1987). *Women, Elections and Representation*. New York: Longman.

David, Miriam (1986). "Moral and Maternal: The Family in the Right," in Ruth Levitas (ed.), *The Ideology of the New Right*. London: Polity Press.

Desai, Meera, and Maithreyi Krishnaraj (1987). *Women and Society in India*. New Delhi: Ajanta.

DeSantis, Marie (1990). "Nicaraguan Women Under Attack," *Against the Current* (September/October): 10.

Directorate of Women's Affairs (1990). "A Paper on the Role of Ugandan Women in Politics," Report to Directorate of External Relations/Permanent Uganda Delegation to UNESCO, April 11.

Downs, Anthony (1957). *An Economic Theory of Democracy*. New York: Harper and Row.

Dubinsky, Karen (1985). *Lament for 'Patriarchy Lost'? Anti-Feminism, Anti-Abortion, and R.E.A.L. Women in Canada*. Ottawa: Canadian Research Institute for the Advancement of Women.

Dublin, Thomas (1979). *Women at Work: The Transformation of Work and Community in Lowell*. New York: Columbia University Press.

DuBois, Ellen, et al. (1980). "Politics and Culture in Women's History: A Symposium," *Feminist Studies* 6 (Spring): 26–64.

——— (1985). *Feminist Scholarship: Kindling in the Groves of Academe*. Urbana, IL: University of Illinois Press.

Dunbar, A. R. (1965). *A History of Bunyoro-Kitara*. Nairobi: Oxford University Press.

Dunbar, Roxanne (1975). "Female Liberation as the Basis for Social Revolution," in Mary Lou Thompson (ed.), *Voices of the New Feminism*. Boston: Beacon Press, pp. 44–58.

Duran, M. A., and M. T. Gallego (1986). "The Women's Movement in Spain and the New Spanish Democracy," in Drude Dahlerup (ed.), *The New Women's Movement*. London: Sage.

Duverger, Maurice (1964). *Political Parties*. London: Methuen.

Duverger, Michael (1955). *The Political Role of Women*. New York: UNESCO.

Echols, Alice (1989). *Daring to Be Bad: Radical Feminism in America 1967–1975*. Minneapolis, MN: University of Minnesota Press.

Eckstein-Diener, Bette (1965). *Mothers and Amazons: The First Feminine History of Culture*. New York: Julian Press.

Edelman, Marc (1988). "Soviet-Nicaraguan Relations and the Contra War," *International Journal of World Peace* 5 (July–September): 45–67.

Edwards, Julia (1989). "Women's Committees: A Model for Good Local Government?" *Policy and Politics* 17(3): 5–17.

——— (1988). "Local Government Women's Committees," *Critical Social Policy* 8(3): 52–64.

Eisenstein, Hester (1983). *Contemporary Feminist Thought*. Boston: K. G. Hall.

Enigrac (1989). *Canciones de la Lucha Sandinista* (Songs of the Sandinista struggle). Managua (pamphlet and two cassettes).

Enloe, Cynthia (1989). *Bananas, Beaches and Bases: Making Feminist Sense of International Politics*. Berkeley, CA: University of California

Enriquez, Magda (1985). "We Women Learned What We Were Capable of Doing," in *Nicaragua: The Sandinista People's Revolution; Speeches by Sandinista Leaders.* New York: Pathfinders Press.

Epstein, Scarlett T., and Rosemary A. Watts (eds.) (1981). *The Endless Day: Some Case Material on Asian Rural Women.* Oxford: Pergamon.

Evans, Judith, et al. (1986). *Feminism and Political Theory.* London: Sage.

Evans, R. J. (1977). *The Feminists: Women's Emancipation Movements in Europe, America and Australasia, 1840–1920.* London: Croom Helm.

Felsenthal, Carol (1982). *The Biography of Phyllis Schlafly: The Sweetheart of the Silent Majority.* Chicago: Regnery Gateway.

"Feminismo y Movimiento Popular en Mexico" (Feminism and popular movement in Mexico) (1986). *Memoria de las Jornadas Feministas* (Memory of feminist journeys). Mexico: Planeta.

Ferree, Myra Marx, and Beth B. Hess (1985). *Controversy and Coalition: The Feminist Movement.* Boston: Twayne.

Firestone, Shulamith (1970). *The Dialectic of Sex: The Case for Feminist Revolution.* New York: William Morrow.

Flora, C. B. and N. B. Lynn (1974). "Women and Political Socialization: Consideration of the Input of Motherhood," in Jane Jacquette (ed.), *Women in Politics.* New York: John Wiley.

Førde, Britt Fougner, and Helga Maria Hernes (1988). "Gender Equality in Norway," *Canadian Woman Studies* 9(2) (Summer): 27–30.

Franda, Marcus (1979). *India's Rural Development: An Assessment of Alternatives.* Bloomington, IN: Indiana University Press.

Freedman, Estelle (1979). "Separatism as a Strategy: Female Institution Building and American Feminism, 1870–1930," *Feminist Studies* 3 (Fall): 512–29.

Freeman, Jo (1983). "Women and Public Policy: An Overview," in Ellen Boneparth (ed.), *Women, Power and Policy.* New York: Pergamon.

——— (1979). "The Women's Liberation Movement: Its Origins, Organizations, Activities and Ideas," in Jo Freeman (ed.), *Women: A Feminist Perspective.* Berkeley, CA: Mayfield.

——— (1975). *The Politics of Women's Liberation.* New York: Longman.

Friedel, Ernestine (1975). *Women and Men: An Anthropologist's View.* New York: Holt, Rinehart and Winston.

FSLN (Frente Sandinista de Liberación Nacional) (1987). *Women and the Sandinista Revolution.* Managua Directorate, La Vanguardia.

Garber-Katz, Elaine, and Jenny Horsman (1988). "Is It Her Voice If She Speaks Their Words?" *Canadian Woman Studies* 9(3/4) (Fall/Winter): 117–20.

Garfield, Richard M., and Sten H. Vermund (1986). "Health Education and Community Participation in Mass Drug Administration for Malaria in Nicaragua," *Social Science and Medicine* 22: 869–977.

Gelb, Joyce, and Marian Palley (1987) *Women and Public Policies.* Princeton, NJ: Princeton University Press.

Gicolini, Cristina Gonzales (1987). *El Movimiento Feminista en Mexico: Aportes para su Análisis* (The feminist movement in Mexico: contributions to its analysis). Master's thesis, National Autonomous University of Mexico, Mexico City.

Gilkes, Cheryl Townsend (1985). "Together and in Harness: Women's Traditions in the Sanctified Church," *Signs* 10(4) (Summer): 678–99.

Gilligan, Carol (1982). *In A Different Voice.* Cambridge, MA: Harvard University Press.

Gittell, Marilyn, and Teresa Shtob (1980). "Changing Women's Roles in Political Voluntarism and Reform of the City," *Signs* 5(3 supplement): S67–78.

Gonzales, Anabel (1979). *El Feminismo en España Hoy* (Feminism in Spain today). Madrid: Zero-zyx.

Graham-Brown, Sarah (1987). "Feminism in Egypt: A Conversation with Nawal Sadawi," *MERIP Reports* (March–April): 27.

Gray, Virginia (1983). "Innovation in the States," *American Political Science Review* 67: 1174–1193.

Grimshaw, Jean (1987). *Philosophy and Feminist Thinking*. Minneapolis, MN: University of Minnesota Press.

Grupo Pancasan (1985). *Pancasan*. Managua: Enigrac.

GUS (Główny Urząd Statystyczny) (1988). *Rocznik Statystyczny* (Statistical yearbook). Warsaw.

—— (1986). *Rocznik Statystyczny* (Statistical yearbook). Warsaw.

—— (1985). *Kobieta w Polsce* (Woman in Poland). Warsaw.

—— (1985). *Rocznik Statystyczny* (Statistical yearbook). Warsaw.

—— (1970). *Rocznik Statystyczny* (Statistical yearbook). Warsaw.

Haavio-Mannila, Elina, et al. (1985). *Unfinished Democracy: Women in Nordic Politics*. Oxford: Pergamon.

Halabi, Rafik (1981). *The West Bank Story*. New York: Harcourt, Brace, Jovanovich.

Hammami, Rema (1990). "Women, the Hijab and the Intifada," *Middle East Report* (May/August): 24–28.

Havens, Thomas R. H. (1975). "Women and War in Japan, 1937–45," *The American Historical Review* 80(4) (October): 921–32.

Hazarika, Sanjoy (1981). "Past Threatens the Future of Indian Women," *The New York Times* December 6, sec. C, p. 5.

Heeger, Gerald A. (1974). *The Politics of Underdevelopment*. New York: St. Martin's Press.

Heinen, Jane (1988). "Women in Eastern Europe Today: Liberation or Patriarchy?" *Against the Current*, 14–20.

Hernes, Helga Maria, and Eva Hanninen-Salmelin (1985). "Women in the Corporate System," in Elina Haavio Mannila et al. (eds.), *Unfinished Democracy: Women in Nordic Politics*. Oxford: Pergamon.

—— (1984). *The Role of Women in Voluntary Associations and Organizations*. Part III of The Situation of Women in the Political Process in Europe. Strasbourg: Council of Europe.

Hiltermann, Joost (1988). "Before the Uprising: The Organization of Palestinian Workers and Women in the Israeli Occupied West Bank and Gaza Strip," Ph.D. dissertation, University of California at Santa Cruz.

Hoff-Wilson, Joan (ed.) (1986). *Rights of Passage: The Past and Future of the ERA*. Bloomington, IN: Indiana University Press.

Holter, Harriet (1970). *Sex Roles and Social Structure*. Oslo: Universitetsforlaget.

Hooks, Bell (1981). *Ain't I a Woman: Black Women and Feminism*. Boston: South End Press.

Hosek, Chaviva (1983). "Women and the Constitutional Process," in Keith Banting and Richard Simeon (eds.), *And No One Cheered: Federalism, Democracy and the Constitution Act*. Toronto: Methuen, 280–300.

Huber, Joan (1990). "Macro-Micro Links in Gender Stratification," *American Sociological Review* 55(1) (February): 1–10.

Humphries, Jane, and Jill Rubery (1988). "British Women in a Changing Workplace, 1979–1988," in Jane Jenson et al. (eds.), *Feminization of the Labour Force*. London: Polity Press.

*Información Costureras: Un Sidicato Nacido de los Escombros* (Seamstress' information: a union born out of the rubble) (1986). Mexico: Información Obrera-Equipo Pueblo.

Instituto I.D.E.S. (1988). *Las Españolas ante la Política* (Spanish women and politics). Madrid: Instituto de la Mujer, Ministerio de Asuntos Sociales.

—— (1987). *Estudio Sociológico Sobre las Actitudes de las Mujeres Ante la Política y al Feminismo* (A sociological study of the attitudes of women toward politics and feminism). Madrid: Instituto de la Mujer, Ministerio de Cultura.

Jaggar, Alison M. (1983). *Feminist Politics and Human Nature*. Totowa, NJ: Rowman & Allanheld.

Jaiven, Ana Lau (1987). *La Nueva Ola del Feminismo en Mexico* (The new wave of feminism in Mexico). Mexico: Planeta.

Jancar, Barbara Wolfe (1985). "Women in Opposition in Poland and Czechoslovakia in the 1970s," in S. L. Wolchik and A. G. Meyer (eds.), *Women, State and Party in Eastern Europe*. Durham, NC: Duke University Press.

—— (1978). *Women Under Communism*. Baltimore, MD: Johns Hopkins University Press.

Jasiewicz, Krzysztof (1979). *Role Społeczne Radnych Wojewódzkich Rad Narodowych* (The social role of provincial council members). Wroclaw: Zakład Narodowy Imienia Osolinskich.

Jayawardena, Kumari (1986). *Feminism and Nationalism in the Third World*. London: Zed Books.

Jenson, Jane (1989). "Paradigms and Political Discourse: Protective Legislation in France and the United States Before 1914," *Canadian Journal of Political Science* 22(2) (June): 234–58.

—— (1987). Changing Discourse, Changing Agendas: Political Rights and Reproductive Policies in France," in Mary F. Katzenstein and Carol M. Mueller (eds.), *The Women's Movement of the United States and Western Europe*. Philadelphia: Temple University Press, 64–88.

—— (1985). "Struggling for Identity: The Women's Movement and the State in Western Europe," *West European Politics* 8 (4) (October): 5–18.

Joseph, Suad (1986). "Women and Politics in the Middle East," *Middle East Report* (January–February): 3.

Kalsoyia-Tournaviti, Niki (1982). "The Feminist Movement in Greece," *Women's Struggle* 15: 12–16 (in Greek).

Kanter, Rosabeth Moss (1977). *Men and Women of the Corporation*. New York: Basic Books.

Karkal, Malina, and Divya Pandey (1989). *Studies on Women and Population*. Bombay: Himalaya Publishing House.

Kawai, Michi, and Ochimi Kubushiro (1934). *Japanese Women Speak*. Boston: The Central Committee on the United Study of Foreign Missions.

Khader, Sami (1988). "Illiteracy among Palestinian Women: Its Incidence, Effects, and Suggested Remedies," *Al-Katib* (The writer) 101 (September): 51–74.

Khaled, Leila (1973). *My People Shall Live: The Autobiography of a Revolutionary*. London: Hodder and Stoughton.

Khalifah, Ijlal (1974). *Al-Mar'ah Wa Kadiyyat Falastine* (Women and the Palestinian cause). Cairo: Modern Arabic Press.

Khorsheid, Ghazi (1972). "The Palestinian Resistance and Social Work," *Shu'un Falastiniyyah* (Palestinian affairs) (January): 104–22.

Kiwanuka, M. S. M. (1972). *A History of Buganda from the Foundation of the Kingdom to 1900*. New York: Africana.

Klein, Ethel (1984). *Gender Politics*. Cambridge, MA: Harvard University Press.

Klein, Vera, and Alva Myrdal (1956). *Women's Two Roles: Home and Work*. London: Kegan Paul.

Kome, Penney (1983). *The Taking of Twenty-Eight: Women Challenge the Constitution*. Toronto: Women's Press.

Kothari, Jajni (1983). "Party and State in Our Time: The Rise of Non-Party Political Formations," *Alternatives* 9: 551–64.

Kubo, Kimiko (1990). "Japanese Women's Participation in Politics." Paper presented at the Fourth International Interdisciplinary Congress on Women, Hunter College, New York (June).

Kuttab, Eileen, and Khalidah Al-Ratrout (1988). "Women's Cooperative Experience:

The Cooperatives of Beitello and Sa'ir," *Developmental Affairs* (East Jerusalem) (December): 24–26.

Lafferty, William M. (1981). *Participation and Democracy in Norway.* Oslo: Universitetsforlaget.

Lamas, Marta (1989). "Las Mujeres y las Políticas Publicas, un Tema que Puede Expresarse desde sus Extremos" (Women and public politics, a topic which may be expressed in extreme form), *Doblejornada,* supplement to *La Jornada,* June 5, p. 10.

Lasser, Carol (1988). " 'Let Us Be Sisters Forever': The Sororal Model of Nineteenth Century Female Friendship," *Signs* 14(1) (Autumn): 158–81.

Latouche, Daniel (1990). "Quebec and Canada: Scenarios for the Future," *Business in the Contemporary World* 3(1) (Autumn): 58–70.

Leacock, Eleanor B. (1972). "Introduction," in Frederick Engels, *Origin of the Family, Private Property and the State.* New York: International Publishers.

Lenz, Elinor, and Barabara Myerhoff (1985). *The Feminization of America: How Women's Values Are Changing Our Public and Private Lives.* Los Angeles, CA: Jeremy P. Tarcher.

Lerner, Gerda (1986). *The Creation of Patriarchy.* New York: Oxford University Press.

Levy, Darlene G., and Harriet B. Applewhite. "Women of the Popular Classes in Revolutionary Paris, 1789–1795," in Carol R. Berkin and Clara M. Lovett (eds.), *Women, War and Revolution.* New York: Holmes and Meier.

Lewis, Harriet (1989). "It is Possible to Agree on Principles: An Interview with Hanan Mikhail-Ashrami," *New Outlook* (June/July): 7.

Limberes, Nickolas (1986). "Mass Voting Behavior: The Factors that Influenced the Conservative Vote During the 1981 Greek Election," *European Journal of Political Research* 2: 113–37.

Lobao, Linda (1990). "Women in Revolutionary Movements: Changing Patterns of Latin American Guerilla Struggle," in Guida West and Rhoda Lois Blumberg (eds.), *Women and Social Protest.* London: Oxford University Press.

——— (1987). "Women in Revolutionary Movements," (unpublished paper).

Łobodzinska, Barbara (1970). *Małżeństwo w Mieście* (Marriage in the city). Warsaw: PWN.

Lorde, Audre (1984). *Sister Outside.* Trumansburg, NY: Crossing Press.

Lovenduski, Joni (1989). "Implementing Equal Opportunities in the 1980s: An Overview," *Public Administration* 67 (Spring): 42–59.

——— (1986). *Women and European Politics.* Brighton: Harvester Press.

——— and Vicky Randall (1990). "Feminist Perspectives on Thatcherism," *Talking Politics* 2(2): 23–34.

Lovera, Sara (1990). "El Coraje Organizado—Invaluable Lección de Jovenes Violadas; El Movimiento Feminista Debe Replantear Estrategias" (Organized courage—invaluable lessons of raped women; the feminist movement needs to reaffirm strategies), *Doblejornada,* supplement to *La Jornada,* February 6, p. 5.

Maier, Elizabeth (1985). *Las Sandinistas.* Mexico D.F.: Ediciónes de Cultura Popular.

Mamdani, Mahnood (1983). *Imperialism and Fascism in Uganda.* London: Heinemann Educational Books.

Manasrah, Najah (1989). "Early Marriage: Temporary Retreat in the March of Palestinian Women," *Al-Katib* (The writer) 112 (August): 24–31.

——— (1988). "Has Women's Status Kept Up with Their Role in Events?" *Al-Katib* (The writer) 97 (May): 4–58.

Mandel, Michael (1989). *The Charter of Rights and the Legalization of Politics in Canada.* Toronto: Wall and Thompson.

Mansbridge, Jane J. (1986). *Why We Lost the ERA.* Chicago: University of Chicago Press.

Marshall, Tyler (1981). "Extra 12 Million Shocks India Census Takers," *International Herald Tribune* May 6, p. 3.

Mayer, Elizabeth (1989). "Encuentros Cotidianos con la Antidemocracia: Un Punto de Vista de Genero/Clase" (Everyday encounters with anti-democracy: a gender/ class point of view), *Doblejornada,* supplement to *La Jornada* September 22, p. 16.

Mayo, Marjorie (1977). *Women in the Community.* London: Routledge & Kegan Paul.

McAdam, Doug (1987). "Gender Implications of the Traditional Academic Conception of the Political," in Susan Hardy Aiken et al. (eds.), *Changing Our Minds: Feminist Transformations of Knowledge.* Albany, NY: State University of New York Press.

McCormack, Thelma (1975). "Towards a Non-Sexist Perspective on Social and Political Change," in Marcia Millman and Rosabeth Moss Kanter (eds.), *Another Voice.* Garden City, NY: Doubleday-Anchor.

McCourt, Kathleen (1977). *Working Class Women and Grass Roots Politics.* Bloomington, IN: Indiana University Press.

McWilliams, Norma (1974). "Contemporary Feminism, Consciousness Raising and Changing Views of the Political," in Jane S. Jaquette, *Women in Politics.* New York: John Wiley.

Meehan, Elizabeth (1985). *Women's Rights at Work.* New York: Macmillan.

Melder, Keith E. (1977). *Beginnings of Sisterhood: The American Women's Rights Movement, 1800–1850.* New York: Schocken Books.

Miller, Sally (1981). *Flawed Liberation: Socialism and Feminism.* Westport, CT: Greenwood Press.

Millett, Kate (1971). *Sexual Politics.* New York: Avon Books.

Milne, David (1989). *The Canadian Constitution: From Patriation to Meech Lake.* Toronto: James Lorimer.

Minces, Juliette (1980). "Women in Algeria," in Lois Beck and Nikki Keddie (eds.), *Women in the Muslim World.* Cambridge, MA: Harvard University Press.

Ministry of Consumer Affairs and Government Administration (1985a). *The Norwegian Equal Status Act With Comments.* Oslo: Norwegian Central Information Service.

——— (1985b). *The Norwegian Plan of Action and Other Measures Related to Equality Between the Sexes.* Oslo: Norwegian Central Information Service.

Monsivais, Carlos (1987). "Notas Para Una Crónica del Feminismo en Mexico" (Notes on the chronology of the feminist movement in Mexico), *Casa del Tiempo* (House of time) 71 (May–June): 13–17.

——— (1986). *Entrada Libre* (Free entrance). Mexico: Editorial ERA.

Moraes, Frank, and E. A. Howe (eds.) (1974). *John Kenneth Galbraith Introduces India.* Delhi: Vikas.

Moraga, Cherrie, and Gloria Azaldua (eds.) (1981). *This Bridge Called My Back: Writings of Radical Women of Color.* Watertown, MA: Persephone Press.

Moreno, Amparo (1977). *Mujeres an Lucha: El Movimiento Feminista en la España* (Women in battle: the feminist movement in Spain). Barcelona: Anagrama.

Mouzelis, Nicos (1978). *Modern Greece: Facets of Underdevelopment.* London: Macmillan.

Mueller, Carol (1984). "Women's Organizational Strategies in State Legislatures," in Janet A. Flammang (ed.), *Political Women: Current Roles in State and Local Government.* Beverly Hills, CA: Sage.

Myrdal, Alva and Gunnar Myrdal (1935). *Kris i Belfolknigsfragan* (Crisis in the population question). Stockholm: Libe.

Nelson, D. N. (1985). "Women in Local Communist Politics in Romania and Poland," in S. L. Wolchik and A. G. Meyer (eds.), *Women, State and Party in Eastern Europe.* Durham, NC: Duke University Press.

Norris, Pippa (1987). *Politics and Sexual Equality: The Comparative Position of Women in Western Democracies.* Boulder, CO: Lynne Reiner.

Obbo, Christine (1980). *African Women: Their Struggle for Economic Independence.* London: Zed Books.

O'Neill, William L. (1969). *The Woman Movement: Feminism in the United States and England.* London: Allen & Unwin.

Overholser, Geneva (1987). "Would Women Govern Differently?" *The New York Times* June 15, sec. A, p. 17.

*Palestine/Israel Bulletin* (1986). "Movement of Democratic Women in Israel," (January): 5.

Palmer, Monte (1989). *Dilemmas of Political Development.* Itasca, IL: Peacock.

Papachristou, A. K. (1982). "The Ideological Function of the Family Law," in *The File of Equality.* Athens: Odysseas, 79–94 (in Greek).

Papageorgiou-Limberes, Yota (1988). "Conventional Political Involvement of Greek Women," *Journal of Political and Military Sociology* 16 (Spring): 31–41.

Paulson, Joy (1978). "Evolution of the Feminine Ideal," in Joyce Lebra, Joy Paulson, and Elizabeth Powers (eds.), *Women in Changing Japan.* Stanford, CA: Stanford University Press.

Pesa, Flavia (1985). "The Image of Women in Palestinian Literature," *Al-Fajr* (The dawn) March 15, p. 11.

Peteet, Julie (1986). "No Going Back: Women and the Palestinian Movement," *Middle East Report* (January–February): 11.

Peterson, Esther (1983). "The Kennedy Commission," in Irene Tinker (ed.), *Women in Washington.* Beverly Hills, CA: Sage, 21–34.

Pfeffer, Naomi (1983). *The Experience of Infertility.* London: Virago.

PFWAC (Palestinian Federation of Women's Action Committees) (1989). *Newsletter* (March).

———— (1989). *Newsletter* (June).

———— (1988). *Newsletter.*

———— (1987a). *Darb el-Mara'ah* (Women's path).

———— (1987b). *The Development of the Palestinian Women's Movement in the Territories Occupied in 1967.*

———— (1987c). *Newsletter.*

———— (1987). *Newsletter* (June).

———— (1987). *Newsletter* (September).

———— (1986). *Masirat al-Mara'ah* (Women's march).

Pharr, Susan J. (1981). *Political Women in Japan.* Berkeley, CA: University of California Press.

Piven, Francis Fox, and Richard A. Cloward (1979). *Poor People's Movements: Why They Succeed, How They Fail.* New York: Vintage Books.

Polish Feminist Association (1987). (unpublished manuscript).

Pomian, Anna (1989). "Political Activism and Its Consequences for Polish Women," *Polish Independent Press Review* August 26, pp. 23–29.

Poulanzas, Nicos (1976). *The Crisis of the Dictatorship: Portugal, Greece, Spain.* London: Humanities Press.

PUWWC (Palestinian Union of Working Women's Committees) (1987). *Newsletter* (June 5).

PWWC (Palestinian Working Women's Committees) (1989). *Nisa'a el-Intifada* (Women of the Intifada) (March 8).

———— (1985). *Nidal al-Maraa Al Amila* (Working women's struggle) (March).

Randall, Margaret (1981). *Sandino's Daughters: Testimonies of Nicaraguan Writers.* Edited by Linda Yang. Vancouver: New Star Books.

Randall, Vicky (1987). *Women and Politics: An International Perspective.* Chicago, IL: University of Chicago Press.

Rawalt, Margaret (1983). "The Equal Rights Amendment," in Irene Tinker (ed.), *Women in Washington.* Beverly Hills, CA: Sage, 49–78.

Regent Lechowicz, Maria (1990). "Political Rights of Women," *Legal Situation of Women in Poland.* Warsaw: Bureau of Women's Affairs.

Report of the Secretary General of the United Nations and the Commission on the

Status of Women (1970). *Participation of Women in the Economic and Social Development of Their Countries.* New York: United Nations.

República de Nicaragua (1964). *Censos Nacionales 1963* (National census of 1963). Population Volume I. Managua: Ministerio de Economia, Dirección General de Estadística y Censos.

Riley, Kathryn (1990). "Equality for Women—The Role of Local Authorities," *Local Government Studies* (January/February): 52–73.

Ringelheim, Joan M. (1985). "Women and the Holocaust: A Reconsideration of Research," *Signs* 10(4) (Summer): 741–61.

Robins-Mowry, Dorothy (1983). *The Hidden Sun: Women of Modern Japan.* Boulder, CO: Westview Press.

Rogers, Barbara (1983). *The Domestication of Women: Discrimination in Developing Societies.* New York: St. Martin's Press.

Rolfsen, Karl (1977). "Sol og Vind og Kvinnesinn" (Sun and wind and women's minds). *Økologi* 8(3): 40–43.

Rossi, Alice (1977). "A Biosocial Perspective on Parenting," *Daedalus* 106(2) (Spring): 1–31.

Royal Norwegian Embassy (1989). "Non-Socialist Coalition Takes Over," *News of Norway* (October/November): 57, 63.

Ruchwarger, Gary (1987). *People in Power: Forging a Grassroots Democracy in Nicaragua.* South Hadley, MA: Bergin & Garvey.

Ruddick, Sara (1988). *Maternal Thinking: Toward a Politics of Peace.* Boston, MA: Beacon Press.

Rule, Wilma (1981). "Why Women Don't Run: The Critical Contextual Factors in Women's Legislative Recruitment," *The Western Political Quarterly* 34(1): 60–77.

Sachs, Carolyn E. (1983). *The Invisible Farmers: Women in Agricultural Production.* New York: Rowman & Allenheld.

Said, Manar (1985). "Maternity: High Risk in the West Bank," *Al-Fajr* (The dawn) March 8, p. 7.

Sano, Noriko (1980). "Japanese Women's Movement During World War II," *Feminist International* 2 (Tokyo): 12–28.

Sayigh, Rosemary (1986). "Palestinian Women and Politics in Lebanon," Proceedings from a symposium on Women and Arab Society: Old Boundaries, New Frontiers. Washington, D.C.: Georgetown University, CCAS.

——— (1984). "The Mukhabarat State: Testimony of a Palestinian Woman Prisoner," *Race and Class* 26 (4) (Autumn): 7–15.

——— (1983). "Women in Struggle," *Third World Quarterly* 5(4) (October): 28–41.

Scanlon, Geraldine (1978). *La Polémica Feminista en la España Contemporánea, 1968–1974* (The feminist debate in contemporary Spain, 1968–1974). Madrid: Siglo XXI Editores.

Schlafly, Phyllis (1977). *The Power of the Positive Woman.* New York: Jove.

Schlegal, Alice (1977). *Sexual Stratification: A Cross-Cultural View.* New York: Columbia University Press.

Schoenberg, Sandra Perlman (1980). "Some Trends in the Community Participation of Women in Their Neighborhoods," *Signs* 5(3 supplement): S261–68.

Scott, Barbara Ann (1989). "Let Women Make Peace for a Change." Paper presented at the International Conference on Women and Peace, University of Illinois, Champaign-Urbana (March).

Sharma, Kumud, Sahda Hussain, and Archana Saharya (1984). *Women in Focus: A Community in Search of Equal Roles.* New Delhi: Sangam Books.

Sheridan, Diana Brown (1988). "Empowering Women's Voice: Strategies of Norwegian Peacemaking Women," *Women's Studies in Communication* 11 (Spring): 37–49.

Sieminska, Renata (1986). "Women and Social Movements in Poland," *Women and Politics* 6(4): 5–35.

Sievers, Sharon L. (1983). *Flowers in Salt: The Beginning of Feminist Consciousness in Modern Japan*. Stanford, CA: Stanford University Press.

Siltanen, Janet, and Michelle Stanworth (eds.) (1984). *Women and the Public Sphere: A Critique of Sociology and Politics*. London: Hutchison.

Singh, Rash Bihari Prasad (1986). *Social Welfare for Rural Development: A Case Study*. New Delhi: Inter-India Publications.

Sinkkonnen, Sirkka (1985). "Women in Local Politics," in Elina Haavio-Mannila et al. (eds.), *Unfinished Democracy: Women in Nordic Politics*. Oxford: Pergamon.

Sipila, Helvi (1973). "Third World Woman, Master of Her Own Destiny," *UNICEF News*. New York: United Nations, UNICEF Public Information Division.

Sivard, Ruth Leger (1985). *Women . . . A World Survey*. Washington, D.C.: World Priorities.

Skard, Åse Gruda (1953). *Kvinnesak Tredje Akt* (The women's cause, third act). Oslo: Women's Rights Organization.

Skard, Torild, and Elina Haavio-Mannila (1985). "Women in Parliament," in Elina Haavio-Mannila et al. (eds.), *Unfinished Democracy: Women in Nordic Politics*. New York: Pergamon.

—— (1980). *Utvalgt til Stortinget* (Chosen for parliament). Oslo: Gyldendal.

Smith, Jane (1980). *Women in Contemporary Muslim Societies*. London: Associated University Press.

Smith-Rosenberg, Carroll (1975). "The Female World of Love and Ritual: Relations Between Women in Nineteenth Century America," *Signs* 1: 1–29.

Sokolowska, Magdalena (1977). "Poland: Women's Experience under Socialism," in J. Zollinger Giele and Audrey Chapman Smock (eds.), *Women: Roles and Status in Eight Countries*. New York: John Wiley, 347–83.

South, J. S., et al. (1982). "Social Structure and Group Interaction: Men and Women of the Federal Bureaucracy," *American Journal of Sociology* 47: 587–99.

Spangler, Evelyn, et al. (1978). "Token Women: An Empirical Test of Kanter's Hypothesis," *American Journal of Sociology* 84: 160–70.

Spear, Percival (1972). *India: A Modern History*. Ann Arbor, MI: University of Michigan Press.

Srinivas, Mysore N. (1987). *The Dominant Caste and Other Essays*. New Delhi: Oxford University Press.

—— (1969). *Social Change in Modern India*. Berkeley, CA: University of California Press.

—— (1960). *India's Villages*. Bombay: Asia Publishing House.

Stacey, Margaret, and Marion Price (1981). *Women, Power and Politics*. London: Tavistock.

Stack, Carol (1974). *All Our Kin: Strategies for Survival in a Black Community*. New York: Harper & Row.

Stamiris, Eleni (1986). "The Greek Women's Movement," *New Left Review* 158 (July–August): 98–112.

Stamm, Liesa, and Carol B. Ryff (eds.) (1984). *Social Power and Influence of Women*. Boulder, CO: Westview Press.

Swantz, Marja-Liisa (1985). *Women in Development: A Creative Role Denied? The Case of Tanzania*. New York: St. Martin's Press.

Swedenburg, Ted (1985/86). "Problems of Oral History: The 1936 Revolt in Palestine," *Birzeit Research Review* 2 (Winter): 33.

Talhami, Ghada (1985). "History of Palestinian Women's Struggle," *Al-Fajr* (The dawn) March 8, p. 8 and March 15, p. 16.

Tarrow, Sidney (1989). "Struggle, Politics, and Reform: Collective Action, Social Movements, and Cycles of Protest," Cornell Studies in International Affairs, Western Societies Papers. Ithaca, NY: Cornell University Press.

Tawfeeq, Basem (1990). "Openness and Frankness Dominate Discussion on Women's Role," *Al-Fajr* (The dawn) December 24, pp. 8–9.

Ten Tusscher, Tessa (1986). "Patriarchy, Capitalism and the New Right," in Judith Evans et al. (eds.), *Feminism and Political Theory*. London: Sage.

Threllfall, Monica (1985). "The Women's Movement in Spain," *New Left Review* 151: 27–49.

Tikoo, Prithvi Nath (1985). *Indian Women*. Delhi: B. R. Publishing.

Tinker, Irene (ed.) (1983). "Introduction: Two Decades of Influence," *Women in Washington*. Beverly Hills, CA: Sage, 7–17.

Tsoucalas, Nicos (1977). *Dependence and Reproduction*. Athens: Themelio (in Greek).

Tsouderou, Virginia (1979). *Women in Politics*. Athens: Phototechniki of Greece (in Greek).

Tuñon, Esperanza (1986). "La Lucha de las Mujeres en el Cardenismo" (Women's fight during the Cardeno era). Master's thesis, National Autonomous University of Mexico, Mexico City.

Ueda, Takashiko (1990). "Feminist Mariko Mitsui Speaks Her Mind Freely: Liberating Women is Assembly Member's Goal," *The Japan Times Weekly International Edition* July 16–22, sec. A, p. 14.

Ueno, Chzuko (1987). "The Position of Japanese Women Reconsidered," *Current Anthropology* 28(4 Supplement) (August–October): S75–84.

UNICEF (1988). *The State of the World's Children*. London: Oxford University Press.

*USA Today* (1990). May 31, sec. A, p. 3.

Uścińska, Grażyna (1990). "Prawo Pracy i Świadczenia Krótkookresowe z Ubezpieczenia Społecznego" (The right to work and short-term social security), *Legal Situation of Women in Poland*. Warsaw: Bureau for Women's Affairs.

Van Loon, Richard J., and Michael S. Whittington (1981). *The Canadian Political System: Environment, Structure and Process*. Third Edition. Toronto: McGraw-Hill-Ryerson.

Van der Ros, Janneke (1986). "Women and Participatory Behavior in Norway: An Overview and an Evaluation of the Equality of Democratic Input." Working paper #8 from the research project, A Feminist Perspective on Democracy in Norway (unpublished).

Ve, Hildur (1984). "Women's Mutual Alliances: Altruism as a Premise for Interaction," in Harriet Holter (ed.), *Patriarchy in a Welfare Society*. Oslo: Universitetsforlaget.

Vickers, Jill (ed.) (1987). *Getting Things Done: Women's Views of Their Involvement in Political Life*. Ottawa, Ont.: Canadian Research Institute for the Advancement of Women.

——— (1986). "Equality-Seeking in a Cold Climate," in Lynn Smith (ed.), *Righting the Balance: Canada's New Equality Rights*. Saskatoon, Sask.: The Canadian Human Rights Reporter, 3–24.

WCSW (Union of Women's Committees for Social Work) (1987). *Fourth Issue of Accomplishments for the Year 1986* (March).

Waerness, Kari (1982). *Kvinneperspectiver pa Socialpolitikken* (Women's perspective on social politics). Oslo: Universitetsforlaget.

Wandersee, Winnifred D. (1988). *On The Move: American Women in the 1970s*. Boston: Twayne.

Watson, Sophie (1990). "Unpacking 'The State': Reflections on Australian, British and Scandinavian Feminist Interventions," in Mary F. Katzenstein and Hege Skjeie (eds.), *Going Public*. Oslo: Institute for Social Research.

Wilson, Elizabeth (1987). "Thatcherism and Women: After Seven Years," in Ralph Miliband et al. (eds.), *Socialist Register 1987*. London: Merlin.

Xiradaki, Koula (1989). *The Feminist Movement in Greece*. Athens: Glaros (in Greek).

Yoder, Janice D., Penny L. Crumpton, and John F. Zipp (1989). "The Power of Numbers in Influencing Hiring Decisions," *Gender and Society* 3(2): 269–76.

————, et al. (1983). "The Price of a Token," *Journal of Political and Military Sociology*
   11:325–37.
Zermeno, Sergio (1985). *México: Una Democracia Utopica, el Movimiento Estudiantil del*
   *68* (Mexico: a utopian democracy, the student movement of 68). Mexico: Siglo
   XXI Editores.

# C O N T R I B U T O R S

JUDITH ASTELARRA was raised and educated in her native Spain and received her doctorate degree in sociology from the National University of Madrid. She is currently in the Sociology Department at the Autonomous University of Barcelona where she teaches and conducts research on women and politics. She has participated extensively in the Spanish women's movement and has written about its history and its impact on the women of Spain.

W. KARAGWA BYANYIMA was born the second of seven children in the village of Ruti in Uganda. She attended Christian missionary schools in her homeland and obtained most of her post-secondary education in England. She has degrees in Aeronautical Engineering from Manchester University and in Engineering from the Cranfield Institute of Technology. She joined the National Resistance Movement in Uganda, was forced to go underground in 1984, and spent over a year with other guerrilla fighters in the bush. After the Movement took control of the government, she worked in the Department of Technology. Currently, she is the Deputy Ambassador to the Permanent Mission of the Republic of Uganda to UNESCO in Paris.

JILL M. BYSTYDZIENSKI was born in Poland and has lived in the United States, Canada, England, and Norway. She was educated at McGill University and at the State University of New York at Albany. She has been involved in the feminist and peace movements and has a longstanding interest in studying women in cross-cultural perspective. She teaches sociology, Canadian studies, and women's studies at Franklin College of Indiana.

SUSAN J. CARROLL is Associate Professor of Political Science at Rutgers University and Senior Research Associate at the Center for the American Woman and Politics (CAWP) of the Eagleton Institute of Politics. She is the author of *Women as Candidates in American Politics* and has conducted research at CAWP focusing on women elected officials, women appointees in both the Carter and Reagan administrations, and women voters.

DORANE L. FREDLAND has had a long-time interest in the involvement of women in the political and economic life of their countries. She studied international relations at American University School of International Service in Washington, D.C., taught at Ehwa Women's University in Seoul, South Korea, and currently teaches women in politics and East Asian politics at Indiana University—Purdue University at Indianapolis.

MELISSA A. HAUSSMAN was educated in U.S. schools and Carleton University in Ottawa, Canada. She is currently teaching in the Department of Politics at Wake Forest University in North Carolina and is completing a doctoral dissertation at Duke University comparing Canadian and U.S. women's attempts to obtain an equal rights clause in their respective constitutions.

YURIKO LING, a native of Japan, studied English and American literature at the Tokyo Womens' Christian University and folklore at Indiana University in Bloomington. She teaches folklore, sociology, and Japanese language at Franklin College of Indiana and at Indiana University—Purdue University at Indianapolis and is also a consultant for KYB Industries, a Japanese company located in Franklin. While residing permanently in the United States, she maintains her Japanese ties through yearly visits.

AZUSA MATSUNO, born and raised in Japan, is currently a graduate student in sociology at Boston University. In Japan, she conducted research in Japanese folklore and studied playing the flute. She has had a longstanding interest in women in politics which was fostered through her attendance at Kinjo University in Nagoya.

ORAYB AREF NAJJAR was born in Jerusalem, Palestine. She began her schooling in the West Bank and later taught at Birzeit University for four years in the 1980s. She received a B.A. in English from the American University of Beirut in Lebanon and worked as a television director at Jordan T.V. before coming to the United States to study journalism at Indiana University. She currently teaches journalism at Northern Illinois University in De Kalb. Since the late 1960s, she has helped to establish children's libraries and distribute books in Palestinian refugee camps in Jordan and in villages in the West Bank. She is co-author of the book *Portraits of Palestinian Women* written with Kitty Warnock.

ESPERANZA TUÑON PABLOS, a native of Mexico City, has been an active participant in the Mexican new feminist movement since the late 1970s. She studied sociology at Mexico's National University and currently is writing a doctoral dissertation on women and democracy in Mexico. She has published a book, *La Lucha de las Mujeres Durante el Cardenismo: 1934–1940* (The struggle of women during Cardeno's regime: 1934–1940), and several articles dealing with women's issues.

YOTA PAPAGEORGIOU-LIMBERES is a lecturer of political science at the University of Athens in Greece and has worked previously as a researcher at the Foundation of Mediterranean Women's Studies in Athens. She was educated at Pantios College of Political Science in Athens, the University of Missouri-Columbia, and Florida State University. She has conducted extensive field work in Greece and has published many articles on women's mass political participation. Her current work focuses on Greek women's involvement in elections and in high public offices.

VICKY RANDALL is Principal Lecturer in politics at the Polytechnic of Central London in the Faculty of Social Sciences. She has been both a participant and student of the women's movement in Britain and worldwide. She is the author of *Women and Politics in International Perspective* (revised edition, 1987) and numerous articles on women, politics, feminism, Thatcherism, and Ireland. She is working currently with Joni Lovenduski on a book on the British women's movement in the 1980s.

JOANNA REGULSKA is Associate Professor of Geography and Director of the Local Democracy in Poland project at Rutgers University in the United States. Her current research includes a focus on the role of women in social, economic, and political changes occurring in Eastern Europe. She is the co-author of *Warsaw: Space, People and Politics* (1990) and has written numerous articles published in U.S. and Polish journals.

BARBARA J. SEITZ has a doctorate in Folklore/Ethnomusicology from Indiana University. She has made numerous trips to Nicaragua, has conducted many informal interviews with women of that country, and has written extensively about the lives of Nicaraguan women. She has been a member and coordinator of several delegations from Bloomington, IN to its sister city, Posoltega, Nicaragua and visited Nicaragua in 1990 with a group of U.S. election observers.